About the Author

Born in 1956, MAUREEN McCORMICK began her career at the age of six after winning the Baby Miss San Fernando Valley Beauty Pageant. She appeared in numerous commercials for brands such as Mattel and Kool-Aid, and performed in early episodes of *Bewitched* and *My Three Sons*, before landing the starring role as Marcia Brady in the groundbreaking sitcom *The Brady Bunch*, which aired in prime time from 1969 to 1974. McCormick is also a singer and voice-over-actor, who has made a number of appearances in television and movie roles during her long career. She recently returned to television as a cast member of VH1's *Celebrity Fit Club*—and won! She lives in Southern California with her husband and daughter.

itbooks

AN IMPRINT OF HARPERCOLLINS *PUBLISHERS*

Here's the Story

Surviving
Marcia Brady *and*
Finding
My True Voice

Maureen McCormick

*it***books**

A hardcover edition of this book was published in 2008 by William Morrow, an imprint of HarperCollins Publishers.

First It Books paperback published 2009.

Designed by Kate Nichols

Library of Congress Cataloging-in-Publication data is available upon request.

ISBN 978-0-06-1490156

09   10   11   12   13   WBC/RRD   10   9   8   7   6   5   4   3   2   1

To Michael *and* Natalie

And to my mother, Irene

Ye shall know the truth,

and the truth will set you free.

—JOHN 8:32

Contents

Contents

x

Part *Two*

Part *Three*

Part *Four*

Prologue

Tell me the honest truth. Do I look funny?

—Marcia Brady,
"Brace Yourself" episode of *The Brady Bunch*

This story begins in the fall of 2006 in Los Angeles. It was the first day of production of VH1's *Celebrity Fit Club*. I was fifty years old, and I was about to get my initial weigh-in. Kimberley Locke, Tiffany, Da Brat, Cletus T. Judd, Warren G, and Ross the Intern from *The Tonight Show* were among the other celebrities participating in season five of the competition weight-loss show. All of them, as well as the production crew, were staring at me as I stepped on the scale.

Until that moment, not even my husband of twenty-one years, Michael, knew how much I weighed. Nor did my seventeen-year-old daughter, Natalie, who had urged me to participate in this reality show. I can't say if my doctor knew my weight. Sharing my weight was tantamount to many other admissions that I was loath to make even to myself. But all that was about to change.

As the numbers were calculated, I felt an overwhelming sense of humiliation. What was I doing? Why? The world was about to know how much I weighed. From that, they could infer much more. I may as well have been naked, caught having sex, or walking down the aisle of an airplane with toilet paper stuck to my shoe. I wanted to put my head in the ground and disappear.

I tried to control my emotions and look unfazed by the results (more than 150 pounds) as cameras captured every nuance of my mortification. My blond-brown hair was pulled back and I wore thick-rimmed black glasses that had drawn surprised comments from the other competitors a few hours earlier. *Wow, cool glasses. I didn't know you wore them.*

Of course they didn't. We'd just met.

Some didn't say anything about the glasses, but I still noticed the expression on their faces. So many other people had given me that same look over the years that I felt like a mind reader. They were thinking the glasses didn't look very Marcia-like. Or if it wasn't the glasses, it was my age, weight, or something else they couldn't immediately reconcile with the long-held image in their head.

I understood.

I had no choice but to understand. A few years before, my husband and I had taken a car trip. We stopped for lunch at a restaurant in a small Colorado town. A large man approached our table, apologized for interrupting our meal, but said he couldn't help it. He said he had to show me something. Then he took off his jacket and rolled up the left sleeve of his flannel shirt.

"What do you think?" he asked.

His upper arm was covered by a tattoo of my face, albeit a younger, thinner me. Beneath it, in beautiful script, was the line I LOVE MARCIA BRADY.

"It's . . . it's nice," I said. "I'm flattered."

There was nothing else to say. For most of my life, I have been followed, and sometimes haunted, by Marcia Brady. I don't have a choice in the matter. Imagine always being shadowed by a younger, prettier, more popular you. Even when I met the other *Celebrity Fit Club* cast members, several of them inadvertently referred to me as Marcia, not Maureen, as in "nice to meet you, Marcia," or "Hi, Marcia, I grew up watching you," or "Hey, it's Marcia, Marcia, Marcia!"

That kind of thing had happened to me so often since *The Brady Bunch* went on the air on September 26, 1969, that I shouldn't have noticed. Except that I did. Every time. I had played Marcia Brady for five years. But I wasn't her in any way, shape, or form. She was perfect. I was anything but that.

As I knew too well, it wasn't Marcia who'd been asked to appear on *Celebrity Fit Club*. She was still a perfect-looking teenager, struggling with the ups and downs of adolescence, and she would stay that way throughout TV rerun eternity. No, the show's producers had asked me, Marcia's imperfect-looking, middle-aged doppelgänger. There was one main reason they had asked me. They thought I was fat. They knew the reaction viewers would have when they saw me.

Is that Marcia Brady? Oh my God, what happened to her?

The better question was what *didn't* happen to her? And did I want the world to know all that, along with my weight?

Those details had been off-limits to other people my whole life. In fact, as I contemplated a decision, my thoughts raced back to a day during the first season of *The Brady Bunch*. It was 1969, and I was thirteen years old. We were shooting the "Brace Yourself" episode, the one in which Marcia feels like her life is over after she gets braces. She feels "ugly, ugly, ugly." Then her boyfriend breaks their date, making her feel even uglier, and she sobs uncontrollably.

What no one knew—not Florence Henderson, Robert Reed, Barry Williams, Eve Plumb, Chris Knight, Mike Lookinland, Susan Olsen, or Ann B. Davis—was that those tears were real. My parents had recently had a terrible fight, which shattered my sense of peace and security. In the fallout, I learned that my mother had a deep, dark secret she'd spent her life hiding from us and everyone else.

Through ignorance and an inability to communicate, her secret became mine, and during the entire run of *The Brady Bunch*, I thought I was going to end up insane, as she did briefly and as her mother did before her. But I kept that to myself, as I waited for that fateful time. I didn't want anyone to know. I tried to be perfect and to make everything seem perfect, as if through a combination of willpower, denial, and control, I could prevent what I thought was inevitable.

So much was going on behind my fake smile. The others made fun of me for the way I frequently spaced out. *Oh, there's Maureen, in her own little world again. Look at Maureen; she flaked out again.*

It wasn't like my fellow Bradys didn't have their own issues. I'd later learn that Bob Reed hated the show and hid his homosexuality, Eve Plumb resented me for getting too much attention, and Susie Olsen despised her pigtails and the fake lisp the producers had her employ to ratchet up her cuteness factor. But as a teenager, I had no idea that few people are everything they present to the outside world.

When the show went off the air, I missed the structure and routine provided by my fictional TV family, and in a way I missed Marcia, with whom I had such a love-hate relationship. She'd given me an identity. Without her, I had to figure out who I was—a next-to-impossible task for someone doing everything she could to avoid the truth about herself.

I sought refuge in seemingly glamorous cocaine dens above Hollywood. I thought I would find answers there, while in reality I was simply running farther from myself. From there, I spiraled downward on a path of self-destruction that cost me my career and very nearly my life. Over the years I battled drug addiction and bulimia. I was treated in a psych ward, went in and out of rehab, and looked to God for answers. I managed to marry a wonderful husband and give birth to a spectacular daughter, yet I never felt as if the light shined on me, not even on the sunniest of days.

I came out of it slowly and in stages. First, I had to acknowledge, and then get help for a longtime struggle with depression. Then I had to come to terms with my mother. And finally I needed to face myself. Once I stopped telling lies and trying to pretend life was perfect, I was able to move on. As trivial as it sounds, I didn't feel like I quit pretending until I made a decision about whether or not to do *Celebrity Fit Club*.

I know—it sounds crazy! It might have been.

But that's what happened. Michael, Natalie, and I were at the kitchen table, talking about the offer. All of a sudden I had a feeling in my gut. Call it being fifty and fatigued. Or being fifty and courageous. Or being fifty and not caring anymore what people thought about me. But for the first time in my life I said, "You know what? I'm overweight. I'm really imperfect. I've had all this shit happen to me. I'm not going to hide it anymore."

"You're going to do it, then?" both of them asked.

"Yup," I said. "Screw it."

I started to write this book after a trip to New York during which I guested on a TV talk show and spoke about my life since childhood. It felt good to be able to open up about these issues. No more subterfuge. No more hiding behind fake smiles. No more pretending my life was like *The Brady Bunch*. No more pretending to be Marcia Brady.

As I sat down at the dining-room table to put pen to paper, I took a deep breath and looked through the sliding-glass doors into the backyard. Up to then, I never thought I would actually write a book about my life until I had a great ending. What did I mean by a great ending? Something neat. A pretty package tied up with a bow. A tale that would get people talking and move critics to praise it as perfect.

Then I laughed at myself. How stupid. Not a single word written yet and I'd immediately fallen into striving for perfection, wanting to write the perfect book and thinking I had to in order for anyone to pay attention. Maureen, I said, get a grip! Hadn't I learned anything through my battles with coke, pills, self-destructive behavior, and depression? I had beaten them. Why did I have to make things so hard on myself?

After that, the book didn't happen right away. Several months passed before I undertook the endeavor again, buoyed by a more reasonable expectation. I'm fifty-two years old. At this moment I am craving coffee and a cigarette. They're about the only vices I have left. No, that's not really true. Lately, I have struggled with food. Despite my success on *Celebrity Fit Club,* my weight has continued to fluctuate, and the satisfaction of fitting into size twos and fours is a fading memory. Right now I'm an eight. My husband, the sweetest, most patient man in the world, has lately dropped hints that I might want to lose a few of those pounds.

I have told him that I will try. But the truth is that, although I'm paranoid about my weight, I would really like to spend all day in my pajamas, drinking coffee, smoking cigarettes, and eating all the See's candy and Baskin-Robbins chocolate mint ice cream that I can get my hands on. Shit, how transparent am I? I just want to fill the empty hole in me. I want to fill it to the brim. I want to fill it to overflowing.

I won't do it, of course.

Instead I am going to fill it through work, and by sharing the events and emotions that caused me so much fear, that brought me harm, that made me strong, and that over time allowed me to realize that I didn't have to be anything more than me, and that being me, being human, being real, and being my absolutely imperfect self, was quite all right.

It's funny. My mother never wanted me to write a memoir. She was adamant about that. It took me a while after her death to realize that this was an extension of the shame she had carried through her entire life, the insidious fear she had that people would find out about her secret. But I saw her in a different light. To me, she was an amazing woman, something I hope my daughter will one day be able to say about me—and if not amazing, I want her to at least be able to say that I tried.

For those reasons, I need to write this book. As you'll see, it hasn't been easy, and it still isn't. I feel guilty about my intellectually handicapped brother living in a facility for adults with special needs, and I'm dealing with a situation of elder abuse with my father. In general, though, I have tried. For the most part, too, I think I have gotten to a really good place. Along the way, I have learned some important lessons, gained some wisdom, and discovered that, while I may not really be the grooviest girl on campus, I am a lot stronger than I ever thought. When people come to my house, they look around at what I hope seems like a comfortable, cozy family home and invariably ask if I have any memorabilia lying around. None of the magazine covers, photos, or gold albums are displayed. Except for a few dolls and stuffed animals I had as a child and a small music box that belonged to my mother, everything has been packed in boxes and in storage for years.

This book is my way of finally unpacking those boxes. My mother's sentiments aside, I am looking forward to sharing the things that have been locked away about her and the rest of my family, about myself, and, yes, even about Marcia and the rest of the Brady bunch.

Here's the story . . .

Part
One

1

The One Day When This Lady Met This Fellow

I wish my mother had been alive for my fiftieth birthday. I think my attitude would have surprised her. Rather than dreading the half-century milestone, I celebrated it. I embraced the idea of getting older. My family was around me all day. At night, they brought out a big cake and I blew out candles. We toasted . . . me!

I said silly things like "fifty is nifty." Several reporters called, wanting to know how Marcia Brady felt about turning fifty. Politely, I reminded them that Marcia Brady was still a teenager, but I, Maureen, created not in Sherwood Schwartz's imagination but in the womb of Irene McCormick, felt okay about it.

And no, I responded to another frequently asked question, I hadn't had any plastic surgery and didn't plan to. I borrowed Flip Wilson's line: What you see is what you get. It wasn't that bad. Despite the punishment I'd heaped on my body over the years, gravity had been kind to me. I didn't have many wrinkles, at least none that were undeserved. I had few complaints.

But those questions got me thinking. Why would I get surgically pulled, stretched, and Botoxed? When I looked in the mirror, I wanted to see me. *The real me—warts, wrinkles, and everything else.* I'd gone through hell and back to get to a place where I could, and indeed wanted to, look at myself—and like what I saw.

My mother had spent nearly her entire life doing the opposite, hiding from her past and trying to avoid the truth. It clouded much that she should've liked. A stay-at-home mother, she was a hard worker, with a good sense of people, good morals, and a good business sense.

Before the end, she came around and was much better and happier for it. By then, of course, much had happened.

My mother was born in 1921 in Burlington, Iowa, a small town along the Mississippi settled by German immigrants. Her father contracted syphilis while serving overseas during World War I, and he passed it on to her mother. She entered a mental institution with extreme paresis and died there without being able to recognize my mother or her younger sister.

A week after she entered the institution, my mom's father locked himself in the garage and breathed the exhaust fumes from his car. He died leaving his two girls inside the house. My mother was ten years old when she lost both of her parents.

She and her sister moved in with an aunt and uncle. They were dedicated, devoted, and loving people. They provided my mother and her sister with a loving, nurturing home, though small-town life being what it was, my mother and her younger sister were still subjected to scorn. A year later, she was diagnosed with syphilis, an event that scarred her more psychologically than physically for the rest of her life.

It turned out she'd inherited the disease at birth from her mother. Following the diagnosis, she was warned not to tell anyone, *ever,* lest she be branded diseased and dirty. She didn't have to be told. From that first moment on, she *felt* dirty and diseased. It was the most shameful thing in the world to her. She was also frightened that she'd end up in an institution like her mother.

She was treated with stovarsol and mercury capsules, though both treatments caused a bad rash and later a more extreme skin condition.

She ate her meals off a separate set of dishes. It was like wearing a scarlet *A,* only worse. At thirteen, she began special treatments at the State University of Iowa in Iowa City to ensure she would never pass the syphilis on to any children she might have. Those treatments lasted for three years and required long and lonely bus rides.

"At the time of her last visit here, on December 28, 1938, she seemed to be in good health, had been taking mercury and chalk fairly regularly, and had been going to her local physician for weekly Bismuth shots," her doctor wrote in a report. "Physical examination at the time of her last visit revealed a well-developed, well-nourished female. She was quite cooperative but acted rather self-consciously."

Despite everything, she did well in school, worked numerous odd jobs, and put herself through business college. She blossomed into a beautiful, intelligent, ambitious young woman. On the one hand, I picture her sitting on those long bus rides to the hospital: alone, scared, praying no one found out about her condition. On the other hand, I marvel at the strength she must have had; though she didn't show it, she was the strongest woman I've ever met.

At twenty, she fell in love and married a soldier who was immediately shipped off to Europe. A week later, he was killed in World War II when a German U-boat sank the transport ship he was on.

Devastated, she moved to the West Coast with her best girlfriend, Mary Crawley. They wanted to live in Hollywood, among the movie stars and fancy theaters. They dreamed of adventure, maybe even stardom. But they ended up fifteen miles away in Westwood, near UCLA. My mom didn't care. She was happy to be out of Burlington and away from the stares and stigma of her past.

My father, Richard, was the youngest of three children born to Joseph McCormick, a bartender in Riverside, New Jersey. His father was a heavy drinker who abused his wife. He lost everything in the Depression and died in his mid-thirties from illnesses related to alcoholism.

My father's mother did the best she could to raise her family, but they were very poor and at one point they had to burn furniture to keep warm in the winter. My dad spent most of his youth in a wheelchair, the result of osteomyelitis. By his late teens, though, his illness was gone. Near the end of World War II, he lied about his age and joined the Coast Guard. One day he was on deck, cooking for his shipmates, and his gas stove exploded, severely burning his leg.

Discharged because of his injury, he moved to Los Angeles and enrolled at UCLA. It was 1945, and he lived in a fraternity house. To earn money, he and a friend started a window-washing business. One day he was washing windows outside a doctor's office, and he began making eyes at the pretty receptionist on the other side. That was my mother. She had gotten a job as a receptionist/office manager for a foot doctor in Westwood.

She smiled back at the nice-looking window washer. A moment later, he walked into the office. He heard music playing on the office radio. Inspired and playful, he asked her to dance. She said okay, got up from her desk, and, in a manner of speaking, they never stopped dancing.

They married six weeks later in a Catholic church in Westwood. My dad's window-washing partner and his girlfriend were the only witnesses. A framed photo of my mother from that day stands in my living room. My mom wore a smart, dark suit and looked as striking as any movie star I've seen. But I'm sure her outfit was old. She never would've spent money on a new dress, not even on her wedding day. She didn't think she was worth it.

She was like that my whole life. She bought clothes on sale at Kmart, wore cheap wigs to cover her very thin hair, and wore the least expensive makeup and shoes. She never felt deserving of anything. Yet she was very beautiful and feminine. Tragically, I don't think she ever saw or felt it.

Not long after they married, my mom grew homesick and she and my dad moved back to Iowa. They lived in a duplex with my mom's sister and her husband. Dad and a buddy opened a gas station. My dad was always industrious. In 1948, they had their first child, Mike. Eleven months later, my mom gave birth to a second son, Kevin. During both pregnancies, as would be the case with subsequent pregnancies, she received extremely painful shots of penicillin directly into her hip on ten successive days to prevent her congenital syphilis from being passed to her children.

After Kevin arrived, they moved to Davenport, where Dad spent a year at Drake University. In 1952, my mother was pregnant again. With a growing family, both she and my father realized there were more economic opportunities in California, so they loaded up their station wagon and drove to San Diego, where my father got his teaching credential at San Diego State College.

They were living in a military-style Quonset hut when my brother Dennis arrived. My mother was overjoyed, but three boys was a lot for a woman who worried about her stamina. In 1953, my dad graduated and found a teaching job in Malibu. They moved to a rustic, one-room cabin on twenty acres of land near Malibu Lake. On their first night there, the entire family slept in a queen-size bed. That was togetherness!

A couple years later, they moved to a more spacious, three-bedroom tract home in Reseda. Mike started kindergarten. Kevin and Dennis were still home with my mother. Mike remembers Dad coming home one night from his after-school job at Builders Emporium with cuts and bruises. He said angry union mobsters had beat him up after he refused to join the union.

Mike also remembers one day when he and Kevin, then about five and four, were playing cowboys with the girl next door. At Kevin's suggestion, they captured her, tied her to a stake, and painted her with mud. That didn't go over well with her father, who knocked on our door that night and demanded an apology.

The boys apologized, but then they had to face my father. For some reason, Kevin was let off the hook. Mike wasn't as lucky. My father whipped him with a belt until he was black-and-blue.

Around this time, my mother entered the hospital. My father gathered the boys together and said she needed to go away for special care. My aunt came out and filled in for my mother. The episode was a mystery for years, until my father revealed that my mother had had a nervous breakdown and received shock treatment. He said that her behavior turned disturbing, and includes an episode where she had complained of seeing snakes coming out of the couch.

I've asked Mike if he remembered such behavior. He didn't. A longtime friend of my mother's told me that my father may have pushed her into that state. My mother's friend Harriet, who died at age ninety-three as I was finishing this book, said they fought often and at times my father hit her.

My mother refused to discuss anything like that, as well as her hospitalization. She pushed it out of her thoughts. For her, it was just one more thing to be ashamed of, one more thing to hide.

In 1954, at the end of the school year, my father built a home for the family in Woodland Hills. He enlisted some of his students to help with the construction. He loved do-it-yourself projects, but that meant cutting corners to cut costs. As such, the home was full of leaks from bad pipe fittings in the cement slab, all of which had to be redone by experts. And for a month after moving in, they lived amid the earsplitting sound of jackhammers as plumbers broke up the floor and replaced the pipes.

Apparently that was a source of laughter in those days, but these were also very difficult times for my mother—indeed, for both of my parents. According to Harriet, their fighting was intense. Harriet was often and I think the only person my mother turned to after such fights. For whatever reason, she was able to show her bruises and bare her soul to her friend.

In fact, when Harriet recalled these moments to me, I remembered seeing my mother full of bruises. As I thought back, I couldn't remember a time when I didn't see her bruised somewhere on her body.

"I asked her why she didn't do something, why she didn't yell for help," Harriet told me. "Your mother said she couldn't. She didn't want the neighbors to hear."

However, according to Harriet, they did go to a Catholic priest for help with their problems. He told them to have another baby. At the end of 1955, my mother got pregnant again. That Christmas everyone talked about how they wanted a girl. They got their wish when I arrived ten months later on August 5, 1956. My mother was ecstatic when she heard the doctor say, "It's a girl."

She named me Maureen. My parents' second choice was Christine. But my mother said I looked more like a Maureen. She also said that I was the most beautiful baby she'd ever seen.

The years following my birth were happy times. We spent many weekends with our cousins from Long Beach. Either they drove up or we visited them. One Sunday, while both families were at our house, Dennis got into my dad's car and released the emergency brake. It began rolling backward down the long, steep driveway. Someone saw it move and screamed. My dad, who was seated about twenty feet away, dropped his beer and sprinted alongside the moving car until he was able to jump inside and slam on the brakes.

We stayed in that home for about two years. Finally my mother had enough of the dirt roads, the mud slides, and other difficulties of rural life in the hills. In 1958, we moved to a neighborhood near Topanga Canyon and Mulholland Drive. We spent the next five years there. It was a great neighborhood, with lots of children, trees to climb, and large backyards where we played.

Soon we added a pet duck and a homemade pigeon coop. My mom used to make a delicious angel-food cake when the duck laid its eggs. Around this time, my parents learned that Denny was intellectually handicapped. He'd had a problematic birth and suffered minor brain damage from a lack of oxygen. My parents had known about this, but had hoped and prayed for the best. But their worst fears were confirmed.

My dad saw this as a challenge, and he took night-school classes on how to teach children with special needs. Kevin's behavior worried my mother, too. Ever since the incident when he tied the little neighbor girl up, others looked at him with a wary eye. My mother wanted to get him help, but my father wouldn't let her. He felt Kevin was fine. Everything was fine.

Yet my dad always wanted a better job, something more, and as a result he moved from school to school, district to district, which infuriated my mother because it meant he constantly lost the tenure and retirement he'd built up. Because it was difficult to support a family of six on a teacher's salary, he moonlighted, selling portrait photography and family paintings for artist Jim Gaines. One day, he suggested they use me as a baby model, and soon clients remarked on what a beautiful child I was.

I loved the attention and posing for the camera in different outfits and jewelry. At five years old, I was able to give the photographer any expression he wanted. Two years later, my parents entered one of my photos in a Baby Miss San Fernando Valley Beauty Pageant. I sang "Getting to Know You" from *The King and I.* I also recited poetry from the book *Little Women.* And I won.

Little did they realize a star had been born.

2

Wind Her Up and . . .

After a picture of me winning the Baby Miss San Fernando Valley beauty pageant ran in the local newspaper, talent agent Pat Domigan of the Jack Wormser Agency called our house and asked if she could represent me for radio and TV commercials. We met at her office. She seemed legit and trustworthy. She suggested I take dance and modeling lessons, but she was convinced I had that special quality that casting directors looked for in kids.

My parents liked hearing that, and while I enjoyed the occasional modeling, I was really a normal kid. I enjoyed playing make-believe. I practically lived in our tree house, and I put on puppet shows for anyone willing to watch. Thanks to my brothers, though, I was more of a tomboy than a girlie girl. I made mud pies, climbed trees, played cowboys and Indians, threw footballs, baseballs, and Frisbees, and joined in games of hide-and-seek. My knees always had scabs on them from skateboarding.

The only hint of an interest in show business was the time I spent with my parents watching all the great musicals on TV, and often after dinner my father asked me to sing favorite songs from *Carousel*,

Oklahoma!, The King and I, and *West Side Story.* He could listen till I exhausted my repertoire. That was fine with me. As the baby of the family, I enjoyed the attention.

Then a short time after signing with Pat, I had my first interview. The strange thing was it didn't come through my new agent. No matter. I thought I would burst from excitement. We were told to be at Paramount Studios early one Saturday morning. It was raining when we left home, and my father stopped at a store in Hollywood to buy an umbrella so my hair wouldn't get wet.

But when we got to the studio, the gates were locked. We waited, thinking they would eventually open up since we had an appointment. They never did. We went to a pay phone and called Pat, who was surprised by what was going on and set us straight, explaining that no one had meetings on the weekend.

The interview turned out to be a cruel setup by an unhappy mother of one of the girls who hadn't won the beauty and talent contest. It was the kind of hoax you hear about on the news today—the revenge-of-the-bitter-cheerleader's-mother kind of thing. We learned a lesson. As we later said, laughing, at least we got our feet wet—literally!

On April 24, 1964, I went to my first legit interview, and I got the job. It was a commercial for Mattel's new doll, Baby Pattaburp. They showed me how to put the doll over my shoulder, pat her, and make her really burp. She was the cutest thing I'd ever seen. Even then, back when I was almost eight years old, my dream was to get married and be a mom. So the doll was like a dream come true.

Four months later, Mattel hired me again to do an ad for their Chatty Cathy dolls. I still have my original Chatty Cathy. My voice was used for the dolls, too. My favorite days were those when I got to go to the Mattel factory in Hawthorne because I usually left with new toys and dolls. Believe it or not, those are still some of my favorite memories.

Before the year ended, I was cast in the play *Wind It Up and It Breaks* at the La Jolla Playhouse. It was directed by Cy Howard, produced by Ray Stark, and starred Mike Connors (later known for the hit series *Mannix*) and Jack Weston. For my first acting job, I could not have worked with a better group of professionals. They gave me pointers and made me feel comfortable and confident onstage.

They also taught me the meaning of the old adage "the show must go on." Shortly after the play opened, I came down with the flu. My parents wanted to keep me in bed, but they were told there were no sick days in the theater. Instead I was given a paper bag and told to run offstage if I had to throw up, then get back out there and be ready to deliver my next line.

There was talk of the play going to Broadway. All of us were disappointed when it didn't happen, but we had a fun wrap party all the same.

I can't imagine that my family would've let me follow the play to New York. My career was still more of a lark amid the comings and goings of our busy family. But there was genuine excitement when my next job was on *Bewitched*, one of everyone's favorite shows. It was the episode titled "And Something Makes Three," and I played Tabitha in a dream Samantha had before she gave birth to the actual Tabitha.

I remember being awed by Elizabeth Montgomery and thinking wow, she's more beautiful in person. I also remember that in my scene I was supposed to wiggle my nose, like Samantha, but I can't remember if they used *my nose* or Elizabeth's.

Trivia, trivia, trivia.

I worked on pilots for *Camp Runamuck* and *This Is the Hopsital*, though neither was picked up, and then I was cast in episodes of *The Farmer's Daughter* and *Honey West*. I also returned to *Bewitched*, this time playing Endora (Agnes Moorhead) as a child, and I followed that with spots on *I Dream of Jeannie* and *My Three Sons*. In fact, I received my first on-screen kiss as Ernie's girlfriend. The funny thing was I had a crush on Fred MacMurray, the boys' pipe-smoking father. I thought he was a cutie.

I made my movie debut in *The Arrangement,* a drama starring Faye Dunaway and Kirk Douglas. Elia Kazan directed, but I only have a vague impression of him as businesslike when it came to positioning me. My best training came on commercials for Pillsbury chocolate-chip cookies (I was the first person to appear on-screen with the Pillsbury Doughboy; I even poked him in his tummy), Barbie's "Color'n Curl" set, Standard Oil, Chevron, Kool-Aid, Gaines Dog Food, White Cloud tissues, the new Twist Barbie, and Mr. Bubble.

My work and various dance and singing lessons I took after school provided me with an escape from growing tension and stress at home, some of which was too nuanced for me to notice but some of which I understood too well. The tension revolved around my brother Kevin, who had a difficult time as a middle child finding his way amid the attention given to me and my brother Denny, who had special needs, and my oldest brother Mike's excellence in and out of school.

Indeed, following Mike wasn't easy, as he got good grades, worked two paper routes, had a job at a TV repair store all through junior high and high school, and set his sights on college. Kevin also tried a paper route, but he was fired after he was caught dumping his papers into trash cans behind a store. After that, his grades dropped and he began hanging around with a bad crowd.

By junior high, Kevin was regularly in trouble. He was suspended from school for poor grades and fighting. He also started to drink and experiment with drugs. He and his friends broke into neighborhood homes for kicks. My mother was concerned, but she was busy with me at the studios or occupied by Denny. Although she pleaded with my father to get him help and separate him from his friends, he refused, arguing that Kevin was in a phase that he'd eventually grow out of.

While Denny would never grow out of his situation, he attended regular school through a program that integrated special-ed students with the regular student population. He was adorable as he hurried to the bus every morning with his books and then came home in the afternoon and did his homework, hoping to get a gold star. He was about one thing—love. All he wanted was a hug, a kiss, or a smile, and he gave as much affection as he got.

Certain friends of mine weren't allowed to spend the night at our house because I had a handicapped brother. Their parents feared he might turn violent. I was infuriated by their ignorance. Denny was the kindest person in the whole world. Then there was the cruelty I witnessed when people made fun of him or called him a "retard." After one such incident at the mall, Denny turned to me and asked, "What's a retard?" Another time he asked, "Maureen, am I retarded? What does that mean?"

We were raised Catholic, and I always wondered how the all-knowing and all-loving God we heard about at church could permit other people to hurt Denny. I had even more questions when my father, after befriending a charismatic local preacher, turned into an impassioned born-again Christian. Almost every night for about six months, he came home and implored all of us to get to know Jesus better.

Then the preacher hanged himself. After hearing the news, my father was devastated and disillusioned. The rest of us were relieved. We didn't have to sit through any more of his dinner-table preaching.

And a lot of good the preaching did. After a year of high school, Kevin dropped out. He took up painting, at which he showed promise, and guitar, but for the most part he drifted around and got into trouble. Mike, who attended junior college and managed a TV repair store, was rarely home. My father started to teach emotionally disturbed students, on top of his other jobs, including ferrying my mother and me back and forth to the studio.

We were a busy family, a close unit but in some ways as compartmentalized as a Swanson's TV dinner. Everyone was excited when I was told that I got the title role in the TV movie *Heidi*. Blake Edwards, whose wife, Julie Andrews, was one of my heroes, was producing, and the project starred Maximilian Schell, Jean Simmons, and Michael

Redgrave. Then out of the blue I was told my role was going instead to Edwards' daughter, Jennifer.

Oh my God was I disappointed. I threw myself on my bed like a little drama queen. It felt like my life was over. My mother sat on my bed, took me in her arms, and promised something else good would come along. I looked up at her through tear-filled eyes. It was clear to me that she didn't understand.

3

The Way We Became the Brady Bunch

Can one be both blessed and cursed by the same thing?

That's the question that comes to mind as I think back to the end of the summer of 1968, when I began interviewing for *The Brady Bunch* at Paramount Studios. As we drove to the studio, I was unaware of the show's brief history in Hollywood. What I later learned was that executive producer Sherwood Schwartz, an Emmy-winning writer and creator of *Gilligan's Island,* had written the pilot two years earlier after reading an *L.A. Times* story about "blended families," two parents with children from previous marriages, but all the networks turned it down.

Then the Henry Fonda–Lucille Ball movie *Yours, Mine and Ours* was a hit in theaters, and ABC remembered Sherwood's pet project. It looked like his perseverance had paid off. Sherwood and director John Rich saw 1,200 boys and girls, then narrowed the field down to 464, and then finally down to two sets of kids—one set with three blond girls and three brown-haired boys and one set with three brunette girls and three blond boys.

I was in the first group, where I was actually the middle daughter.

But Sherwood decided to go with younger children, and I was moved into a new threesome with Eve Plumb and Susan Olsen, where I was the oldest. I wonder how my life would've been different if I'd played Jan. Then it was down to the hair color of the parents. Once Sherwood and the network decided on Florence Henderson as the mother, they chose us. She was blond, and so were we. (And back then it was natural!)

During the audition process, I recognized Eve Plumb from other tryouts and Susan Olsen and I had met in passing at an audition for the Elvis Presley movie *The Trouble with Girls* (neither of us got the part). But my first real introduction to my Brady sisters came at the screen test we did for Sherwood and John, where we answered questions. It felt more like a personality test than an audition. In retrospect, Sherwood was gauging our chemistry together.

It was evident to us that we hit it off and I guess to him, too. Soon after that final interview, my agent called with good news. It was then that I also learned my brothers were to be played by Barry Williams, Chris Knight, and Mike Lookinland. I couldn't wait to meet them.

Later I found out that actress Joyce Bulifant had been first in line to play Carol Brady, that is until Sherwood saw Florence's screen test and went with her. He had also wanted a young Gene Hackman to play Mike Brady, but the executives at Paramount thought he lacked TV experience and instead went with Bob Reed, who was still under contract to the studio after having starred on the series *The Defenders*.

Our first run-through was at the Lucille Ball rehearsal hall on the Paramount lot. That's where everyone met. Sherwood made the introduction by saying, "This is your new family." I liked the sound of that—*my new family*. Even better, I liked the looks of the three boys, all of whom were supercute.

The first day of shooting took place on Barry Williams's fourteenth birthday. There was a party on the set. Barry was the most enthusiastic of the six kids; the most ambitious, too. He was ready for his Johnny Bravo moment. Chris was shy. Eve was quiet. Susie and Mike were young. It seemed like a friendly group. Everyone except Bob seemed glad to be there.

I don't know what it was about Bob that I sensed. He'd come off the E. G. Marshall drama *The Defenders* to find himself the head of the Brady household with six kids, a dog, a cat, a housekeeper, and an unrealistic plot. He was a stickler for realism, so the show tortured him from the get-go. But I recently went back and watched the first episodes, and in the scene when I hug my new dad for the first time, I saw genuine affection in my eyes—and Bob's.

I was fascinated to see that in me. It was more than acting. All of us really were making deep connections, like a family.

Then there was a six-month wait between the time we finished the pilot and the news that ABC had picked up the show—and to borrow a line from the show's theme song, "that's the way we all became the Brady Bunch." We began shooting that summer, and as I later wrote in a high-school essay, "*The Brady Bunch* became a big part of my life, with Paramount Studios as my second home and the people I worked with my second family."

When we returned to work, I and all the other kids were asked to bring a couple of personal items from home to help decorate our new bedrooms on the set. I brought a stuffed giraffe and the Miss Baby San Fernando Valley trophy I'd won years earlier. Funnily enough, my beauty pageant trophy ended up on a shelf in the boys' bedroom. That was fine with me. I wasn't interested in replicating the non-Brady-like chaos of my real house. I liked this new arrangement.

One day my mom and I rode to the studio with Susie Olsen and her mother. Susie started to read a book that I'd brought and got carsick. When we stopped outside the studio to give the guard our names, she threw up all over the gate. A short time later, Eve Plumb and her mother arrived. Her mother reported that a kid had vomited all over the front gate.

Susie's mom nonchalantly asked how she knew it was a kid.

"You can see what they ate for breakfast," Eve's mom said.

We also laughed at Mike, the youngest, whose hair had been dyed red for the pilot but was now dyed black, and sadly for him, it ran in black-streaked drivels down his face as he perspired under the hot lights. I remember Chris teasing me. The flirtations started right away. I was titillated by the fact that the boys were dressing, and undressing, in a room right next door to us. That drove me crazy as we got older.

A typical day began at five A.M. when I woke up and got ready. At five-thirty, my mother and I caught a ride to the studio either from my father or with the Knights or the Olsens. At the studio, we went into hair and makeup and then worked with our tutor until we were needed on the set. The day ended around five P.M. It took about an hour to get home. After dinner, I studied my lines until bedtime and often fell asleep still wearing my makeup.

In those early days on the set, we were constantly under adult supervision, usually a combination of parents, producers, and a tutor. Our girls' dressing room resembled a crowded hair salon. I remember Susie's mom constantly fussing with her daughter's pigtails, and Eve's mother carefully brushing her daughter's long blond hair. Of course I brushed mine as much as, if not more than, anyone.

I heard the boys' side was less animated. Barry's parents were sweet, classy people. Chris's mom, Willie, was a tough New Yorker. And Mike Lookinland's parents seemed the most Brady-like, though they divorced years later. As for my mother, she got along with everyone, but she preferred to stay in the background and away from the gossip that everyone liked to swap.

I loved the familiarity of being on the set every day. It became a second home, including the mischief. Eve and Susie teased me for pressing my ear against the wall that separated our dressing room from the boys. But I wanted to hear their conversations, especially if they were talking about us—but really me! I wondered if Barry liked me. I sure wanted him to. That would come later.

Susie and Mike had the first on-set romance. They snuck off into the doghouse and made out. Once Eve and I threw Mike into our dressing room and locked him inside with Susie. By the time we shot the eighth episode, "A-Camping We Will Go," Susan and Mike had professed their love. I officiated at a fake marriage ceremony outside our dressing room, asking if he took her as his *awfully* wedded wife.

In August, I celebrated my thirteenth birthday on the set. Finally a teenager, I was ready for big changes. One morning on the way to the studio, Susie's mom mentioned that her other daughter, Diane, who was my age, had gotten her period for the first time the night before. I was so jealous I couldn't contain myself.

"I want mine!" I blurted.

I had to wait until the next season for that special moment, and when it finally happened I was blocking a scene, wearing white pants. I sprinted to the dressing room, followed by the wardrobe lady, my mother, Eve's mother, and others, everyone whispering, "She started her period." It felt like an exclamation point.

When I noticed Eve that first season getting boobs, I had a minor girlie fit. She was younger than me by two years. Although it was barely noticeable (and not even anything producers had to hide yet), I thought it was unfair that she should start to pop out before me. With three mothers standing by as I had my meltdown, I received plenty of advice and consolation. Mine would come, they said.

I could only hope and pray it came soon.

The first of our eventual 117 episodes premiered on Friday, September 26, 1969, airing at eight P.M. on ABC. I watched it at home. After dinner, my whole family gathered around the TV set. It was the first time I remember all of us watching anything together since Robert Kennedy's assassination the previous year. The mood in the room was decidedly happier while watching *The Brady Bunch*. I think my brother Denny was the first person to ever turn to me and say, "You're Marcia Brady!"

And so I was, but I can't say I was 100 percent happy about it. To be honest, I was slightly embarrassed after the generally poor reviews came out. I wished I could have been on a hipper show. Even though *The Brady Bunch* became a Friday-night staple, the show's ratings put it only in the top thirty. There was much more buzz about the series that aired opposite us on CBS, *Get Smart*.

At that time, television was transitioning from the conservative 1960s to the more progressive 1970s. *Laugh-In* was the country's top-rated show, followed by *Gunsmoke*, *Bonanza*, *Mayberry R.F.D.*, and *Family Affair*. *Room 222* and *The Courtship of Eddie's Father* also debuted that year. My favorite was *The Mod Squad*, the detective series starring Clarence Williams III, Peggy Lipton, and Michael Cole, who I thought was the dreamiest guy on television. I also thought Peggy Lipton was the epitome of pure, natural beauty.

When I found out *The Mod Squad* shot near us on the Paramount lot, I put myself on high alert every time I walked outside our stage. One day Eve and I were walking to lunch at the commissary when I saw Michael Cole coming toward us. My heart raced. I looked into his eyes as we passed, then I stopped, breathless, and asked Eve if she had seen what had happened.

"What?" she asked.

"He looked at me!"

"Really?"

"Oh my God!"

A thousand fantasies were born right there. I remember thinking if he ever asked me out, I was going to say yes. And if my parents said I was too young, I'd sneak out of the house anyway. In reality, I don't think Michael even slowed his step as he passed the two of us.

By this time, I also had a crush on Barry. I realized that he thought every girl had a crush on him—and to be fair, most of them did—but he liked me, too. We flirted shamelessly as we got to know each other. Nothing explicit would happen between us for a couple of seasons, but Sherwood Schwartz and his son Lloyd, also an executive producer, watched the two of us closely, wondering not *what if* but *when*.

To me, it felt like something might happen when we shot the camping show. It was our first time on location, and I tried to imagine what it would be like if Barry and I actually shared a tent overnight. The closest we came was a scene when a tent collapsed on all six of us kids. For a few moments we were close together in the dark. Suddenly there was a lot of pushing, touching, and giggling. My fingertips found Barry's arms and chest, and I felt someone's hands touch my arms and legs.

Several weeks later we shot "Vote for Brady," the episode in which Greg and Marcia run against each other for student-body president. It was one of my favorite episodes because Barry and I had so many scenes together. I also liked working closely with Bob Reed in the "Father of the Year" episode. I always had a thing for older men, including Bob, who had a lovely daughter, Caroline, from a previous marriage. I had no idea he was secretly gay. I used to imagine running off with him.

What was with us Brady kids? The following year Barry developed the hots for Florence, took her out on what he considered a dinner date, and gave her a good-night kiss. That was weird. Florence was married (though her husband spent most of the time in New York) and more than twice Barry's age. I want to believe she thought his puppy love was cute and she decided to play along. If you ask me, it's still weird.

My life couldn't have been any better. I remember spending the weekend at Eve's family's beach house and lying out in the sun with her and her beautiful older sister, Flora. We were gossiping about the boys, the show, and a thousand other subjects that interested teenage girls. Before bed, we brushed our long hair like two princesses. I could hear the surf outside. As I drifted off to sleep, I thought my life was perfect. It was like a dream.

Little did I know the nightmare was about to begin.

4

Brace Yourself

Fighting was a part of the McCormick household whether or not anyone acknowledged it, and generally we didn't. My parents were both loving, family-oriented people, and that's how we kids preferred to think of them. But the truth is, they fought. Their fights often flared into roof-shaking scream fests. My mother was stubborn and opinionated, and my father had a temper. Generally, their reasons for losing their cool with each other had to do with stress from situations with Kevin, Denny, my schedule, one of my father's various jobs, or money.

I was midway through production of that first *Brady* season when their fighting reached a whole new level, changed our family, and created emotional scars in me that I've dealt with for the rest of my life. It started after my mother found a receipt from a nearby hotel in my father's coat pocket.

Something preceded her discovery; she must have had a reason for searching my father's pockets. I was never privy to that information. In any event, she waited for him to get home from school and then all hell broke loose. Although their bedroom door was closed, I still heard the details clearly. Dad had had an affair with Kathy Pointer, a woman all of us had met. She was the mother of a student he tutored at night, and they'd been to our house for a barbecue. My father had taken her to the Canoga Park Inn, a lodge near our house.

Then my mother stormed from the bedroom, went into the kitchen, and grabbed a bottle of wine. Until then, I'd never known her to take a sip of alcohol. She planted the bottle on the counter, poured herself a glass, and gulped it down. She drank a second glass, ignoring my father as he stood next to her, accusing her of spying on him. My mother yelled at him for trying to turn the tables, then stormed off, trying to get away from him.

She stormed from room to room before pushing through the front door. From the front lawn, she turned and screamed at my father in the doorway. She didn't care if any of the neighbors heard, something she ordinarily worried about whenever they raised their voices. Then she sat on the curb, buried her head in her hands, and cried so hard her entire body shook.

By the time I ventured out to help her, she'd stopped crying. She looked at me through dazed eyes as I helped her up and back inside. The house felt cold and lonely that night. My brother Mike, now enrolled at UCLA, was managing an apartment building in Westwood. Kevin had gone out with his friends. Denny and I tried to comfort each other. We watched TV together, and every so often he turned to me and, as if reading my mind, said, "Dad had an affair with Kathy Pointer."

It was unfathomable. I thought for sure my parents would divorce. But a few nights later, while my mother was in her bedroom, my father called my brothers and me into the living room, acknowledged his affair, and then said there were reasons he'd gone outside the marriage, reasons that were justified by circumstances that us kids weren't aware of but were probably old enough to understand.

He went on to explain that he and my mother didn't have a normal husband–wife relationship. He made that admission hesitantly, as if gauging our reaction. It definitely crossed new boundaries in terms of the information about intimacy shared in our family. After a pause, he said they didn't have *any* such relationship and that in order to satisfy what he described as basic needs, he had to go someplace else.

"You don't know this about your mother," he said, "but . . ."

That's when I learned—when all of us learned—facts about my mother and her family that she had kept hidden her entire life. My father told us my mother's mother—our grandmother—had contracted syphilis, passed it to her daughter, and subsequently died from it in a mental institution. He said that my mother had been treated so that none of us would get syphilis, but he added that she'd also suffered a breakdown and received electroshock treatment when the boys were little.

My father presented and spun facts to his advantage. It was all about what he had tolerated for years. We didn't hear any of my mother's side of the story. None of her torment and shame. I can't imagine the devastation my mother must have felt as she listened to this from her bedroom. I know that after hearing that story, I never felt the same about my father, my mother, or myself.

I wish I could say that after my father's talk I ran to my mother and threw my arms around her, rejuvenating her with my unconditional love. Sadly, that didn't happen. At some point that night I did seek her out and attempt to make her feel better, but I was really more interested in looking at her for signs of syphilis.

Suddenly she was a curiosity to me. The next time the two of us were in the backseat of Susie Olsen's mother's car, I realized that I was staring at her the same way, searching for a sign or a symptom. I wanted to know what the syphilis looked like. She never brought it up, never offered an explanation, never uttered a word about it. It would be many years before we ever broached the subject.

In the meantime, my relationship with her underwent a sudden, very subtle, but dramatic change, and so did my perceptions about myself. It was all due to ignorance and the inability of any of us to discuss this seismic jolt our family had received. Following my father's revelation, I felt embarrassed about my mother. It's terrible to admit even now. But I didn't like being around her in public, especially among the other mothers on the *Brady* set. I knew she didn't fit in with them, and now I thought I knew the reason. It was because of her syphilis. I figured everyone could see it.

Granted, I had yet to see signs of it—later, I would learn she did suffer long-term effects, including bad eyes, thin hair, and physical frailty—but I was sure other people noticed.

Even worse, I took the few facts I knew and used them to convince myself that I was also infected with syphilis. I ignored my father's claim that my mother had received treatments to prevent transmission. I told myself that it ran in the family. My mother's mother suffered from syphilis, then she passed it to my mother, and thus it made sense that I was infected, too.

I knew exactly what that meant. Like my mother and her mother before her, I was destined to go insane. Both of them had ended up in mental institutions. It was only a matter of time, I reasoned, before the same thing happened to me.

I wasn't entirely wrong. By believing that I had syphilis, I inherited all the same emotional problems that had plagued my mother, namely the debilitating psychological side effects of carrying around a secret. I was suddenly filled with dread, shame, and fear, feelings that grew worse over time. When I went back to work, we were shooting "Brace Yourself," the episode in which Marcia gets braces. It was a story about self-image.

How fitting! My self-image was in crisis mode. Susie remembers me as suddenly different. According to her, the change was subtle but noticeable. It was like I had my head in the clouds. My attention drifted. Chris Knight even made fun of me a few times for that reason.

But I *was* different. I remember being in the dressing room, the same as always, except this time I felt as if everyone was looking at my mother and me. I felt as if they could see signs of the syphilis in both of us (it felt obvious to me), but I wasn't going to say anything in case they couldn't. Then the producers sent me to an orthodontist to get real braces put on my teeth. I was against that idea; why stand out even more?

When I returned to the set, Barry, Chris, Eve, and the others said my teeth were going to be marked for life. I really felt, as Marcia said in the script, ugly, ugly, ugly.

If only they knew what was going on with me, I thought.

I was required to cry in several scenes, and I summoned the tears easily. It was the first time I'd cried since witnessing my parents' fight and convincing myself that syphilis had made me a ticking time bomb. Little did anyone on the *Brady* set know my tears were real and it felt so good to cry.

At the end of January 1970, the show took a brief hiatus as producers waited to hear if the network was going to pick it up for a second season. This also gave the writers time to finish scripts for the remaining episodes. During the break, I traveled to Washington, D.C., with TV host Art Linkletter and three other child actors for a TV special called *A Kid's Eye View of Washington*.

With cameras following, the four of us toured the sites of our nation's capital and got a bird's-eye view of the corridors of government. Among our stops were John F. Kennedy's gravesite at Arlington and the Smithsonian, where I tried on the 98.6-carat Bismarck sapphire. Armed guards stood around me as the necklace was placed around my neck. We also took an aerial tour of the city in the presidential helicopter.

The highlight of this amazing trip was a face-to-face with the president of the United States, Richard Nixon. He met us in the Oval Office. The whole thing was carefully choreographed for the TV special. Each of us was supposed to ask President Nixon a question. We rehearsed them before arriving at the White House and we continued to practice as we waited for the president.

Then President Nixon entered the room. I remember thinking he looked exactly as he did on TV, something people probably said about me. He wore a suit and tie and appeared to be relaxed and friendly, though he still seemed stiff. I assumed he had been briefed about our questions and had prepared answers. I said that I was concerned about the state of the world and I wondered what kind of shape he thought it would be in when I was old enough to vote. Then one of the other kids asked him to name the first president of the United States. Nixon replied, "Abraham Lincoln."

What?

I quickly glanced at my mother and the welfare worker/teacher from the show, Frances Whitfield, who had accompanied me on the trip and were standing off to the side. Other nervous glances were exchanged.

Then President Nixon realized his error and said, "Oh my gosh, no. It was George Washington."

All of us laughed. It proved that presidents, as Art Linkletter might've said if that slip had been shown on TV, also say the darnedest things.

The last show of the first season was "The Possible Dream." In it, Marcia loses her diary, in which she has written about her dream of becoming Mrs. Desi Arnez Jr. Desi guested on the episode, and, oh my God, he was so cute. I didn't have to act when I said I had a crush on him.

Then the first season was finished. I hated saying good-bye even though I knew we would be back for another season. My eyes were full of tears as my mother and I drove away from the Paramount lot. The following week I was supposed to return to regular school for the remaining two months of the school year. That also meant returning to my real life as Maureen, not Marcia—and I wasn't sure that was a good thing.

5

Marcia, Marcia, Marcia!

I felt out of place returning to Hughes Junior High for the last few months of eighth grade. I wasn't interested in schoolwork, and I felt out of step socially. I had friends, but there was still the problem of feeling on display. Other girls stared, and I heard comments about my clothes. People whispered behind my back as if I didn't have ears. *Look, she's the one who plays Marcia Brady.*

I used to go through the day wishing I was back on the set, and then, when I was at home, I wished I was someplace else. Mostly I wished I was more like my brother Mike, older and living on my own. When he had returned from Europe the previous year, my parents told me that he had to pay rent unless he went back to school. He turned into a dynamo of ambition, enrolling in UCLA, getting a job in their film and TV department, and managing an apartment building.

I envied his independence. At home, I resented my parents for ruining my comfort and the trust I'd had in them. They had a difficult time recovering from my father's affair. He openly resented my mother, and she had major trust issues that she didn't try to conceal. Since nobody talked about these problems, I was left to figure them out for myself. It caused me to look at my home life in a different, more critical light. Maybe I compared my family too closely with the Bradys', but I knew things at home were kind of weird, definitely not normal, and I blamed my mother.

She didn't cook or clean—nor did she have an Alice to do it for her like Carol Brady did. She wouldn't spend money or throw anything out. We had stacks of newspapers and magazines throughout the house. I hated the mess. I didn't want to bring friends home or invite anyone to sleep over. Why didn't anyone else care?

My mother was on top of things in other ways that I wouldn't know about or understand for years. For all her worrying, or perhaps because of it, she was an astute businesswoman, with an especially sharp eye for real estate. After stretching my father's income, she invested any leftovers in rental properties. She also took care of the money I earned. I had no idea. Most of the time I wondered why she was content with worn furniture and items she and my father bought at garage sales. Why, I wondered, wasn't she like other mothers who bought new clothes and got their hair done?

Was that the reason my father had an affair?

I wondered.

One night my father came home and declared himself a changed man, the result, he said, of seeing Jesus.

I saw my mother roll her eyes. I didn't know what to think.

My father explained that he had been talking to the mother of a student he tutored at the clinic he ran after school when all of a sudden he saw her face morph into that of Jesus, who then spoke to him. Again, I didn't know how to react, whether to think he was crazy or the coolest guy in the neighborhood. My mother looked skeptical. My father leaned forward and reiterated that Jesus had spoken directly to him. It wasn't a vision, he said. It was real.

"He said, 'Who are you to judge lest you be judged?'" He inhaled deeply and looked at us—my mother, Kevin, Denny, and me. *"Who are you to judge lest you be judged."*

None of us had to worry about interpreting the meaning of this experience. My father explained that he'd made certain assumptions about this woman based on her appearance and lack of money. But Jesus had warned him not to make false judgments based on superficial observations. What did he really know about her? Didn't she work hard? Didn't she want a good education for her son?

"So who am I to judge?" my father asked.

After that night, my father went through a phase where he regularly preached to us, as if we needed saving. At dinner, he talked about his rebirth as a Christian. Some nights he spoke in a calm voice. Other nights he was moved to tears. My mother vacillated between engagement, anger, and boredom. Denny wasn't able to comprehend it. Though I should've been freaked out, and who knows, I may have been, I can't really remember, I do recall being affected by his persuasiveness. This was particularly true when, as weeks went by, he applied this argument to his affair.

He was right, I thought. Who was I to judge?

Though some nights my father got so worked up talking about Jesus at the table that we thought he might cross over into crazy land, I eventually came around and believed him. I also excused him for straying with Kathy Pointer. I blamed my mother. In thinking back, it amazes me that I didn't apply my father's who-was-I-to-judge theory to her. As far as I was concerned, she was responsible. If not directly, she was at fault circumstantially. It was the disease, the syphilis.

It pains me to write it even now, but I looked at her as if she were infected, dirty, weak, and responsible for passing the disease on to me.

As all that unfolded, I gave an interview to a fan magazine. I provided a list of my "turn-ons," including shopping for new clothes, ice-skating, dancing, Michael Cole, old-fashioned dolls, singing, jumping on a trampoline, happy people, and flowers. It shows that I was a typical teenage girl in so many ways. It wasn't just a part I played on TV. I really was that person.

But there was more to me than those photos in *16* and *Tiger Beat* magazines let on. More than anyone knew—or would ever know. There was a deeper, darker layer, someone known only to me. I was resigned to keeping it that way, just as my mother had been, just as I was resigned to the fact I would eventually go insane.

After the dismal hiatus, I was bursting with anticipation when production for the second season of *The Brady Bunch* started in the summer of 1970. As I returned to the studio, I felt like I was finally going back home, the place where I felt more comfortable and normal. There really seemed to be magic to the big iron gates that separated Paramount from the outside world. It was a figment of my imagination, but I felt like whatever problems I had were checked at the guard gate. Even the three hours of school we kids attended daily was better than a full day of regular school.

Stage 5 was filled with hugs and kisses as we reunited. All the Brady kids, as we were dubbed, looked a little older after the break. Barry seemed to have filled out some, maybe even grown taller. As much as Eve and I were friends, I didn't want her boobs to be bigger or her tummy to be flatter than mine. Our stomachs both had a little round pooch and her boobs hadn't grown any more noticeable, so I was happy to see mine still had time to catch up.

Our first show that season was called "Going, Going . . . Steady." In it, Marcia set out to snag bespectacled bug collector Harvey Klinger. Nothing against Bill Corcoran, who got the part (and went on to have a busy directing career as an adult), but after ending the previous season by making eyes at Desi Arnez Jr., I was hoping for another pop star. My disappointment was short-lived. A week later we were on to another episode—and I'm sure I had another crush.

Older men also intrigued me: Fred MacMurray, Bob Reed, and Michael Cole. I also thought Barry Williams's father was cool, too. Then I developed a thing for Jack Klugman and Tony Randall, the stars of *The Odd Couple*. Who didn't adore them? Their series was shot on the Paramount lot. On more than a few occasions I chatted with them as we stood in line to get food at a cart near our sets, and I left thinking wow, that Jack Klugman is neat.

As we got into the year, I also liked our script supervisor, Alan Rudolph, who went on to assist Robert Altman and then direct and write more than twenty films, including *Welcome to L.A.* and *Made in Heaven*. In his mid-twenties, he never knew I liked him. His father, Oscar, was one of our regular directors. He was a sweet man, but before each take he turned to us kids as if we were circus animals and chirped, "Up! Up! Up!" We used to make fun of him.

My favorite show that second season was "The Slumber Caper," a Brady classic in which a sleepover Marcia has planned is canceled after she gets in trouble at school for allegedly writing an insulting caption about her teacher on an art project. Would Marcia do something like that? Never.

After she appeals to her father, the slumber party is back on. Her brothers break out the itching powder, and then one of her friends ends up confessing to having sabotaged Marcia's art project with the nasty caption. The best parts in the episode happened off camera with the girls who played my friends: Bob Reed's daughter Carolyn, Sherwood's daughter Hope, and Florence's daughter Barbara.

Yes, nepotism was alive and well on the Brady set—and that was fine with me. We were around the same age, and all of us got along famously. We joked endlessly between takes, gossiped (I revealed that I always felt sexy when I wore my pajamas on the set), and laughed hardest upon discovering that each one of us had a crush on Barry. If only he had known. I remember getting into my sleeping bag and wishing he could join me for some cuddling.

Barbara, Hope, and I stayed friends away from the set and had several slumber parties that summer. I was awed by the home the Hendersons had rented. It was in Beverly Hills, and it had a beautiful swimming pool. It still comes to mind when I picture a mansion. One afternoon Barbara and I were lying out by the pool when Florence joined us.

Florence loved to swim, and she looked terrific in a bikini. I used to stare at her figure, impressed. She was a little bit of a closeted sexpot. This time she underscored that impression by whipping off her top. I hid my surprise as she chatted with us, went for a dip, and then sat in the sun.

After a few more times at their house, I was used to her going topless. In fact, it was the rare occasion where she didn't. She had great boobs, too. And they were real!

I n August, I celebrated my fourteenth birthday—and the arrival of more of a womanly figure when I looked in the mirror. My excitement was short-lived, though. I was bummed out when the new fall TV lineup started in September and ABC's Friday-night lineup, which was kicked off by *The Brady Bunch,* included two new shows that I thought were much better, *The Partridge Family* and *That Girl.*

Like every girl my age that I knew, I fell in love with Marlo Thomas. I thought in a few years I could be just like her, just like *that girl:* an actress, with my own apartment, cute clothes, and a boyfriend like Donald Hollinger.

I had a harder time with *The Partridge Family.* After seeing it, I said to myself, "Where the heck did that show come from?" Not only was it another family sitcom with a brood of kids, they also sang. And they were cool! If not cool in the counterculture sense, they were definitely cooler than us. It made me jealous. Furthermore, I thought Susan Dey was the hippest-looking chick I'd seen since Peggy Lipton. If I could've snapped my fingers, I would've turned myself into her and then grown up to be Marlo Thomas later.

I don't remember any of the other Bradys talking about those new shows. On the set, Bob Reed waged a one-man war with Sherwood and Lloyd to keep the show from losing all credibility. He was always clear. Even if people watched, the actors couldn't be insulted with scripts that defied reality. For Bob, the litmus test was always reality.

Did it look real? Was it real? It was to his credit as an actor that he gave the silly comedy as much believability as possible. But it was a daily fight, and every so often he would blow up or send off a scathing memo to Sherwood, as he did after an episode titled "The Impractical Joker," about the "downgrade of quality," "inconsistency in style and performance," "loss of time due to rewriting," and "bad performances by frustrated actors."

Poor Bob. He wanted to make it Shakespeare. He used to go outside and smoke through his frustrations. During our last season, he would take extended trips to a tiny bar just beyond the studio gates. Florence had a different attitude. She was there for a good time—and a good living. She was a free spirit. She and Bob were very different, yet they had great chemistry.

Ann B. Davis was an island of calm amid waters that were always churning with something. She was a two-time Emmy winner for her work on *The Bob Cummings Show,* a master when it came to comedic timing. No one in the cast hit their mark as often. It was rumored she didn't like working with kids. I never thought that was true; she couldn't have been kinder to me. She was just quiet. Between scenes, she sat in a chair off to the side, working on a needlepoint project, happy as a lark.

Like Alice, she observed all the shenanigans that went on around her. Barry, now sixteen, rode a minibike around the lot. He also had a pack-a-day cigarette habit. He didn't think anyone noticed when he snuck away for a smoke. Susie later told me that Eve was jealous of the attention I got and felt as if she were in my shadow. If that was true, I had no idea. Eve was my best friend. We spent hours in the dressing room discussing fashion, music, and our favorite Beatle (mine was John, and I believe she liked Paul).

I spent that Christmas in New York with Florence and her family. She and her then husband, Broadway producer Ira Bernstein, lived in a magnificent apartment across from Central Park. It was the best trip of my life, and I would've felt the same way even if we had done half as much shopping. At the end of the second season, Eve's family invited me to go with them to Europe. I thought I was living the life of a jet-setter. But my parents said no; they were scared to let me travel that far.

I was envious when a postcard from Eve arrived in the mail. It was from Paris. She wrote the note in French. She said the city was *très intéressante* and that she and her family walked along the Champs-Élysées. *Quelle distance!* She said it was warm but windy there, and French was hard to understand but . . . *ça, c'est la vie!*

I finished ninth grade at Hughes. Feeling more grown up and worldly, as well as less academically inclined, I fell in with a fast crowd. I dated a couple boys and had my first kisses on the hill behind the school. Those affected me. As we started the third season of the show, I remember giving Susie's older sister tips on how to pick up boys on the beach. Listening, Eve laughed at me. She asked what I knew about guys. I told her about my make-out sessions behind the school. Susie asked what it was like.

"Great," I said.

We were growing up.

We began the third season by shooting a three-parter about the Bradys vacationing in the Grand Canyon. The story was typical: The Bradys were stranded in a ghost town, Bobby and Cindy got lost at the bottom of the canyon, and then we helped out an Indian boy who saved the day. It was fun to be on location. Barry described these road-trip episodes as being "as close to *Easy Rider* as *The Brady Bunch* would ever get." Too bad; I could have gone for a skinny-dipping scene with Barry. Unfortunately there were too many parents around for anything like that to happen.

Glenita, our wardrobe lady, was heavily into turquoise, and she draped Florence, Eve, Susan, and me in jewelry. I thought the beads made me look like a hippie, closer to the way I imagined Susan Dey to be. It was during that trip that I noticed my boobs were finally and noticeably bigger than Eve's, though she was curvier. As the season progressed, we tried to wear our skirts as short as possible. When they got too short, Glenita or Lloyd let us know we needed to change. Still, when I rewatched some of those episodes, I glimpsed Eve's and my underpants a few times.

We cranked out the episodes, one a week for more than half the year. We had no idea which ones would take on a life of their own or which lines would be repeated for decades. To me, the episode entitled "Her Sister's Shadow" was just one of many, the fifty-fifth we had made over three seasons. Even the story line was vaguely repetitive: Jan was jealous of her seemingly perfect sister Marcia. But Act One of that show will be remembered in the annals of Brady history for that moment when a frustrated Jan turns away from her older sister and says, "All I ever hear is Marcia, Marcia, Marcia!"

Who knew? None of us had any idea that that line, written by veteran comedy scribe Ben Starr, would take on a life of its own. Ever since that show aired, I can legitimately say, "All I ever hear is Marcia, Marcia, Marcia."

I'm serious. People in airports have passed me and said, "Hi, Marcia, Marcia, Marcia." Waitresses have asked, "What can I get you, Marcia, Marcia, Marcia?" I have heard it in bathrooms, the grocery store, on Fox News. I've heard it adapted to Martha Stewart: Martha, Martha, Martha! I lost track long ago of the number of women who have stopped me and said, "I'm sorry to bother you, but can I just say it?"

Midway through the season, we shot one of my favorite episodes of all time, "Getting Davy Jones." As the head of Fernwood Junior High's Davy Jones Fan Club, Marcia is responsible for getting the impossibly cute lead singer from the Monkees to appear at their prom, and after various miscommunications and lots of worry, she comes through. The show on which Jones actually made an appearance had aired from 1965 to 1968. The made-for-TV band officially broke up shortly before we taped the show, but they were still extremely popular, and Davy's arrival on the set created a buzz greater than any other guest star we had on the show.

Of course I was thrilled to be the one who got to interact with him. I can see why Eve could get jealous. Davy was a lovely guy, and it was a big deal to have a pop star of his caliber on the set. I noticed Barry watch him the way one might if looking for pointers. Though excited to be the object of his affection, or rather attention, I didn't show it. I'd learned to play it cool around stars.

My heart fluttered when he kissed me at the end, I'll admit it, but Peter Tork was always my favorite Monkee. That was the difference between Marcia and me. She was predictable, a straight arrow. My taste was quirky, offbeat, and different. At fifteen, I felt ready to experiment.

6

Time to Change

Barry was ready to experiment, too. One look in his eyes and I knew he was thinking his moment had finally arrived. I'm not talking about jumping my bones. That happened later. No, we were three-quarters of the way through the third season when we arrived at episode 64, a show that was Barry's unofficial coming out as a singer—and I was all for it because the rest of us were along for the ride.

Titled "Dough Re Mi," the show featured Greg writing a song that he was certain would turn him into a pop star. The song was called "We Can Make the World a Whole Lot Brighter." When he didn't have enough money to buy studio time, his siblings split the cost in exchange for singing backup. Then there was a second twist: Peter had a lousy voice. But Greg solved that problem not only by writing another song, "Time to Change," but also by incorporating his brother's adolescent squeaks.

Genius!

Suddenly the Brady kids had two songs. It wasn't enough for an album, but you only needed two for a 45. It looked like we were taking on the Partridges. Thinking about it, wouldn't it have been funny if the two families had toured together and Alice and Reuben Kincaid had fallen in love?

Anyway, it was clearly a ploy by Sherwood and Lloyd to expand the Bradys into other businesses. The previous year we'd recorded a Christmas album. It tested the water. After this episode, it was decided that we would record another album, this one straight-ahead pop and rock, and then tour. Barry was thrilled. All of us were excited. I felt like every dream I had was coming true. As for the bad stuff I worried about, well, this seemed to confirm that it didn't apply in this world of make-believe.

In reality, it was Marcia Brady taking over my life or vice versa, me associating my identity more and more with Marcia. I didn't think I was Marcia. It was just my point of reference. Everything I did revolved around Marcia. She consumed my life in a way that would leave me rudderless and wondering who I was years later when the show ended. Life really was Marcia, Marcia, Marcia. I got up, went to the studio, put in a full day, came home, and memorized lines. If we weren't shooting, I was doing PR or attending events. Now the schedule included singing. That was fine with me. I loved to sing. I had done it professionally on commercials since I was little, and I knew my voice sounded good.

We went into the studio and recorded an album featuring the two songs from the show and covers of a handful of recent soft-rock hits including "American Pie," "Day After Day," and "Me and You and a Dog Named Boo." Professional singers were brought in to cover Chris's parts (in real life, he had a terrible voice) and sweeten our vocals, though I thought Barry and I pulled off our solos with total credibility within the range of our abilities.

As soon as we finished the season, we began rehearsing for a tour. Then we hit the road. Barry took it very seriously, worked extremely hard, and got upset at me for not seeming to embrace it to the same degree as he had. I was trying, though not hard enough to satisfy him. He was driven.

"Do you know what we could become?" he said to me one day during a break in rehearsals.

I did. I loved the singing and dancing as much as he did, and I even thought it might be a new career. It seemed possible. Eve's father was in the music business. David Cassidy was huge. Others on TV cut albums and performed. So it was easy to get swept up in that kind of talk. This opportunity fascinated my brother Kevin, who'd taught himself to play guitar and mused about the two of us writing songs and cutting our own album. We'd talk about that idea for years.

My interest in boys took a more serious turn around this time when I began going out with a guy named Joe. He was my first serious boyfriend. He had blond hair, dark skin, and amazing eyes and lips. On top of all that, he drove a Corvette. He was what we called a hot guy. He ran with a different, older crowd than I was used to. I liked being with him, but I always had the feeling I wasn't fast enough for him.

It turned out I was right. One day a friend of mine said that he found out Joe was dating another girl at the same time as he was dating me. In other words, I was being two-timed. Infuriated, I wanted to confront Joe and let him have a piece of my mind. But then, as I thought about it, I got curious about who this other girl was who interested my boyfriend as much if not more than me. I wanted to see my competition.

My friend drove me to her house, and we sat in his VW van at the end of her driveway, waiting until she came in or out. Within a short time, she walked out of the house. I was ready for a confrontation, except she looked nice. I got out of the van, went up to her, introduced myself, and we talked. The darnedest thing happened. Carin—that was her name—and I became best friends.

Both of us dropped Joe. Carin and I became inseparable. I met her friends. They were Encino girls, wealthier and faster than my crowd in Woodland Hills. Her parents welcomed me as if I were a member of the family. I adored her mother. It was a very different household than mine. Carin taught me to smoke, and one night, as we sat around in her bedroom, she gave me a frank talk about the facts of life. She was quite detailed in her description.

J oe Seiter and Ray Reese, veterans from the Osmonds' tour, produced our show. The moves were slick, but our mothers made our costumes. We also traveled in station wagons rather than limousines. Like most things Brady, it was a mostly homespun effort. But you couldn't start out any bigger than us. Our first public performance was a benefit for the American Guild of Variety Artists at Caesars Palace in Las Vegas. Ed Sullivan hosted, and the headliners included Sonny and Cher, Lily Tomlin, Danny Thomas, and Edwin the Elephant. Naturally, we followed the elephant—and yes, thanks to Edwin, we had to watch our step on the stage.

I was enamored of Sonny and Cher. I couldn't take my eyes off Cher. It was the first time I had been around a woman who thoroughly mesmerized people, who commanded your attention with her looks. We were introduced to her backstage. She was with her daughter, Chastity, a tiny blond cherub with her mother's expressions. Eve held Chastity's hand and sweetly asked, "Can you say *elephant*?"

Before she could respond, Cher cracked, "She can say a hell of a lot more than elephant, that's for sure."

We also appeared on *The Mike Douglas Show*. Liberace was his co-host that week, and he fell in love with us. He looked at Susie and said, "Doesn't she have the cutest lips?" People applauded. "Say something," he said.

"Something," Susie said, getting a big laugh.

Afterward, Liberace invited us to his show and then said he wanted to take us on tour as his opening act. But our tour was already lined up, and Tony Orlando & Dawn opened for us. (Side Note: I had a mad crush on Tony, who could've tied a yellow ribbon around me without complaint.) We officially opened our tour at the San Bernardino Orange Show, an annual event hosted that year by *American Bandstand*'s legendary Dick Clark. We followed that with state fairs and concert halls all over the country: Savannah, Raleigh, Knoxville, Atlantic City, Portland, Seattle, San Francisco.

It was our first real taste of stardom, of our popularity beyond our neighborhoods at home. Until then, we had been pretty much stuck to the Paramount lot and doing magazine interviews. That changed as we traveled across the country. It was like Bradymania everyplace we went. In San Jose, we were scheduled to make an appearance at a mall, but the crowd was so large the architect was called to see if the balconies could support the weight. A town in the South closed school for the day. At various stops, I had hair torn out of my head, beads ripped from my costume, and at one stop in the South fans pushed past security and knocked over our Winnebago.

With parents and welfare workers watching us closely, we didn't stray or get into trouble. But Eve and I still managed to sneak off to smoke cigarettes. We thought we were being clever by spraying our mouths with Binaca. Only Chris Knight's mom, Willie, knew about our nasty habit, and she didn't care. She even bought us packs. Eve paraded around the dressing room without any clothes on. Susie and I were floored by the sight of our long-legged sister fluttering about stark naked. She also farted all the time. When we asked her not to do either one, she tossed back her hair and said, "Oh, get over it."

Our show was fast and busy, with lots of lineup shuffles and costume changes. We changed clothes in makeshift rooms off to the side of the stage, boys and girls next to one another separated only by a flimsy curtain that offered glimpses of the other side through thin separations in the panels of hanging fabric. I remember a lot of intentional flashing between camps—and some unintentional glimpses, too. I saw legs, some butts in their tighty whities, and bare chests—but never any full frontal.

One night as I hurried back onto the stage after a quick change into my yellow beaded halter costume, I was greeted by a blinding burst of flashing camera bulbs. That was normal, but this instance seemed more intense. I had a feeling something was going on. I looked down and saw that one side of my halter had slipped, completely exposing one of my boobs. I wanted to die.

Every night Barry and I dueted on the James Taylor/Carole King classic "You've Got a Friend." He always came out onstage by himself and did the first verse. Then I joined him. We stood on opposite sides of the stage, inching slowly toward the center. Finally, we turned and sang to each other. It was choreographed to be a romantic moment, and there was so much sexual tension between us we didn't have to pretend. The crowd loved it.

But one time when Barry turned to face me, I saw tiny rivers of black dripping from his hair down his face. It was his hair dye. Under the hot lights and with all the sweat, it was melting off his hair. I cracked up so hard that I couldn't get out the words to the song. What struck me as even funnier was that he had no idea it was happening, and he gave me dirty looks as he sang. I knew he wanted me to pull myself together. But I couldn't. He was so serious, so into his act, so involved in the effort to make himself the next David Cassidy, and yet his face was streaked with black hair dye. Although I apologized afterward, he was angry at me for a long time—maybe for a whole day. But all was forgiven by the time we regrouped for season four.

Like the previous season, we began with a multiparter on location. Instead of the Grand Canyon, though, we went to Hawaii. Hawaii was one of my dream destinations. I freaked out with excitement. My family didn't go on vacations. When I was four, my parents took off for the weekend and the house nearly burned down after the lint in the dryer caught on fire, and they never left us alone again.

The flight over the Pacific went by quickly, but I worried for the duration of the five-and-a-half-hour flight about wearing a bikini on camera. What almost sixteen-year-old girl wouldn't have felt the same way? I thought I had good legs, shoulders, and boobs, but I was self-conscious about my hips. I also had a little pooch. No matter how much I dieted or how many sit-ups I did, I never had a flat stomach.

Everything else was pretty good. Why couldn't I have a flat stomach, too?

Florence had one. So did Susan Dey and Peggy Lipton. (It would be interesting to know how those women felt about their figures; all I saw was perfection versus my imperfection.) Everyone I admired had a flat stomach. Nowadays I would give anything to have the stomach I had back then. I was nuts to have spent one second worrying about it, but hey, I had bikini scenes to do. The funny thing was, I ended up holding a towel in front of my stomach in every shot in which I wore a bathing suit.

Anyway, we stayed at the Pink Royal Hawaiian Hotel in Oahu. The surroundings took my breath away. I had never stayed anywhere as beautiful. And talk about romantic! There was the air . . . the water . . . and Barry's blue eyes.

As soon as I stepped off the plane, I started to think about him more intensely, in the way I had fantasized for a long time. We had spent the past three and a half years staving off the desire of a mutual attraction despite the intimacy of working closely with each other every day. We had gone out to dinner plenty of times, played guitar together, and early on we had even sort of double-dated with Florence's daughter and Barry's brother Scott.

An actual romance had yet to happen, though. Heck, till that point, we had never even kissed. Maybe it was the intoxicating effect of the tropical air, but I knew Hawaii was going to be different, and it was.

It was our second full day on the island, and we had finished work but were all still gathered on the beach when Lloyd Schwartz came over to Barry and me as we chatted and suggested that the two of us take a walk together down the beach. Lloyd gestured toward the hotel, which was visible in the distance. I think he wanted us to have some fun, though I don't believe he knew the force of our attraction. Barry and I looked at each other, grinned, and strolled off.

Our shoulders bumped and touched as we walked. Wordlessly, we fell into a slow, easy step and stared at the gorgeous sunset. It was a picture-perfect Hawaiian moment. When we felt comfortably away from the set, he slipped his arm around me and I slid mine around his waist. As we neared our hotel, we turned toward each other, and kissed. We couldn't hold back any longer.

It was our first kiss, and it was long, passionate, and deep. It was wonderful, too, though as we continued to kiss and press against each other so closely that we could feel each other's body heat, a part of me—a tiny part, admittedly—said to myself, "Oh my God! I'm kissing my brother. What am I doing?"

I didn't care.

I knew exactly what I was doing. Barry was a good kisser. Lloyd Schwartz may have regretted it later on when he spotted us back in the hotel. Though Barry and I snuck off for several more private moments, Lloyd kept a close eye on us the rest of the trip, making sure nothing serious happened on his watch.

It didn't matter. I knew that I would go back home not feeling like it was time to change, but the fact was that I had already changed. But of course I had no idea the extent to which that would be true.

7

The Mine Shaft

Our romance carried back to the mainland. For our first show back in L.A., an episode entitled "Today I Am a Freshman," Barry and I had more than the usual number of scenes together, and we couldn't have been happier. I'm sure all eyes were on us; however, we were oblivious. There was so much electricity between us that I felt the hair on my arms stand up every time we got close to each other on the set. I thought about Barry even when I had scenes with other guys. I used to ask myself how I could ever look in eyes other than his liquid blues and feel such love.

We had real feelings for each other, but at our ages—I turned sixteen in August, and he was eighteen a month later—and given our unique situation, our relationship turned out to be more of an on-and-off-again game. That was trying whenever I saw Barry's new girlfriend of the month; they were always beautiful; but I wasn't ready to be tied down to a single guy, not even one I liked as much as Barry.

At that point, I was dreaming of my own adventures—and planning one, too. The previous summer, while I had been out on tour, my brothers Mike and Kevin had ventured off to Europe for a seven-month journey. It had started out as Mike's trip, and my parents persuaded him to take Kevin. When they left, there were four of them—Mike, his friend Milt, Kevin, and his buddy Drew.

Until that time, my brothers had been close for much of their life, though Mike hadn't seen much of Kevin while he'd been at UCLA. Once they got to Europe, Mike was alarmed when Kevin and Drew just wanted to get drunk every night. Mike and Milt wanted to travel and meet girls. After a month, Milt returned home. He couldn't take it any longer.

Mike, Kevin, and Drew traveled through Spain and France. Mike smoked pot with the other two, but he drew the line when it came to other drugs. Kevin and Drew wanted speed and various pills. They also talked about doing heroin, but Mike never saw either of them do it.

While he was in Spain, Mike had fallen in love with a German girl named Hella. Missing her and tired of the druggie life in Paris, he drove to northern Germany and visited Hella for the next few months. When he returned to France to check on Kevin, he nearly got into a fight with Drew, who was so drunk he couldn't walk. Kevin and Drew were also out of money.

After lending them cash, Mike returned to the United States. A short time later, Kevin and Drew followed—they needed money for plane tickets wired to them. Kevin was different when he got back. The whole family dynamic changed as Kevin came and went without any apparent direction. By contrast, Mike was focused and in love. His girlfriend visited the summer I returned from Hawaii.

I liked Hella immediately. She was cute, blond, and European. She breathed a new and different kind of life into our family. She took a strong interest in me, probably since I was the only girl and offered a fun perspective on my brother. I loved talking to her and listening to her German accent. I opened up about my desire to see the world. I'm sure I sounded very naive, maybe even silly. But Hella understood.

Before leaving, she invited me to visit her on my next break in the fall. She promised to show me a good time and take me on a trip.

Finally, in late September, I flew to Germany. Hella picked me up at the airport and drove me to her house in the country. As soon as she got on the autobahn, I thought I was going to die in a car crash. Like everyone else, she drove wildly fast—much faster than the law allowed in Los Angeles. But it proved to be a fitting start to the trip, like a rocket taking me to a new planet.

We stayed at her house for a few days. It was pure 1970s European vacation; every day I saw something that made my eyes bug out, made me feel older and more mature, or both of the above. Everything was free and open. I can't remember where we were, a summer-resort-like spot, but I saw people walking around naked. But that was merely a warm-up for our next stop.

Hella took me to Amsterdam, where—well, just oh my God. I uttered those words so often that they became meaningless. For the first time in my life, I got drunk. I also went into my first gay bar, where a couple of young men seemed to recognize me but didn't care as they hurried off to the dance floor. One especially flamboyant and friendly guy wanted my opinion on his nail polish. He also had me smell his perfume. Since I had already gotten past my shock at seeing guys dancing and kissing one another, I snuggled in for a sniff and made friends.

The next day Hella took me to a lesbian bar. I was fascinated—not just with the women but with what I referred to as "the other side" of life. I think it was a fascination with people who were able to be themselves, something I wasn't able to be even at sixteen. How, I wondered, did these women know who they were? How were they able to figure out what they wanted and liked? Some were gorgeous, too. I don't know why that struck me, but it did. Several flirted with me.

"They like you," Hella said, laughing.

I laughed, too. I was having fun.

Was I also intrigued? Yes. It was impossible not to be intrigued in that environment. It was intoxicating. Hella literally had to grab me and pull me out. As I told her, I wanted to stay there all night.

"Really?" she said.

"Just to watch," I added.

I returned full of stories about the places I'd been to and the action I'd seen in the bars and on the streets of Amsterdam. I thought I sounded grown up, but it turned out I wasn't as worldly as I thought. One day on the set I was describing the gay bars to Florence and Barry. I was my usual gushy self, boasting how I had flirted with gay men *and* women. I was touting my acceptance of homosexuals. I think I even said something along the lines of how amazing it was since I had never met anyone who was gay when suddenly Barry interrupted.

"You know Bob is gay, don't you?" he said.

Florence nodded.

I stared at the two of them, shocked. "What?"

"He's gay," said Barry.

I turned to Florence for confirmation. She nodded again.

"I'm not kidding. I've tried to get him excited in bed scenes," she said. "He's not interested."

Apparently I was the last one, or rather the only one, on the set who didn't know about Bob. Eve shrugged when I mentioned it to her. She didn't care. She gave me her get-over-it look. Susie said she'd found out the previous season. I was incredulous. I don't know why, but I would still need a few years before I stopped dreaming that the two of us would run off together someday.

I also needed to work through the episode "Greg's Triangle." The plot was exactly as it sounds, with a little cheerleading drama concerning Marcia to complicate matters. Basically, Greg had two beautiful girlfriends. One was played by actress Tannis Montgomery, and the other role went to Rita Wilson, who went on to star in movies and marry Tom Hanks. From my perspective, Barry simply enjoyed himself way too much around both of those girls. Even though we were on again and off again, I got jealous. On the set, I felt proprietary. I gave him dirty looks the entire week.

Then I was swept up into something new. After returning home from Europe, Mike opened a nightclub. He had talked about it for a couple years, observing, correctly it would turn out, that the West Valley lacked a cool nightspot where you could hear great live music, hang out, drink, and dance. There were numerous places like that in Hollywood and on the Sunset Strip, but none near us.

Like my father, Mike had a knack for coming up with good ideas. Unlike my father, he had better follow-through. Not that my father was irresponsible. It's just that Mike was tenacious; he stuck with things for a longer time. I have to give credit to my father, though. He urged Mike to pursue his dream; he was even the one who went out and found a space for the club in Calabasas.

Just like that, it seemed, the idea of this nightclub turned into a reality and it took over our lives. Mike was ready, too. He was living at home, but serious about Hella, who came out and stayed with him. Mike had about $7,000 in savings. He borrowed $3,000 from the teachers' union. My parents lent him $10,000. And I chipped in another $5,000. With that initial sum, he started the Calabasas Mine Shaft.

Along with his friends plus Hella, Mike set about turning an old schoolhouse into a nightclub. It had a great vibe, and it got even better as the work was completed. Then, a month before the opening, the County of Los Angeles required Mike to pave the parking lot in order to get the permits needed for business. Out of money, Mike was desperate. He went to his friend Milt, who promised to invest but then backed out, though he suggested approaching his nephew Craig.

That turned out to be a good call. Although Craig was, at twenty, underage, his father owned a construction company. In exchange for his father paving the parking lot, Mike gave Craig a 20 percent silent partnership in the club. Work was completed, old barn wood was used to build the stage, and my father and Kevin put the finishing touches on the back patio. My mother came up with the name the Mine Shaft; Mike had wanted a Western theme.

Once all those ingredients were in place, Mike hired kids to pass flyers out across the Valley and beyond, from malls to beach parking lots. As a result, the Mine Shaft was well known before the front doors were ever unlocked.

Maybe too well known. On the very first night, two rival motorcycle gangs, the Hell's Angels and Satan's Slaves, showed up and a fight broke out in the barroom. One guy's ear got cut off. The LAPD and the sheriff's department arrived on the scene, as did several ambulances. It was a hell of a way to say welcome to the neighborhood. But the club was packed from day one; it was an instant success.

The club held 310 people inside and another 100 on the patio, yet my brother estimated nearly 2,000 people filtered through on a typical weekend. Wolfman Jack nearly used it as a location for his *Midnight Special* series. L.A. scene maker Rodney Bingenheimer also frequented the bar, no doubt drawn by the rockers who hung out there, including members of Led Zeppelin, Fleetwood Mac, the Eagles, and America.

Mike and Hella, who got married amid the hullabaloo, lived in the back of the club with their friends Tom and Emilie. Mike worked days around the club, cleaning and doing yard work, making repairs, receiving deliveries from vendors, and picking up supplies. Against his better judgment, he gave Kevin a job at the club. My parents pressured him. It turned out to be the beginning of the end of Mike and Kevin's relationship. Kevin was unreliable; he only showed up at night to drink with his friends and ask for his paycheck.

There were more problems. Six months after the Mine Shaft opened, a rival bar sent over a posse of bouncers to cause trouble. They jumped Mike and beat up Kevin with brass knuckles. Mike then hired his own group of guards, all of whom were black-belt martial-arts fighters. Drugs also made their way into the scene. The smell of pot was prevalent even though it was against the law, and people toked openly in the parking lot.

Mike worried about that, aware that on any given night undercover cops might be at the club. Cocaine was an even bigger concern. Early on, after a tip from some of the bartenders, my brother caught Kevin's friend Craig dealing coke from the club. Craig didn't deny it. When Mike ordered him to stop, Craig threw around his 20 percent ownership and friendship with Kevin, and continued to deal. Everyone knew it would end up a problem, and it did.

I went to the club on weekend nights and enjoyed a glass of wine. It was very European of me—and also against the law, since I was underage. But that was conveniently overlooked. I usually took Carin or other girlfriends of mine. My brother says he was so busy that he didn't know when I was there. That was probably true. I kept my presence low-key by staying in the back or hiding out in a nook on the patio or losing myself in the crowd on the dance floor.

After I got my driver's license, I set my sights on getting an Audi. My parents took me to the dealership in Encino. As we walked around the lot, my father emphasized to the salesman that he wanted me, his only daughter, in a car that was extremely safe. He kept saying the word *safe*. As a result, I drove off the lot in a large diesel Mercedes. It was a beautiful car—chocolate brown on the outside, with a beige leather interior—but at the time I was disappointed. I didn't think it was cool. From the way it drove—and the way I felt driving it—I might as well have been in an eighteen-wheeler.

But a few months later, I got into a wreck. I left the studio, turned right onto Gower from Melrose, pulled out a cigarette, and reached down for a lighter. The next thing I knew, I had plowed into a car that was making a left turn in front of me. I never saw it. On impact, my face slammed into the steering wheel. After the initial shock, I saw that I was covered in blood and my nose was killing me. I looked in the rearview mirror and saw it was huge and swollen.

Then I worried the light blue outfit I had on was ruined. That was the least of my problems, though. An ambulance arrived. And so did Susan Olsen and her mother, who were on their way home. They calmed me down and notified my parents after the ambulance took me to the hospital.

The emergency-room doctor, who must have spoken to my parents on the phone, recommended an immediate operation on my nose. As a result, my parents showed up in the ER carrying several photos of what my nose normally looked like. My mother wanted to make sure the surgeon kept it looking the same. After more discussion, though, my mom suggested we get a second opinion. It was good thinking. It turned out my nose wasn't broken, and it eventually healed on its own.

Ironically, my accident occurred on a Friday, and that night's Brady episode was "The Subject Was Noses," the show in which Marcia, right before the school dance, gets hit in the face by a football. Looking at her throbbing, Jimmy Durante–size proboscis, she shrieks, "Oh, my nose!"

Although that's one of the more famous *Brady Bunch* episodes, it's not one of my favorites because of the memories I have of making it. Practically everyone on the set from the prop man to Lloyd Schwartz threw a Nerf football at my face, trying to get it in the perfect spot. Chris Knight was the one whose toss made the final take, and I couldn't have been happier when the director finally said, "Perfect! Print that one!"

Besides my parents, the person who worried most about my driving was Katherine Jackson, the strong-willed matriarch of the Jackson family. I'd met the Jackson 5 about a year and a half earlier when they visited us in the recording studio where we were doing the voices for the *Brady Kids* animated series. Michael was a fan, and we became friends—as friendly as one could get with Michael.

But I think Michael really liked me. He called me and then I started driving over to his house, where we hung out and talked about TV and music. He let me watch him sing and dance in their studio, which was a thrill, as I had been a fan of the Jackson 5 for years. Having performed onstage myself, I envied his talent. Once we went ice-skating and he held my hand as we glided around the rink. I wondered if he might try to kiss me, but he didn't. After another outing, he did give me a kiss good-bye. But it was only a gentle peck on the cheek.

Michael's parents made me nervous. I was a little afraid of his father, and his mother struck me as the strong, silent type. I became even friendlier with Michael's sister LaToya than I was with Michael. She was fun and had a good sense of humor. She used to confide in me about how strict her parents were. It was funny. We were shopping buddies, and when I picked her up, she always said she couldn't wait to get out of their house.

I was also friendly with Susan Cowsill, a member of the popular family singing group whose pop hit "The Rain, the Park and Other Things" was one of my favorites. We met at the Hollywood Professional Children's School, where I enrolled for eleventh grade instead of returning to Taft High. The two of us used to skip out of class and prowl the hot stores like Judy's and Pigeons. Sometimes we bought six-packs of beer at a nearby liquor store, drank one or two at the Griffith Observatory, and then returned to school tipsy. Thank goodness there weren't paparazzi like there are today.

I did something to Susie that I still regret. It happened one day when we were at the mall. I'd driven the two of us and a friend of hers. We were browsing in Pigeons, and we decided to shoplift. It was for kicks. To this day, I don't know if all three of us stole something, but I put a T-shirt in my purse, continued to shop as if nothing was wrong, and then walked out with the other girls.

As soon as I stepped through the doorway, the store alarm went off. It was right after electronic sensors were introduced. Once I heard the siren, I took off and ran through the mall as if I were an Olympic sprinter. I was afraid of getting busted, the headlines that would appear if I were caught shoplifting, and the damage that would do to my girl-next-door image.

I'd never run as fast in my life. Nor had I been as scared.

Unfortunately, Susie and her friend were caught. While police dealt with them, I hid in my car for hours. I lay on the backseat, careful not to raise my head in case someone was looking through the parking lot. I didn't want to go home either, in case the cops were waiting for me there. It was like an episode from the show, something so surreal Bob Reed would've complained it made no sense. It didn't. I felt like a fugitive from the law.

When I finally did go home, I pretended nothing was wrong. But Susie's parents had already called and spoken to my parents, who relayed the information Susie's parents had given—all accurate—and said they agreed with them, that if I had stolen anything I needed to turn myself in. On *The Brady Bunch,* this would be the moment where Marcia breaks down in tears and admits the truth. But this was real life, my life, and I vehemently denied doing anything wrong.

I'm sure everyone knew I was lying, and consequently my friendship with Susan ended. Sadly, I haven't seen her since the moment when I fled from the mall. It was stupid, cowardly. If I had the chance, I'd apologize to Susan, own up to being a jerk, and ask if she would forgive me.

Even now, when I hear a security siren go off in a store, I reexperience that surge of anxiety, and then it changes to guilt. That was thirty-six years ago! It's a painful reminder of what was the first of a long line of mistakes.

8

To Be or Not to Be Brady

When we shot "A Room at the Top," the final show of the fourth season, the tension between Barry and me was at an all-time high. Lloyd Schwartz directed this episode, which revolved around Greg and Marcia both wanting to turn the attic into their own bedroom. I couldn't read the word *bedroom* in the script without conjuring up fantasies of the two of us. It was as if *bedroom* had turned into a code word for something illicit and wonderful.

Barry wasn't much better. Shooting the scene where we sat next to each other on the bed was more than either of us could handle. We couldn't keep our hands off each other. After more than a dozen takes, Lloyd, frustrated at the time it was taking, walked over to the bed and told Barry to make a fist.

"Keep that much distance between the two of you," he said. "I don't want to see you touching."

He didn't see us the following season. When we returned for the fifth season, Barry received his own dressing room, separate from Chris and Mike. It was something he'd lobbied for since the third season, and in what would be our final season, he was finally rewarded, as he should've been. At nineteen, he was an adult, and he deserved star treatment.

Of course Barry turned it into a bachelor pad. I was impressed by the sofa, thick carpet, and great sound system. We rolled around on the sofa and the floor, fumbling with each other's clothes, but every time we got to a crucial point, we seemed to be interrupted by a knock on the door and then the knowing voice of the assistant director saying, "Barry, we're ready for you."

I was ready to lose my virginity to Barry, and it might have happened one night at his house if not for his parents busting in on us as we listened to music and made out in his bedroom. We'd gone swimming beforehand. Even though we wore swimsuits, I felt as if we were naked. I am sure his parents sensed that we were hot and heavy and crazy. In the fall, we had another perfect opportunity to do it when Bob Reed flew all of us kids to New York and took us to Europe on the *QE2*.

The trip was a generous gesture of affection from Bob. And as I just said, it was also an incredible opportunity to finally go all the way with Barry. Except that I wasn't into him on that trip. As always with us, the timing was off. If it wasn't a parent or adult walking in on us, it was usually that he was dating another girl, though in this case I was dating other guys—and I didn't two-time.

Still, that cruise was a blast. Eve and I shared a room. We drank rum and Cokes on board the ship, and once in Europe we enjoyed wine. We could have called ourselves the Boozy Bunch. I think the trip was Bob's way of saying thanks, it's been great working together. By that fifth season, he had mostly given up fighting for better scripts. His passion flared up occasionally, and he went after Sherwood. But it was known that if the show came back for another season, the producers planned to do it without him.

Bob wasn't alone. Touring and being together nonstop over the past couple years had taken its toll. We were cranky and petty with one another. Egos got bigger and I sensed tension among some of the parents, who were jockeying for more screen time for their kid as they began to eye post-*Brady* careers. In a very real sense, it was much like the stuff that goes on in families.

Like Bob, we also wanted more mature scripts. Barry and I still played kids living at home even though he was nineteen and I was seventeen. It was as if we lived in a time bubble. It was 1972! Our home was untouched by the world around us. Imagine if the writers had dealt with Greg worrying about the draft, Carol and Mike spicing up their sex life by skinny-dipping with the neighbors, Marcia hiding a boy in her bedroom, or Jan staying out all night after seeing a rock concert.

What if Mike and the boys had sided with George McGovern and Carol and the girls with Richard Nixon in the 1972 presidential election? It could've been great if, like America, the Bradys had undergone some changes.

It happened off camera. Barry smoked weed. When we shot at a theme park in Cincinnati, Susie got drunk for the first time. And you know times have changed when your little sister starts to get a buzz. I rebelled quietly by taping a show without wearing a bra. I convinced Eve to go braless, too. It was also our subtle way of telling the producers that we were too old for the same old stuff.

We got away with it on a show or two. Then one day Lloyd noticed while he was watching dailies. Nothing was ever formally said to us. There were no dictums stating Maureen and Eve must wear a bra on shows. But apparently it was a no-no. Every time we came on the set for a scene, Lloyd made it a point to say something to us, then put his hand on our backs to see if we were wearing bras.

Most of us thought the show would run another year since it was holding its own in the ratings. Then all of us got a call from Sherwood saying that the network had decided not to renew. As we counted down the remaining shows, I felt both bittersweet and excited about the new opportunities that lay ahead. In truth, I was ready to move on, and in my own way I had already started to do so.

Earlier in the year, I fell madly in love with Freddie Lopez, a friend of the guy my girlfriend Carin dated. Freddie, in his early twenties, was gorgeous. "I can't get him off my mind," I wrote in my diary. He ran an import-export business, and he seemed mature and worldly. I debated whether I should lose my virginity to him. "He's damn good-looking and wonderful to be around, but I feel as if he's giving me the rub-off since he feels no sex will come of our relationship.

"I don't know," I continued, confused. "I feel it is a great time for me to break my virginity and enjoy that part of my life. My desire is very much there, so why should I keep it to myself?"

There was a reason. It turned out Freddie was seeing another girl!

"I can't believe it," I noted after his painful admission. "He said it was a heavy relationship."

After Freddie, I dated Steve Hartunian, another great-looking guy. He was hot in a totally seventies way. He had long, sandy-brown hair, wore his shirts unbuttoned to the middle of his bronzed chest, and drove a Corvette. He was a player, too. He had a roving eye, which made me never feel quite pretty enough. I don't know why I always went after those type of guys; it always ended in disappointment. And that's how it was with Steve. (P.S. I don't *think* I lost my virginity to him, not in a strict interpretation. But I can't be sure, since some of our fooling around may have qualified.)

I wasn't with Steve anymore when my father tried to interest me in a guy named Robert. Normally my parents didn't meddle in my love life, but this was different; in fact an odd, and as it turned out, frightening situation. Robert came into our family, and my life, after writing my parents a letter from his home in Florida, saying he had ideas about how to take over my fan club and help my career.

What impressed my parents and especially my father is something

I'll never know, but my father corresponded with him several times and then invited him to Los Angeles. Once in Los Angeles, he befriended my parents further. They thought he was brilliant. He was in his late twenties, smooth, and smart. One day he took my mother on her first shopping trip to Beverly Hills, and she returned gushing like a schoolgirl after her first date. He bought me an expensive set of luggage. My father was the one who really liked him. He invited Robert for dinner, and the two of them schemed for hours at a time.

It's scary to think back on how easily he ingratiated himself. Once he was "in" with my parents, Robert became more ambitious. Instead of taking over my fan club, he tried to move in as my manager. At some point, he confided to my father that he had fallen in love with me and wanted to get married.

That should've been a tip-off. But it wasn't.

I didn't like Robert. I'd been sheltered from any stalkers or weirdo fans of mine. If they existed, I never knew about it. But Robert made me uncomfortable. I would never have come right out and called him a con man, but my antennae were up. Then one night after dinner, Robert made his move. Again, I don't know what he said as he talked with my father, but at some point, my father pressed me to spend some time alone with Robert, and he basically pushed him into my bedroom.

"Talk to Robert," he said. "Listen to what he has to say. Get to know him."

It creeped me out to have Robert in my bedroom, but there was nothing I could do about it. We sat on the bed, and Robert moved quickly. He took my hand (that was weird), then put his arm around my shoulders (even weirder), and then, a few moments later, he tried to kiss me. With that, I pushed him away and hurried out of my room.

He followed, probably anxious to hear what I was going to tell my parents. Upset, I told my parents that it wasn't working out. The expression on my face emphasized the point. Once Robert left, I insisted they get rid of him. I flatly said I didn't want him involved in any part of my life.

My father delivered the news to Robert. Fortunately, we never heard from him again. Later, we found out that Robert was a convicted felon who had been released from prison shortly before he'd come out to Los Angeles. We surmised that he might have written my parents from jail or right after he got out. From what we heard, he returned to Florida, violated his parole, and was put back behind bars.

I felt lucky that all he'd tried to do was kiss me.

The Brady Bunch ended without fanfare or celebration. Bob Reed was so infuriated by the script that he didn't appear in the final show. As I think back, after five years, during which time we literally grew up with one another, made out with one another, got drunk with one another, and so on, it was oddly unemotional. Maybe it was because all of us knew that in one way or another we'd always remain . . . a family.

I had this notion of being free; it was more like being unmoored. I returned to Taft High for my senior year. I stuck close to Debbie, Julie, and a few others who'd been my close friends since junior high, but my reentry was still difficult. I didn't have any interest in academics. Nor was I prepared for the work required to graduate. To help me study, Debbie and Julie introduced me to White Crosses, tiny pills that they said would help me stay up as I crammed information into my head.

The pills put me in such a good mood that I started taking them on Friday and Saturday nights. It was like they peeled away the layer of disquietude that had gradually resurfaced after I no longer had my life as a Brady to keep it at bay. I didn't consider any deeper connections, like maybe the transition to Maureen from Marcia might be more difficult than I ever imagined; it was just that those little pills let me laugh.

As the senior prom neared, we also popped them to lose weight. I wasn't fat, but I always seemed to be five pounds away from being happy with myself. If I took a pill in the afternoon and another one at night, I could go till dinnertime without eating much. Within a few days, I shed those extra pounds.

I wish I could've shed the senior prom, too. It's funny to think back on all the different stories fan magazines published featuring me giving advice to other teen girls about boys, dating, and dances, as if I were an expert, and then my senior prom turned out to be a disaster. It was because I set my hopes on going with Phil, one of the school's most popular guys. Then he asked my friend Debbie.

I was so sure I was going with Phil that I brushed off the few guys who hinted that they wanted to ask me. I'd had this vision of the two of us lighting up the ballroom as we walked in. It was so vivid that it seemed real. By the week of the prom, though, I didn't have a date. I was destroyed. Finally, Debbie arranged for me to go with Phil's brother so we could double-date.

I agreed, mostly because I still wanted to be around Phil. But I felt like the word *loser* was stamped on my forehead.

On prom night, Debbie and Phil rode in the cab of Phil's truck while Phil's brother and I sat in the back and bounced up and down on the freeway. My hair was a windblown disaster by the time we arrived. I got out of the truck looking like I had survived three weeks at sea in a hurricane. Bummed, I got drunk on Mateus rosé wine and cried in the bathroom.

I didn't understand how I'd turned into a lame chick who couldn't get a date to the prom. Until them, I hadn't dealt much with reality.

After graduation, I moved into my own apartment. My father and mother found me a one-bedroom condo in Woodland Hills. He rationalized it as a good investment. Regardless, it was a bold move since I wouldn't turn eighteen until the end of the summer. But I wanted to have more control over my life, and though I didn't say this part, I also wanted to get away from the craziness at home.

The problems there were more upsetting than unbearable. They revolved around the Mine Shaft. After reaching the end of his rope with Kevin, Mike put his friend and the club's manager Bill Antil in charge of Kevin. A month later, Bill fired Kevin for not showing up for work. As Mike said, Kevin thought he could do what he wanted because his parents owned part of the club.

In the meantime, everyone else worked their butts off. As a result, Mike paid back all of the loans. My parents gave Kevin a portion of their income from the club, though he wasn't to work there. They bought him a condo in the same building where I lived; in fact, it was on the second floor, almost directly above mine. They also bought him several cars; he seemed to get into a lot of wrecks. They encouraged him to paint and do something with his artistic skills.

Basically, they wanted him doing something productive, and they tried to set him up the best way they knew how. They may have given him too much. With Mike and me doing well, they felt bad for Kevin. They wanted to help him find himself. Kevin didn't seem to get it. He continued to hang out at the club every night. Mike knew that he and Craig were using coke. Craig was also still dealing. That was way too risky.

Finally, Mike and my parents told Craig that they were buying him out of his percentage of the club. They gave him $20,000 and forced him out. Craig, who'd also been receiving income and profits for about two years, agreed, and his interest in the club was dissolved.

Kevin was upset at the way Craig had been treated. Then, about a month later, Craig filed a $100,000 suit against the club, saying he was forced out under duress. (He settled with Mike for $5,000.) A month later, Kevin brought a $1 million lawsuit against my parents—not the club or Mike—claiming they'd cheated him.

My parents were extremely hurt, and my mother was even more worried about what friends and family would say if they found out. Mike and Hella pleaded with Kevin to reconsider, and he eventually dropped the suit. But three months later, Craig started a new, competing nightclub called Star Baby, and Kevin worked for him.

Interestingly, a week before that club opened, the Mine Shaft caught fire and burned to the ground. The sheriff's and fire departments both determined the blaze was caused by arson. We found out that Craig's father, who'd moved to Nevada, had been accused of burning down projects to collect insurance. Mike and Hella felt strongly that Craig and Kevin were responsible for the fire.

My father didn't want to consider that theory. But my mother had her suspicions. One thing has always struck me as bizarrely curious. A paraplegic named Eddie worked at the club. He and his wheelchair were as much of a presence as the beer tap. Everyone knew him. Ordinarily he would have been at the club at the time the blaze swept through the place, and most likely he wouldn't have been able to get out in time. But my brother Kevin had come by early and taken him home.

No one ever brought that up. The Mine Shaft was rebuilt, though it never recovered. Mike also ran into problems with the landlord, eventually selling for slightly less than the debts he incurred while the club was closed. A few years after the fire, Craig was found dead in a car without any clothes on. Along with my parents and Mike, I suspected that drugs were involved. That was another mystery.

But we knew one thing for sure. The *Brady* era was definitely over.

9

Not So Happy Days

It was a sign of the times when I heard that my friend Julie was going to pose for *Playboy*. She was one of my two closest girlfriends from high school. I actually heard the news from my other friend Debbie. I was stunned. Julie had been brought up in a strict Mormon household. But as Debbie and I talked about it, my attitude was Why not? She was a beautiful girl.

"Would you ever do it?" Debbie asked.

"No," I said, laughing nervously.

I did other things, though.

Indeed, my life after Marcia Brady was a whirlwind of experimentation and searching that evolved into a grim spiral of avoidance, denial, and self-destruction. The roller coaster began with a visit to Debbie, who was going to college in Santa Barbara. At a dinner she arranged for me to meet a few of her friends, we gorged ourselves on pizza, chips, and desserts. It was more food than I'd eaten in my entire life, and afterward I felt sickeningly full as well as guilty.

But one of Debbie's new friends explained that she knew a way to get rid of everything we'd eaten. Eyes lit up around the room. Really? How? It was easy, she said. You made yourself throw up.

She explained how to do it, and one by one we went into the bathroom, stuck a finger down our throats, and threw up in the toilet. After some initial fear, I had an easy time of it. I felt better immediately. I had no idea it was dangerous.

I forced myself to throw up a few times later on after bingeing out of nervousness and anxiety. It was like a trick I could do when I needed help regaining control of my emotions. I'd get wound up because of work—or the difficulty getting it. The kind of serious acting jobs I hoped for after *The Brady Bunch* didn't come easily or quickly. I pictured myself going into movies. I had a reservoir of deep and dark emotions in me, and I was ready to show the world there was more to me than Marcia. I wanted to be known for serious work and winning awards.

But nothing came from the auditions I went on. People wanted to meet me, it seemed. Some asked me out. Others just wanted to look at me. There always seemed to be so much promise. Then it failed to materialize. Little by little, like waves and wind reshaping a rocky shoreline, that process, the cruelest part of Hollywood, chipped away at my confidence, sense of self, determination, and hope. "Almost breaking through," I wrote in my diary. "But it doesn't want to shine . . ."

> *I know there's life all around*
> *Though in places hard to find*
>
> *My phone—it's still not busy*
> *But I'm waiting—I'll be here for a while*
> *Breaking through is not easy*
> *That blossom has yet to bloom*
> *Maybe tomorrow*
> *Or the day after next*
> *Things don't always come that soon*

Kevin and I, neighbors in our condo complex, hung out, playing guitar, writing songs, and dreaming of a recording career. Well, he dreamed, and my father encouraged it. But I found myself more aware of Kevin's inability to find a satisfying direction in his life. The two of us went to Hawaii, where we killed time under the guise of getting healthy and in shape. In reality, we drank lots of fruit juices and ran on the beach. I wasn't much of a pot smoker yet, not like Kevin anyway, but we also sampled some of the local pot, the Maui Wowie.

> *Today—I find my own*
> *With shades of yellow, others gray*
> *I've strummed my words—they're dry now*
> *My drawings—gradually find their way*

Gradually, I seemed to find my way too. I landed a part as a heroin addict on an episode of *Harry-O*, the smart detective series starring David Janssen as former-LAPD-officer-turned-private-eye Harry Orwell.

I patterned my character after my brother Kevin's friend Ron, a long-time heroin addict who'd battled a serious drug problem when both of them were in high school. It was my first serious, adult role, a great showcase for me, and felt like I took a step up the acting ladder when my effort earned praise from the *Harry-O* director, as well as from David Janssen.

I carried that confidence into my next job, a guest spot on *Happy Days*. I played one of three girls that Richie, Potsie, and Ralph pick up after they go cruising for chicks.

The atmosphere on the set was relaxed and warm, and I had fun meeting Henry Winkler and Ron Howard. Both of them were among the nicest, warmest, and most genuine people I'd met. I was impressed by the way they were handling stardom with effortless grace.

I was embraced by the show's director, Jerry Paris, who wanted to set me up with one of his sons. I didn't want to say no because he also intimated that he might have ideas that could help my career. I met his son, and we went out on a few dates. But when they didn't work out, I never heard from Jerry again.

Around the same time I also met a well-known producer whose office was on the Paramount lot. One day he introduced himself, and I was surprised that this man whom I'll call J.M. knew who I was. He was at least twenty years older than me, very successful, and in a different league. A short time later, though, his secretary called and said J.M. would like to meet with me.

I was even more shocked when I went to his office and all he did was gush about my talent and charisma. He made me feel like a million dollars. He also arranged for me to audition for a new series. I didn't get the part, but I heard from him immediately afterward. He said not to worry, he wanted to create a series for me.

My own series?

Coming from J.M., that was a big deal. He had the clout to make such a thing happen. He promised we'd get together soon to discuss it. I'd never felt as good about being rejected.

Soon after, we met for lunch at the Paramount commissary, which turned out to be a regular spot for us. That lunch led to another and another. We always sat at his corner table. Sometimes I felt odd being there with him. I wasn't always clear on the purpose, as those lunches, despite discussions about my series, gradually came to feel more personal than professional. But J.M. said he needed to get to know me as part of his research.

I didn't know much about J.M. personally other than that he was in his forties, married, and a father. He also had a thick accent that he was able to thicken for comedic effect. But I liked spending time with him. He was smart and entertaining, personable and warm. He made me feel good about myself. I wouldn't go as far as to say I was seduced, but I was thoroughly charmed by the attention he gave me.

I didn't analyze it, either. To be honest, I couldn't think beyond the show he promised. My show. Our show. The show I inspired him to create. Whatever. It made me like putty in his hands. And I started to feel his hands. During our lunches, I noticed he began to touch my arm when he wanted to emphasize a point. It was easy to confuse that sort of gesture with simple, innocent warmth. His leg also occasionally rested against mine under the table. Once he put his arm around me as we walked back to his office. Another time he held my hand as we walked back to his office. Even though it didn't feel right to me, I didn't pull away.

I told myself that we were friends; we were making the connection he needed to write a show for me. People in show business were more overtly affectionate than in a normal office workplace. I conveniently avoided thinking there might be something else going on.

Like many young actresses, I was, despite my years in the business, gullible and way too eager and open for someone with influence to help usher me to my next dream. Thus I was easy prey.

In the meantime, I shot an episode of *The Turning Point of Jim Malloy*, a series based on John O'Hara stories starring John Savage. I also went out on a handful of auditions. I tried not to think about the day when my own show would launch. Finally, J.M. called with an update. He was getting close on the series, and since he was writing about my apartment, he wanted to come to my place to see what it was like and make sure it was true to my character.

Fine, I said. Whatever he needed.

We set a date for him to come over to my place after work. He brought a magnum of chilled champagne. I wasn't displeased when he showed me, but I wasn't expecting it either. He said it was to toast our show.

J.M. popped the cork and poured us glasses. We sat next to each other on the sofa and clinked glasses. When they were empty, he refilled them. He glanced around my apartment, commenting on a few things. He also talked enthusiastically about the show and me. I didn't know which was more intoxicating, the champagne or his compliments.

At some point, he asked to see my bedroom. I admit that I was tipsy and turned on as I got up and led him down the hall. Once inside, it felt like the temperature in the room went up about a hundred degrees. Suddenly he turned toward me and said that he wanted me. I didn't know what I wanted. But before I could figure it out, he pushed me down on the bed, not hard, but firmly, and began to kiss me. I started to kiss him back. But it felt wrong, and when I felt his hands under my shirt it felt really wrong. I said stop and pushed him off me.

An extremely awkward moment ensued during which we exchanged confused and at least on my end partly apologetic stares, then several words, and finally without saying anything more J.M. went into the other room, put on his jacket, and left. I don't know why I felt compelled to apologize; my naiveté may have made me slightly complicit. But I felt taken advantage of and used.

In any event, I was relieved and grateful when he went away. Later that night I cried myself to sleep, wishing I could wake up and have the world the way it was before J.M. knocked on my door.

I guess I wasn't as special as J.M. said. After that night, he quit calling. Our lunches stopped. And my show, our show, if it ever existed, faded into an unpleasant memory. It took a while to get over my disappointment and the pain of feeling used, but I was glad I didn't sleep my way into a show. That wasn't a role I desired. I didn't ever want to be one of those actresses.

Still, I worried about what would happen when J.M. and I crossed paths at the studio, which I knew was inevitable. I was on guard every time I was on that lot, poised to duck around the corner and avoid what I knew would be an uncomfortable confrontation. The funny thing was the one time I wasn't looking out for him was the time when I heard his voice.

"Hello, Maureen."

When that happened, it was like a switch flipped inside me. One minute I was walking along a sidewalk amid soundstages and the bustle of studio workers, and the next minute I was transported back into my bedroom.

Talk about great acting. I hid the fact that I was freaked out just hearing his voice. Instead, I offered a warm but wary hello, the same as his, and kept going.

At home that night, though, I had an anxiety attack, something I hadn't experience before. I went into the kitchen and stuffed every morsel of food I could find into my mouth. Afterward, I walked into the bathroom and vomited.

E ach time I saw J.M. after that was a little easier. He was always friendly and our hellos turned into a few short, polite sentences.

How are you? Good.

You look good. You, too.

As time passed, I pushed those not-so-happy days to the back of my mind and only recalled them (always with a private shudder) when actress friends talked about powerful men hitting on them. A couple years went by before we saw each other again, and when we did, he invited me to lunch. I didn't know what to say. My hesitation was the result of seriously mixed feelings.

He repeated his invitation. I assumed he finally wanted to talk to me about what had happened. I didn't know if there was much to say or if it was necessary. For the sake of closure, though, and because I'd once really liked and admired J.M., I made myself go.

The first few minutes were uncomfortable. Our conversation was forced and polite as we caught up. Then J.M. apologized. He still believed in me, he said, and wanted to make amends by helping my career. He gave me his company's phone number and made me promise to call. I thought about it a few times, but I never picked up the phone.

I didn't trust him. Years later I ran into his secretary and she also apologized.

The worst part about the whole encounter was that I didn't trust myself anymore—and looking back, that was the most damaging part of the whole thing.

10

Wonderland Avenue

I looked for something different, a proving ground, something that
would show me off to the Hollywood community in a new light,
and I found it in a production of Jean-Paul Sartre's *No Exit*. The
play was about three people thrown together in a room that turns out
to be hell—and hell, of course, turns out to be other people.

Veteran actors Vince Cannon and Marian McCargo Bell occupied
the top spots on the marquee of the small theater in Beverly Hills. My
name was underneath in smaller letters. That seemed appropriate to
me. I was in a work mode. I told Tracy Roberts, the play's director and
a renowned acting coach, that I looked forward to the challenge of being onstage without any second takes or safety net.

The two of us had a long talk about acting, the work I had done,
and the work I hoped to do. I spoke to her about some of my frustrations to that point. Because of the nature of the play, she got me to
open up further about my nonacting life. We got into a pretty heavy
conversation. She stared at me with an intensity that almost lifted me
from my chair. I'd never been studied like that.

"You surprise me," she said.

"Is that good?" I asked.

"It's not good or bad," she said. "I'm surprised."

"What do you mean?"

She smiled.

"There's more to Marcia Brady than we know."

"Right," I said, with a slight, self-satisfied grin.

Besides rehearsals, preparations for the play included heavy-duty conversations about life among Tracy, Vince, Marian, and myself. Since I didn't come from a family where we talked openly or communicated easily, I was initially reluctant to share my thoughts. Rather, I was intimidated. I was younger than the others, had fewer real-world experiences, and little formal education. What did I know about life compared to my more seasoned co-stars?

I was especially impressed by Marian, whose life was the stuff of fiction. She grew up back east, where she was a top tennis player in the 1950s. She married an advertising executive, moved to L.A. and had four sons before divorcing in 1963. Three years later, she began acting in the movies *Dead Heat on a Merry-Go-Round* and *Buona Sera, Mrs. Campbell* and also the TV series *Perry Mason, Hogan's Heroes,* and *Voyage to the Bottom of the Sea.* In 1970, she married a widowed congressman with three boys of his own.

Essentially, she was dramatically different from my mother, and I was flattered when she took an interest in me. One day she said she wanted to introduce me to an up-and-coming young actor. She said he was handsome and sweet. Moreover, she said that she thought we'd look good together.

I gave my okay, and she arranged for Eric to come by the theater one afternoon a few days later. Even before we were formally introduced, I recognized him from across the backstage area by her description. Eric was blond, with a great build, and a smile that lit up the room. Then Marian introduced us, and I realized she was a good matchmaker. We hit it off immediately. He came back that night for the performance, and afteward we went for a drive in his car, an AMC Pacer.

It was a cute car with some zip and a slick backside. I remember it because that was also my impression of Eric—cute with a slick backside.

He took me to his house, which was off Coldwater Canyon and along a street that wound through the hills and then past a large gate. Getting there in the dark seemed like an adventure. We finally stopped in front of a breathtaking ranch-style home. He parked at the end of the driveway and began leading me around back. I was able to peek inside a couple windows. It looked very elegant.

"Watch your step," Eric said.

We were going around back and needed to follow a brick path. He held on to my arm—a good thing for me since I continued to glance around. The property included a pool and tennis court and was set amid a rustic landscape that overlooked the Franklin Reservoir.

"You live here?" I asked.

"I'll show you where I live," he said.

This was his parents' house, he explained, while leading me around the side and up private stairs that stopped at the entrance to what by then felt like a separate house. Before entering, we turned around and looked at the view. The moon cast the property in a soft light. I saw the swimming pool and tennis court below us. Giant trees were on either side. It was magnificent.

"Come on in," he said. "This is where I live."

Eric lived in what I initially assumed was the guest room, except it was much larger than a room. It was more like a guest wing. It had its own entrance, and included a bedroom, living room, and full bathroom. It was connected to the main house, but Eric could lock the doors and make it completely private if he wanted. I put my hands on my cheeks and said the only thing that came to mind—wow!

We spent several hours together, talking and listening to music. He told me about his family. I'd already gathered they were quite wealthy. He mellowed out with a joint. We also made out. I let myself be swept away. At one point, I opened my eyes, looked over his shoulder, and

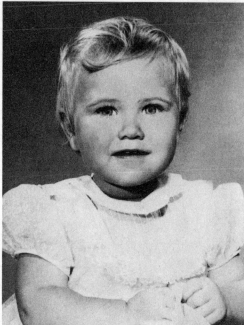

Baby Maureen, eighteen
months old.

My father, Richard
McCormick.

My dad's father, Joseph McCormick.

My dad and his mom, Nana.

Above, left: Granddad Theodore, Grandma Helen, and my mother, Irene.

Above, right: My mother, age 22, 1943.

The wedding of Richard and Irene McCormick.

Young Maureen, 1959.

Young Maureen with her dolls, 1959.

New bathing suit.

With Dad at the ocean.

Denny joins me and Judy Anderson for tea in the backyard.

The house on top of the hill in which I was born. "The do-it-yourself house."

With Christine Machette, who was also in the Baby Miss San Fernando Valley beauty pageant, 1963.

Getting ready for the role in *Heidi*, 1968.

Taping the one hundredth episode.

The Brady kids and their parents.

The Grand Canyon, 1971.

The Grand Canyon episode.

Mom and me at home during the Brady years.

Hawaii—*from the left:* Frances Whitfield (set social worker), Willie Knight (Chris Knight's mom), my mom, and Dee Olsen (Susan Olsen's mom). *Top, right:* Mildred Schwartz.

Barry and I were inseparable while on the Hawaii shoot, 1972.

Bobby's all tuckered out.

Ann B. Davis and me in Hawaii. Vintage Maureen, hiding her stomach.

Chris Knight and me, 1972.

Visiting Marine One, 1970.

Debbie Anderson and me; high school buddies, 1973.

Me and my prom date, 1974.

The Valley Girls, 1978.
Clockwise from top left: Kathy
Miller, Judy Kaufman, me,
and Carin.

With Steve Hartanian, 1973.

Left: My condo in West
Hollywood, "the Pink
Palace," 1978 or 1979.

Circa 1986.

Carin and me, 1988.

Kevin and me in "Heavenly Hana," 1975.

asked myself how did I get here again? I felt like Cinderella and that I was in a fairy tale.

It was late when Eric took me back to my car in back of the theater. I drove home, replaying the night in my head. I had to thank Marian.

The play ran for a couple more weeks, and Eric came to the theater every day. We went out for dinner following each performance, and talked into the night. I fell for him quickly. At the end of the first week, I spent the night at his place and I didn't have any doubt afterward that we had made love.

I woke up knowing that I was in love with Eric. There was no other way to explain how I felt. One day those words came out of his mouth, too.

Within a couple weeks of the play ending, I moved into his place. I was spending all my time there, so why not? My parents were livid. They didn't believe in living together, and they thought I was too young at 18 to make such a commitment.

We continued to argue about it long after I made the move. I called them old fashioned and claimed they didn't understand me. It created a real strain.

On the other hand, Eric's parents embraced me as if I were a member of their large family. They had a passel of children; Eric was right in the middle. After I moved in, we quit dating and hung out at his house. There was no reason to go anyplace else. Eric's family employed a full-time chef, who served us steak and eggs in the morning and snacks by the pool.

The lifestyle was ridiculously luxurious—and fattening! I gained so much weight I started to wear overalls to cover up my tummy.

Eric's mother laughed when she saw me patting my belly one day out by the pool. She was a Grace Kelly–type, who was as comfortable in shorts as she was full-length gowns. Eric's stepfather was a powerful but charming and debonair businessman. He was dashing in his own way.

With all those boys at the table, playing tennis and jumping in the pool, Eric's family reminded me of a camp where the campers had come as little boys and never gone home.

"This is like a dream," I repeatedly told Eric, who still probably had no idea how truly overwhelmed I felt by his family and their way of life.

I was embarrassed to take him to my family's home. How was I supposed to explain the mess in each room? This is the junk my mother hordes? Nor did I picture introducing him to Kevin or Denny, who was at any moment liable to blurt out, "My father had an affair with Kathy Pointer" or "My sister is Marcia Brady."

There was too much to explain or, from another angle, there was too much I didn't want to explain. Although Eric and I talked about everything, I kept certain things off-limits. I didn't see the point in telling him about my mother's condition, her mother's sad fate, or that deep down I believed I also inherited syphilis and would end up going insane like my grandmother. Those subjects were private, too personal.

One of the things I loved about Eric was the way being with him spirited me away from all of those fears, insecurities, and embarrassments.

One day Eric said he wanted to take me to his teacher's house. I had no idea what he meant by "his teacher." He hadn't mentioned anything about an acting class or that he was studying with anyone. It could have been a point of conversation had I been more inquisitive, but I followed him into his Pacer and drove through the canyon to meet his teacher.

Eric turned on Wonderland Ave., a marvelously named street that twisted and turned up Laurel Canyon. Dwellings of every type, from shacks to mansions, dotted the street. He turned into a driveway and stopped at the gate. When it opened, I couldn't believe my eyes. In front of me was a stone cottage set amid a perfectly manicured lawn, flower gardens, pond, rocks, and a wishing well. It was a rich hippie's interpretation of Lewis Carroll's *Alice in Wonderland*.

"Oh my God, this is amazing."

"Wait," said Eric. "It gets better."

He was right. We walked inside and my mouth dropped as he took me on a mini-tour. The house was fabulous, all stone and polished wood, with ferns and plants—how I imagined the Hobbit would have lived if J.R.R. Tolkein had set him in Los Angeles in the 1970s. Except it would turn out that the home's owner, Bill, whom Eric introduced as his teacher, was more like Smaug, the volatile, powerful, controlling, manipulative dragon with all the treasure in his dark cave.

Initially, though, Bill impressed me as friendly and upbeat. Thanks to my connection to Eric, he greeted me warmly and invited me in as if we were old pals. In his mid-thirties, blond and fair-skinned, he had the shape of someone who lived well and didn't often deprive himself of many pleasures. We liked each other right way. I also liked his wife, a cute, slender woman with long brown hair. She dressed like a chic flower child. Then again, so did I. Jeans, work shirts, peasant tops . . . it was all de rigueur for the times.

Bill ushered us into the living room. A handful of people—mostly guys, but a few pretty girls—were already lounging there. Eric knew everyone and introduced me as we sat on a sofa. After taking in the furniture, the large stone fireplace, the wood floors, and Oriental carpets, my eyes fell on the large glass coffee table and the pile of white powder in the middle of it.

"What's that?" I asked.

"You don't know?" said Eric.

"No."

"It's cocaine," he said, with a laugh.

"That's cocaine?"

"Yes."

This was a heavy-duty scene camouflaged as a party. It was as if someone had harnassed a cloud and pushed it onto the table. There must have been a pound, maybe more, of white powder. Though I didn't realize it then, displaying it like that was the ultimate power trip. It was out in the open, but there was no mistaking that Bill controlled it. Even I on my first visit picked up the vibe. The happy-making powder belonged to him, and you only did it at his discretion.

But Eric snorted a line and asked me if I wanted to try one. Bill also encouraged me. I was hesitant, but only because I didn't know how. I wanted to try it. I was curious. With others encouraging me ("you're going to love it," they said) Eric guided me through my first line.

"I don't feel anything," I said. "The inside of my nose burns. Otherwise—"

"Do some more," Eric said.

Sometimes I wonder how my life would've been different if I'd said no and never done another line again. But that's not what happened. I snorted several more lines and soon I understood what everyone in the room had tried to explain. The conversation, the music, everything was suddenly better. And so was I. It was as if I'd stepped out of my normal shell full of insecurities and worries and into a different and far cooler, mellower, and more fun skin.

I felt great.

Someone made the first of many Marcia Brady cracks: "God, if America only knew Marcia Brady was getting high."

Hours later, I was still doing lines. Eric and his friends noted how I went from a novice to doing more than any of them. I shrugged. Why stop?

I wanted more, more, more—and just my luck, there seemed to be an unlimited supply.

Eric and I got home as the sun was coming up. I was exhausted, but in a good way. I felt like my eyes had been opened and my mind expanded. I thought I understood why Eric referred to Bill as his teacher, and I was eager for my next lesson.

I didn't have to wait long. Eric took me back again the following night and from then on we spent the majority of our time at Bill's. It was like we were sucked from the real world into that self-contained scene, which, as I quickly learned, had its own social order. Bill sat on top. He was a major coke connection to a strata of rockers, movie stars, TV actors, and children from Hollywood's wealthiest families.

Bill had several guys working for him, and they also had an elite clientele. By hanging out at his house, though, Eric and I were in the red hot center of it. So were Eric's friends: Andy, Clark, Braden, Conrad, and Tony. Like Eric, they were good-looking children from some of Hollywood's most privileged and powerful families, including a studio president, an accountant, an Oscar-winning producer, a network bigwig, and an agency honcho.

I was clearly from a different world when they spoke of homes in Malibu and Colorado, trips to Europe, and boats kept at the marina. The great common denominator was our time to hang out and party. We played backgammon, talked, and did coke. Our lives centered around Bill's stash. It seemed I was able to do more than anyone else. It earned me the nickname "Hoover," like the vacuum cleaner.

After complaining of trouble going to sleep, someone turned me onto quaaludes and I got in the habit of using them to come back down. I was able to get a prescription from my gynecologist, who also provided refills.

All that partying made me careless. When I missed my period, I had a scary suspicion as to why, but I still waited more than a week just to be sure. I bought a home pregnancy test and it came back positive. I sat Eric down in the living room and started to tell him the news, but I broke down before getting all the words out.

Eric held me until I calmed down and assured me things would be okay. We knew we weren't ready to have a child, and I wasn't prepared to carry a baby to term and give it up for adoption. That left one option. I needed to get an abortion.

Eric and I didn't discuss it in depth, but we discussed it enough so that we reassured each other we were making the best decision for us. That didn't mean it was easy for either of us. Eric agreed to pay for it, since my parents handled all my finances and I wasn't about to ask them for money.

As for how we were supposed to arrange for the procedure, and who was going to do it, well, that was another complication. I felt too guilty and embarrassed to ask even my closest friends. So one day I made call after call to doctors and hospitals, using a fake name and voice to inquire, and I panicked when I was unable to find anyone to do the procedure. I remember sitting on Eric's bed and thinking, Oh my God, I am going to have to have this baby.

Finally, I turned to my gynecologist, the one who gave me quaaludes, and he agreed to perform the abortion. Good news had never made me feel so bad.

Eric drove me to the hospital, where I changed clothes, laid on a bed, and was wheeled into a room where several other girls waited just like me. I'd never been in a hospital before. Eric stayed by my side, comforting me. I was scared of the procedure and even more frightened of being recognized.

When it was my turn, I was grateful they didn't call my name. A nurse came and wheeled me into another room. Eric waited outside. I put myself in another headspace and followed instructions. As I think about it now, I was present but not really there. It was like an out of body experience. Afterward, Eric took me back to his place, where I spent the next couple of days in a fog.

I knew it wouldn't be like this for long, and it wasn't. As soon as I felt ready, we went back to Bill's.

11

A Friend of the Devil

The circumstances may have been less than ideal, but Eric and I came through the abortion together, closer, and eager for more privacy and space. He responded by buying an old, two-story Spanish-style home in Laurel Canyon. We moved there from his parents' home without anyone in either his or my family knowing the circumstances that led us to go out on our own.

Aside from the pleasure of nesting, we adored one thing above all else about the new home, and that was its proximity to Bill's. That should have been a warning sign to both of us, but who bothered to think like that when all of us seemed to have so much fun? Caravanning as a group in our BMWs, we went to the biggest concerts of the day: Fleetwood Mac, Chicago, Crosby, Stills and Nash, and the Jefferson Starship. We had the best tickets. We commandeered corner tables at the Roxy and the Troubadour nightclubs, snorting lines off the table.

In those days, everyone did. But there was a difference. Bill sold most everyone their coke, making our all-access pass something to be envied. We took a private jet to see the Eagles. He flew us to a place in

Northern California where his coke was made or stored; there were large trash cans filled to the top with white powder; we returned to Los Angeles with new supplies for his business. On several occasions, we traveled to Telluride, Colorado, where we skied all day and partied all night. Back in Los Angeles, Bill hired a young contractor named Harrison Ford to build an indoor hot tub. No ordinary hot tub, there was a button next to it. When pushed, a secret stash box rose from out of nowhere.

I took it for granted when someone took off their clothes and slipped into the Jacuzzi or made out with someone else's girlfriend, as began to happen. As long as Bill approved, anything went. In a way, we were like a cult—good people corrupted by bad drugs. Bill drove a BMW 3.0 CS. I bought the same car. I don't think any of us realized the sway he had over us.

One day Eric, Bill, and several others introduced me to a new drug—mushrooms. Bill had bags of them around the house. I had seen them before—ugly, brown, dried-up stems and tops in plastic bags—but didn't know what they were. Now enlightened, I followed the guys into the kitchen. All of us were going to trip, I was told. Bill made a milk shake, then blended in a handful of *'shrooms.*

"Ah, the magic ingredient," he said, smiling at me.

Bill poured me a large glass, then let others take their own portions. I chugged it down, the ice cream tasting sweet and cold in my mouth. Looking back, I shudder at how blindly and blithely I consumed it, asking no question.

It was a little while before I felt anything, but then all of a sudden, *wham,* I began to hallucinate. Whatever pleasantness I initially experienced faded as I got higher and higher. It was like being on a rocket-powered express elevator that kept going up without stopping. Both out of my mind and out of control, I went into Bill's garage and climbed into the front seat of his car, where I imagined myself shrinking to the size of a molecule and caroming through space.

"Mo, are you okay?"

It was Eric. I recognized his voice.

"Maureen, can you hear us?"

No, that was Bill.

"Mo!"

I could hear them, but I could not respond. My brain would not function. I was a molecule.

"I'm so fucked up," I said.

For all I know, I may have been on the threshold of insanity—that's how high I got. Eric, Bill, and Clark picked me up out of the car and took me to Andy's house. Bill probably wanted me out of his house in case something bad happened. At Andy's, someone put a tiny spoon up my nose and told me to snort, thinking coke would counter the mushrooms. Eventually I came down, but I needed a couple of days before I felt like myself again—whatever that was.

"How was it?" Bill asked when I saw him next.

"How was it?" I said. "It scared the hell out of me. That's how it was."

He laughed as if he knew something I didn't.

"It will be better next time," he said.

"How do you know?"

"I just know."

"Is that why Eric calls you his teacher?"

Bill laughed, then took me in his arms and kissed me gently on the cheek, in the soft part just above my neck. I don't know whether I heard him whisper "don't tell Eric" or I imagined it, but when he let me go, I swear to God that I saw a twinkle in his turquoise eyes, a devilish glint that was pure evil—I just didn't recognize it.

By early 1976, after Eric and I had been together slightly more than a year, I started to hear noises. They came at night when I was up doing coke. While Eric could stop and go to bed, I couldn't. As a general rule, I did not stop doing coke until it was gone, and thanks to Bill, we usually had enough to keep me up for two or three days of round-the-clock tooting.

It was during the wee hours while I was hunkered down with my stash and backgammon board that I first heard the sounds outside. The first few times I ignored them. When they persisted, I told Eric, who said they were nothing. But if they were nothing, why did they keep occurring?

The logical thing would have been to investigate—open the door, look out the window, ask if anyone was there, or shout "go away wolves" (we did have coyotes and deer in the yard). But when you're holding half an ounce of coke, you don't do the logical thing. No, instead I convinced myself the police were hiding behind the trees and bushes, waiting for the right moment to stage a raid.

I was completely paranoid. MY response? I took my baggie of coke and my backgammon board and scooted into the closet, staying there until I knew from the sound of chirping birds that it was daylight, and thus safe to come out. Sometimes I didn't come out, though. I hated it when Eric opened the closet doors and found me knotted up on the floor.

Around this time I was haunted by recurring nightmares. There were two of them, actually, both disturbingly real. In one, I was falling from a dangerous height. Sometimes it was from a roof, other times it was from a high building. The sensation was the same in each situation: I was out of control. I always woke up before hitting the ground, feeling anxious, frightened, and as if I had escaped with my life.

The other dream was worse. In it, I had killed someone. It was always right after the fact. I never knew exactly how I had killed the person—or any other details, like whether it was a man, woman, boy, or girl. I was just filled with the dread of having done it. In one variation, Bill and Andy helped me bury the person. It was so real to me that the next time Eric and I went on a hike in the hills near our home,

I kept an eye open for signs of the clearing where we had buried the body.

After enough of these nightmares, I wondered if I had actually committed such a crime. I didn't think so, but I honestly didn't know. All I knew was I didn't want to go to sleep.

Eric didn't realize the extent to which the coke had changed me. Neither did I until I was confronted by an important decision. One day Eric came into the living room. I was playing the guitar. I had been up for three days. I was fried. I may have taken a quaalude to help bring me down; I don't remember. All I recall is feeling on edge, my insides like broken glass.

After listening to me play, Eric got down on one knee and put a small jewelry box in front of me.

"What?" I said. "No! You didn't."

Staring up at me from behind a Cheshire-cat grin, he professed his love for me, his desire to have babies, and be together always, and then, finally, he asked the question I had imagined him asking back when he romanced me on the night we met: "Maureen McCormick, will you marry me?"

The diamond-and-emerald engagement ring fit perfectly, but the idea of marrying Eric did not. It was an odd thing that I couldn't explain. But as a teenager, I had told myself that I wasn't going to sleep with the man I married until our wedding night. That didn't mean I planned on staying a virgin, obviously. It meant that the man I wanted to marry and spend the rest of my life with would be so special that I would torture myself in the best way possible, and I hadn't done that with Eric.

Although we made love that night, I tormented myself after Eric fell asleep. Late the next morning, he found me in the kitchen. He was in such a good mood. But as we made breakfast milk shakes, he noticed that I was a million miles away. He asked if something was wrong. Hesitantly, I said, in fact, there was.

"What? What's going on?" he asked, switching off the blender.

Tears streamed from my eyes. I took off the ring and gave it back to him, explaining that I couldn't marry him.

Eric stared at me, stunned. He might as well have seen a ghost; in a way, he had. He asked what had changed between last night and the morning. I struggled to explain my decision while avoiding the real reason for the shocking turnabout—that though he had once seemed like the man I would marry, I no longer loved him enough to make such a commitment. Sadly I loved cocaine more.

We shouted at each other. Eric picked up the blender and poured the milk shake all over me. I ran out of the house. He ran after me and we went at it in the front yard, screaming, grabbing, flailing, and pushing each other until we got to the point of killing each other or walking away. We walked away.

I could not imagine a worse way to end a relationship with someone about whom I cared so deeply.

Eric and I didn't speak for a long time and gradually I lost track of him as our lives went in separate directions.

Years later, I found him through the Internet and emailed him hello. He then called and we caught up. After we broke up, he'd come down with a virus that doctors weren't able to treat. It took him a long time to heal and get his strength back. He credited his faith for returning him to health.

When I asked what sort of faith, he simply said it was faith that things could and would get better if only he believed it. It was, he said, like he began his life all over again, a whole new chapter. Indeed, he was happily married, the father of two children, and the owner of a successful business.

"It's been a journey," he said. "I've learned a lot of lessons."

As for me, I still needed more time before I'd learn my lessons.

A few weeks after we broke up, I discovered that I was pregnant again. Although Eric and I still talked, if you can call it that, I did not tell him the news. I was afraid he would convince me to have the baby, and I had already made up my mind to terminate the pregnancy.

With no place to turn for help, I went home to my parents. Although I knew they'd disapproved of me living with Eric, I still wanted to go there. It was as if a survival instinct took over. I simply didn't have the strength to handle the situation on my own and I knew that no matter what the situation, they would take care of me, and they did. That's what makes looking back on my drug addiction so painful. I fell in love with coke because it let me escape my anger toward and embarrassment about my family, and yet they were the ones I turned to in this time of need.

I told my parents that I was pregnant and needed their help. I also said that I had broken up with Eric. For reasons I'll never quite understand, I didn't tell them about my drug problem. Maybe it's because I didn't see it as a problem yet. Also, it was scary enough to sit across from my Catholic parents and admit that I was pregnant and wanted an abortion.

My father reacted with a passiveness that reminded me of the way he had dealt with Kevin's problems. Despite his religious beliefs, there were no staunch objections or reprimands. It was my mother, though, who surprised me by stepping up and nursing me through the entire procedure.

With so many frailties and secrets of her own, I think she understood me more than I ever realized, certainly more than she was able to articulate. I think that's where her strength came from; without being able to say so, she didn't want me to have to experience the kind of pain she had known all her life. Little did she or anyone else know about the dark thoughts that had tormented me since my teens, when I first learned about her syphilis.

Then again, maybe she suspected as much. We were birds of a feather in that department. Who knows how different my life would have been if we'd been able to speak openly.

12

No Minor Vices

Once I was up and about, I moved into a condo on one of the lower floors of a Wilshire Boulevard high-rise in West Los Angeles. My parents had purchased it for me as an investment a few years earlier and rented it out, though it had recently become vacant. I didn't want to go back to my old place in Woodland Hills. I felt like I had outgrown it and needed a fresh start.

Work, the one thing about which I was most passionate, had been sporadic while I was with Eric, and I wanted to get back to it. So I was excited when I was cast in an episode of *The Streets of San Francisco*. Better still, it shot in San Francisco, giving me an excuse to get out of town. Before I left, my friend Carin, knowing my thing for older men, joked that I'd probably have a fling with the show's star Karl Malden. She had a point that made me laugh.

As it turned out, I got involved with Richard Hatch, the handsome actor who stepped in after the show's original colead Michael Douglas won a slew of Oscars for producing *One Flew Over the Cuckoo's Nest* and left to pursue a movie career. The episode was titled "No Minor Vices," and I played a teenage call girl who's the subject of an investigation after some of her johns are murdered. The culprit turns out to be her father. Richard and I started flirting on the first day. He invited me to lunch, which ended up including a full bottle of red wine.

I returned to work with a serious buzz and learned my scenes had been switched while we were at lunch and I had to work with Karl. I hated myself for not being in a condition to work with an actor of his caliber. It was emblematic of so much that was to come. I cheated myself as much as him. But I had other worries, like standing straight and walking without falling down. Our scene was outdoors. I spotted a line in the sidewalk, and after the director yelled "action," I followed it to my mark.

Later, Richard assured me that no one could tell I was tipsy. Such a relief. We were in his apartment, an amazing little place in the city, where we began an affair lasting several months. He saw me in Los Angeles on weekends and I flew up to San Francisco a few times. I had no delusions about where the relationship was going or how long it would last. All the girls were into Richard and vice versa.

It was a classic rebound fling, except that in addition to being hot, Richard was also genuinely nice. I had fun being with him, and it was a time when I needed to feel good about myself. He was into health foods and working out, something I wish would have had a more lasting influence on me.

Between visits with Richard, I got a part in the movie *Pony Express Rider,* the story of a young man (played by Stewart Petersen) who joins the Pony Express while searching for his father's killer. I served as the love interest, Rose of Sharon. The movie was shot in Kerrville, Texas, a beautiful, rugged area of oak-covered hills and green valleys. Again, I enjoyed getting away from Los Angeles even though I ended up with some nasty chigger bites on my legs from wearing a wide hoopskirt.

I relearned how to ride a horse, something I'd enjoyed as a kid when my father was an investor in a Malibu stable. I did my own stunts and got hurt when a horse dragged me a few hundred feet across the ground, but I didn't complain, not with costars like Slim Pickens, Dub Taylor, and other veterans of great Westerns looking on. Those men like tough women, and nothing made me prouder than hearing them cheer *"atta girl"* as I dusted myself off.

By the end of that bicentennial summer, I was back in Los Angeles and hanging out with the crowd at Bill's. Work had kept me away from there, but I hadn't severed ties and in fact had kept up with the same crowd, minus Eric, who'd drifted away on his own. I was drawn right back into the routine. My use was even more intense than before, and so were my friendships with Bill, Andy, Clark, and Tony.

Life got crazier. One day Clark threw a party at his parents' home and patched together white bed sheets in the backyard to make an enormous movie screen, then projected the triple-X-rated film *Deep Throat*. He thought only the people in the backyard could see it, but it turned out passersby on Sunset Boulevard could see the other side of the sheet, and soon hundreds of people, strangers, came streaming into the yard through the bushes and over the wall to watch the movie.

While all this was going on I was upstairs in Clark's brother's bedroom, going through his dresser in search of more cocaine.

Without Eric, I worried that my access to Bill might dry up. Why I worried, I don't know. I hadn't been given a reason. But I got anxious when I thought about being stranded with no supply, and so I started dating Tony. Tall, light-skinned, with long, brown hair, Tony was the son of a famous Hollywood songwriter. He was trying to make it in the music business, too, though he didn't need to work. He had plenty of money, which he spent on drugs.

Though Tony and I did not have anything in common, nor did I feel any passion when we were together, the drugs made him attractive to me. Of course I told myself otherwise. Addicts are the best liars on the planet. Ours was a crazy, coke-driven relationship that burned, as we did, for days, then crashed in a heap of singed flesh and synapses, tangled in bed but uninterested in sex.

We were dating in October 1976 when Florence Henderson, Susan Olsen, Mike Lookinland, and I appeared on the *Donny and Marie* show, one of ABC's most popular variety shows. Donny and Marie worked with an impressive seriousness. They were everything I wasn't. But I felt a measure of comfort around my former *Brady* costars, and the skits we did made few demands.

I was at Bill's the night it aired. My agent called a couple days later and said the show's ratings were so huge that ABC president Fred Silverman ordered *Donny and Marie* producers Sid and Marty Kroft to put together a *Brady Bunch* variety special. In fact, he'd already scheduled the special at the end of November. It was almost unheard of. Likewise, we had only about six and a half weeks to put a show together.

Marty Kroft phoned each of us to express his enthusiasm and discuss the show. Everyone signed on except for Eve. Having won raves in the gritty issue-oriented TV movie *Dawn: Portrait of a Teenage Runaway,* she was intent on pursuing a serious acting career and putting the Bradys in her past. Several of us tried talking to her, but she was adamant.

Though I was disappointed I wouldn't be seeing her, I respected her decision. I was even envious.

The rest of us, though, threw ourselves into a frenzied period of meetings, fittings, and rehearsals. Aside from the affection we had for one another, we also shared a genuine enthusiasm for the wacky endeavor itself. Of course the money was good and welcomed, but we were, oddly enough, swept up by a collective hope that the show would turn into something big, like the next *Sonny & Cher* variety show and we could go on tour and . . . well, it was crazy.

Crazier still was Bob Reed. After fighting with producers through every season of *The Brady Bunch,* he was the most excited of all. We joked that it was the first time any of us could remember him wanting to do something *Brady*-related. But he sang and danced without caring that he was lousy and the show itself was worse. His inner Dorothy had found her calling.

One day, as I stood next to Florence in rehearsal, I leaned in and asked how I could not have seen he was gay. Suddenly it was obvious.

Years later he told Barry that although he knew he was terrible and slow to learn the dance steps, he had fun. Great attitude. Barry, who had recently starred in a Broadway production of *Pippin,* was also in his element. Florence, the musical-comedy pro, held us together. As for Chris, the poor guy was tortured by two left feet and even less singing ability, but he was game for anything. Likewise Mike and Susie. I fell in between Bob and Barry and Florence. I worked my butt off and secretly fantasized that the show, if it took off, might rekindle a singing career for me.

Fat chance. The Krofts and writer Bruce Vilanch threw together a fractured and downright weird concoction of material, starting with our opening performance of the hits "Baby Face" and "Love to Love You Baby" (yes, our version of Donna Summer's disco classic). As we worked it onstage, the Kroffette Dancers and Water Follies performed a synchronized ballet in a giant swimming pool in front of us. And that was merely the first couple of minutes.

For the next hour, we mixed the barest bones of a story set in the Bradys' home with skits and musical numbers. Florence sang "One" from *A Chorus Line.* Barry and I did a fifties-inspired rendition of "Splish Splash" with Donny and Marie. Bob dressed in a bunny suit. "Peter" and "Marcia" fought over the phone. Barry delivered an overly earnest "Corner of the Sky" from *Pippin.* And most of the guys were pushed into the pool. Finally, the show closed with all of us onstage, debating what to sing as a finale. Unable to agree, we performed about six songs in different combinations, finally closing with "The Hustle" and "Shake Your Booty."

Never had a variety show contained such . . . variety.

But the special was another ratings hit, and ABC ordered eight more episodes starting in January 1977. Lee Majors and Farrah Fawcett provided the sizzle on the first show, and subsequent guest stars included Tina Turner, the Hudson Brothers, Milton Berle, Rip Taylor, Vincent Price, Charo, Redd Foxx, and the Ohio Players.

I did coke throughout those shows. It was the first time I'd showed up for work high. I never should have crossed that line, because once past it, I kept going. One day I showed up strung out after three straight days without sleep. After that, I often showed up late for rehearsals. When no one said anything, I figured they didn't know. Years later, I found out that all of them knew I had a problem. They just didn't know how to approach me about it.

Florence knew Chevy Chase, who was making a movie on the lot. One day she passed on the word from Chevy that his friend Steve Martin wanted my phone number so he could ask me out. Of course I gave permission. I was flattered. Steve Martin was like a rock star, not just a wild and crazy guy but a wildly funny and, from what I understood, a wildly intelligent guy, too.

So he seemed on the phone. We arranged to meet for dinner at the venerable Hollywood restaurant Musso & Frank's. Both of us brought a friend to make it more casual. After dinner, we went back to Steve's apartment, where we talked and made out. I remember him being a very good kisser. But I was insecure and either high or spaced out (most likely both), and I didn't laugh at his jokes.

Though Steve was too polite and confident of his talent to say anything, I'm sure my inability to carry on a normal conversation or respond intelligently put him off. We never spoke again after that date. I've always regretted my behavior because he impressed me as an extraordinary guy. I would've enjoyed a second date. I used to think if the circumstances had been different we could've hit it off.

I took my bad habits onto my next job, the movie *Moonshine County Express*. It was a redneck action picture directed by Gus Trikonis, Goldie Hawn's first husband. Susan Howard, Claudia Jennings, and I played three sisters who took over the family's moonshine business after our daddy was murdered. Figure-revealing crop tops, short shorts, and fast cars compensated for a thin plot.

The movie was shot in Nevada City, California, an old gold-rush town north of Sacramento, where we decamped in Victorian-style hotels that hadn't seen as much action since the boom times in the mid-1800s. It was only a few days before people found out who had coke, who had the quaaludes, and who had the pot. Our crew was more like a pharmaceutical convention than a movie. Aside from John Saxon, Susan Howard, and a few other straight arrows, I could barely go thirty minutes without someone asking if I wanted a bump.

Claudia and I became instant best friends after discovering both of us had a great capacity for snorting coke. I didn't recall that she had appeared in the "Adios, Johnny Bravo" episode of *The Brady Bunch* in 1973, which was strange, because she was a hard one to forget. A sexy redhead, she had been *Playboy*'s 1970 Playmate of the Year, then landed a part in the steamy adaptation of Jackie Susann's *The Love Machine*, and worked steadily on TV and in B-movies, including the cult roller-derby favorite, *Unholy Rollers,* whose editor was Martin Scorsese.

She was disappointed after losing the part of *Wonder Woman* to Lynda Carter, but, as she told me, that was show business; you had to deal with the bruises. *Sniff. Sniff.* We traded stories, and I learned she'd started doing drugs after injuring herself on the movie *The Great Texas Dynamite Chase*. She also lived with songwriter Bobby Hart, his kids, and a bunch of animals. *Sniff. Sniff.*

As we got to know each other better, I confided that there seemed to be quite a few lesbians among the crew. How did I know? *Sniff.* *Sniff.* Several had hit on me, including one woman who had been quite up-front and graphic.

"What did you say?" Claudia asked, grinning.

Sniff. Sniff.

"I said I was flattered, but no thanks."

Laughing from embarrassment, I told her how I had a close friend who was straight but had recently gone through a phase of dating other women and tried to talk me into experimenting as well. She'd argued that every woman had it in her to make love to another woman. *Sniff.* *Sniff.* However, as I told Carin and then repeated to Claudia, I didn't have a single stirring that would make me switch teams.

"But I'm a terrible flirt," I admitted. "Guys or women—I just love people."

Sniff. Sniff.

At one point, Claudia and I got close to the movie's cinematographer, Gary Graver, who regaled us with stories of his friendship with Orson Welles and even talked about all of us making a movie together. In its own way, the promise of working with the legendary figure was as intoxicating as the drugs that fueled such conversation. All of us would make a great film together! *Sniff. Sniff.*

Then Claudia and Gary began having an affair. Since I liked him, too, I became jealous and terribly insecure, wondering why he hadn't wanted to be with me. Everyone was desperate for a special connection that would make them feel desired, pretty, or talented, even if it was only for a night or two, and that applied to me, too.

Well, one night after I dropped a seductive hint, it turned out he did want to be with me, and for a brief time, the lucky guy shuttled between the two of us. Such was life on that movie set. *Sniff. Sniff.* After returning to Los Angeles, though, I went back with Tony. Claudia stayed with Gary until I introduced her to Bill. Then they had a fling, which changed the dynamic of our friendship.

That happened when everything was about coke, and that's what everything was about at Bill's. Friendships shifted and suffered. Jealousy popped up for no reason or because someone misinterpreted a comment when they were high. And we were high all the time there. We were one another's friends, lovers, and torturers. I slept with Bill, too. I did it only a few times—and always for the same reason: I wanted coke.

The atmosphere at Wonderland Avenue was subject to the availability of cocaine and therefore we were all under the control of Bill to one degree or another. Relationships got even more tangled, and people cheated and stole from one another. Even with all the coke I got from Bill, I scooped up more and took it home with me. Bill's associates once accused Andy of stealing several ounces. They held him at gunpoint and threatened to kill him.

The scene essentially ended when Bill went to jail after getting busted with a van full of Thai sticks. That in itself was a fluke. He'd stopped in front of a liquor store on Sunset Boulevard. While he was inside, cops walked by, smelled the load of potent marijuana, and nailed him when he got back into the van. I also heard Bill's main coke supplier ended up in prison on Rikers Island.

At various points, it could've been me in cuffs. I did an episode of *The Love Boat,* and I couldn't have been happier when I found out it involved an actual cruise to Mexico. My manager, Doug, and his wife, Jill, also wrangled a trip. They partied as much as I did, if not more. After my Bill connection dried up, in fact, Jack bought coke for me. *The Love Boat* turned out to be a nonstop party as we traveled down the coast, somehow managing to also shoot a TV show.

On the day we docked in Puerto Vallarta, Robert Hegyes, who'd played Epstein on *Welcome Back, Kotter, Love Boat* regular Lauren Tewes, and I arranged to get off the boat and go to the beach. At the last minute, I changed my mind and decided to go into town with my manager's wife to shop and drink margaritas.

It turned out to be a good move. While we were partying, Bobby and Lauren were busted for pot. As it turned out, it was a set-up by a crooked cop who planted dope on them, hoping to extort cash from the TV production.

The situation was fixed after only a brief delay in production. It was frightening. Later that night, while sitting up on the deck I said to my manager, "Oh my God, that could've been me." In true Hollywood fashion he replied, "What do you mean *you*? It could've been me!"

It seemed like the close calls were getting closer. Sometime after that cruise Carin and I went on a binge with Andy and Clark. We booked a suite at the Century Plaza Hotel for the weekend, and then we obliterated ourselves with coke and quaaludes. At one point, Carin passed out in the bathtub. She appeared to OD. We were too scared to call an ambulance. Instead we yanked her out, stood her up, and kept her awake until she seemed to be out of danger.

It freaks me out to think of what might have happened if she'd died—or more to the point that she *could have* died because we were too worried about ourselves to call for proper medical attention.

How messed up!

How selfish!

Like most druggies, though, we never considered the danger until it stared us in the face.

And even then . . .

Part
Two

13

Vacation in Hell

I t's because you were Marcia Brady."

My agent put the news bluntly. I had auditioned for the girl-friend's role in the movie *Midnight Express,* the based-on-a-true story of Billy Hayes's escape from a Turkish prison after getting caught trying to smuggle drugs out of the country. The first reading had gone well and they had called me back several times. Each time, my chances looked better and better. For any actress, it was a terrific part: multi-layered, demanding, and transformative. For me, it was also an oppor-tunity to redefine myself as an actress. But then the part went to actress Irene Miracle, who would receive a much-deserved Golden Globe nomination for her work.

I was crushed when I heard the news and even more depressed after learning the reason was that I was too closely identified with *The Brady Bunch* to take on such a heavy role. I was told the producers and direc-tor Alan Parker feared audiences wouldn't accept Marcia Brady in a movie about drugs.

It was the first time I felt cursed by my *Brady Bunch* past. What was I going to do about her? Was Marcia going to haunt me for the rest of my life? Was she going to hold me back? All of a sudden I hated her. If only they had known the truth, I thought. If only they knew the real me.

I poured my heart out to Claudia. She was getting over a disappointment of her own after losing out to Shelley Hack as Kate Jackson's replacement on the TV series *Charlie's Angels.* Disillusioned and depressed from that setback, she would, over time, give up drugs and straighten herself out only to die tragically about a year later when a van plowed into her VW bug on Topanga Canyon Boulevard.

Eager to work and prove myself, I was thrilled when I landed the movie *Take Down,* the story of a high-school English teacher with lofty academic airs who's forced to coach the school's wrestling team. The fine actor Edward Herrmann played the teacher whose high standards and snobbishness put him in conflict with a senior on the wrestling team, a misunderstood kid with a secret problem that could prevent him from graduating. Lorenzo Lamas filled that part, and I played his girlfriend.

It wasn't *Midnight Express,* but it was a good part in a film that had truly moving and inspirational moments. I also hoped I might even get in some skiing when I learned we were shooting in Provo, Utah. That didn't happen. Early on, Lorenzo and I were busted by the director/producer Keith Merrill as we tried to sneak off for a day on the slopes. He couldn't risk us getting hurt.

Keith was a smart, passionate, interesting man who was a Mormon and gave all of us Mormon Bibles at the start of production. I ignored his efforts at converting us. I could have used some guidance, though. Coke was prevalent among the crew, and I quickly found out who was holding and vice versa. It's scary to think back on. One night I had an affair with a lighting guy in a sauna. I wasn't one for one-nighters, but he had coke and I wanted some.

It wasn't long before I fell into a routine, staying up several nights in a row without sleep, then taking pills to bring me down enough that I could get a few hours' sleep and go to work without looking like I'd just been dragged underneath a freight train. One morning, after spending a couple days and nights locked in my room, locked in the sauna, doing coke, drinking, taking downers, and whatnot, I called in sick. I couldn't make it to the set.

Hearing I had the flu, Keith and one of the other producers had me taken to the hospital. There I was given a shot of something the doctor said would take away my nausea and whatever other symptoms I'd manifested or made up. It turned out I had an allergic reaction to the medication. Not immediately, though. I made it back to the set and started to shoot a scene with Lorenzo. We were seated next to each other in a car. There were cameras, lights, and crew everywhere.

All of a sudden my neck began to throb, then the inside of my throat swelled, and I couldn't swallow. I began to gag—and panic. I felt like my neck was going to shut off the rest of my body. I was rushed back to the hospital, where I received an injection to counter the allergic reaction.

That episode scared the hell out of me. I'd thought I was going to die right there on the set. It should have opened my eyes to my drug problem. It didn't. Back in Los Angeles, I made my account to friends as dramatic as possible, and it really was. I didn't have to exaggerate. But the punch line was pure fantasy: I blamed the ER doctor for not being more careful.

After the movie, I worked on an episode of *Lou Grant,* the newspaper drama starring Ed Asner. Some weeks were saner and more sober than others, and I'm glad that was one of them. I got to work opposite Nancy Marchand, the graceful veteran actress who portrayed the newspaper's owner. In the episode, I played her niece, who she discovered couldn't read.

It was a fully developed role, which is tough to do in a sixty-minute show, and I felt so good about myself—a strange experience—when afterward both Nancy and Ed complimented me on a terrific week. Ed topped it off with a bear hug. Those were really lovely, talented people, and I'm glad I was present for them. It could've easily been very different.

And so it was on my next project, the movie-of-the-week *Vacation in Hell*. It was the story of five tourists—four women and a man—who stray from a group holiday in a tropical paradise and get lost in a jungle where a killer begins hunting them. Director David Greene, whose credits included *Roots; Rich Man, Poor Man;* and *The Trial of Lee Harvey Oswald,* gave the production a certain stature. Aside from me, the cast included Priscilla Barnes, Barbara Feldon, Andrea Marcovicci, and Michael Brandon.

This movie was filmed in Hawaii and was fun from day one when we shot the opening scene with the four of us, having gotten lost in the ocean, walking up on the beach and beginning our harrowing adventure. An even bigger real-life adventure brewed offscreen as the cast and crew figured out which ones of us were partiers, and suddenly it was as if a wildfire of sex and craziness swept through the production. That was my experience at least. From the first day, Michael Brandon and I began to flirt. Born in Brooklyn, he was ten years older than me, dark-haired, handsome, a little quirky, and a gifted actor. He was just my type.

He adored women. I noticed he flirted with every female in his line of vision, and they generally found his charm and humor irresistible. But I was the one on the set who eventually got him, and we had a hot and heavy affair throughout the movie. We were also high throughout the production. But *Vacation in Hell* was one of those productions where nearly everyone, unless they were older and obviously straight like Barbara and Priscilla, seemed to some degree to catch party fever.

One day we were shooting a scene on the beach and all of a sudden Andrea, a beautiful, sexy woman with a Broadway background, turned to me and said she missed her dog. My simple acknowledgment wasn't enough for her. She carried on about it, explaining she wanted me to understand that she *really* missed her dog, and then she asked me if I would bark for her.

"Bark?"

"Yes, like a dog."

I looked deep into her eyes to see if she was serious. She was. So I barked for Andrea, who petted my head, smiled, and thanked me for helping remind her of her beloved pooch. Much later I wondered whether that whole scene had been a subtle attempt to embarrass me in front of Michael, who also liked her and may have gone back and forth between us during the movie until he settled on me.

I lusted after him like no one in my life. It was a combination of the drugs and Hawaii, I'm sure, but it was hot and heavy and romantic. When we did scenes together, I imagined him naked, and inside I felt like I was on the verge of bursting out of my clothes. The passion was pretty amazing.

And so was the coke. I was doing it every night, all night, and soon that round-the-clock lifestyle took a toll on me. One morning I didn't show up for work. I was dead to the world and stayed in bed through my alarm and past my call time. I was still in bed when I heard a knock on my door. I didn't answer, figuring they would go away. A moment later, the phone rang. After an annoying number of rings, I picked it up and heard a stern voice say, "Maureen?"

It was Pat Finnegan, who along with her husband, Bill, was producing the movie. The two of them were serious, respected producers. Pat said she had knocked on my door and not gotten an answer. I apologized and said I didn't feel well. She wanted to see me and said to let her into my room.

I was out of it as she pulled a chair up to my bed and stared at me. My skin was pale, my eyes were bloodshot, and I looked like crap.

"Maureen, we *need* you on the set today," she said. "You're in the scenes we're doing."

"I can't," I groaned. "I've got the flu."

I described my symptoms for Pat. It was the same excuse I'd used on *Take Down*.

"I really feel nauseous and like I'm going to throw up any minute," I said.

Pat took a deep breath.

"We'll get you something for that," she said. "You'll be fine. But you've got to come to work. We need you."

I continued to come up with excuses for why I couldn't make it. Finally, Pat sat forward and looked me sternly in the eyes.

"Look, Maureen, I know what you're doing," she said. "I wasn't born yesterday. I'm not naive. But you need to come to work. This morning. We have to do this scene—and we are going to do this scene."

There was no use arguing any further. Pat was the boss. I stayed in bed for a few more hours, waiting for my head to clear and trying to feel straight. I stalled for as long as possible, then went to the set and struggled through the scene and the rest of the movie.

Back in Los Angeles, I moved in with Michael. He shared a large house in Brentwood with a guy whose girlfriend was actress Debra Winger. The four of us spent a lot of time together at the house. Debra was fun, as well as brilliant, charismatic, opinionated, and intense. She gave off a powerful, going-places vibe. I wasn't surprised when she became a superstar.

It was through Michael that I was introduced to the Playboy Mansion. He knew people there, and we were invited to parties. On one occasion, I saw Steven Spielberg with his than girlfriend, actress Amy Irving. Another time Michael pointed out legendary producer Robert Evans lounging poolside amid a bevy of topless bunnies. One night we met Sammy Davis Jr. After the party wound down at the mansion, we followed him up to his house off Benedict Canyon.

A number of other people also made the late-night trip to his place from the mansion. I couldn't believe I was at Sammy's house, nor could I believe what I saw there. He had a bowl of amyl nitrates on his coffee table. They were called poppers, and they were big in the disco scene; a blast sent a numbing shiver through your head and made you tingly. Michael and I disappeared into one of the bedrooms with several of them, got crazy, and then took some home with us.

The Playboy Mansion's lush grounds included rolling grassy hills, a monkey cage, strolling peacocks, and rooms with pinball machines. The action took place around and in the swimming pool. It was most animated in a secret hot tub known as "the grotto." The grotto was legendary for its anything-goes hookups. I never got naked in it or took off my top, as was common, but I partied in the steamy pool.

Michael and I inevitably broke up. Our lifestyle wasn't conducive to longevity, and I was too insecure and unbalanced for a normal relationship. Michael was able to stop partying and resume a regular life. I didn't have the same discipline. If there was coke, I had to stay up and do every last flake even if it meant going without sleep for days. Nothing else mattered.

Like the time Michael found me in the living room after one such jag totally unaware that the two of us were scheduled to meet David Greene and the Finnegans at a recording studio to do voice-overs for the movie. When I said I wasn't up to it, he grabbed me and very clearly and forcefully said it wasn't an either-or situation. I was too messed up to care. I said that I'd reschedule.

"No, no, no, you don't get it," he said. "You can't blow this."

"I can't go," I said.

And I didn't. I stayed at Michael's, where I continued to get high. Then David Greene called and said he needed me. There were costs involved with the studio time and deadlines, he explained. It didn't register with me. I still didn't leave the house, and that was the beginning of the end of so many things. Michael was disappointed and embarrassed when he came home. He said they found someone else to dub my part, which depressed me and led to a fight.

That was more and more typical of me. Anger was the only way I knew how to express the innermost awareness I had that I was fucking up. After that, Michael and I went downhill. One day, while swimming laps in his pool, I kicked too hard against an underwater light, broke it, and sliced my foot open on the glass. It wasn't a pretty sight. Blood was all over the pool and the deck. Michael drove me to the emergency room, which I thought was sweet.

For Easter, he bought me a stuffed bunny. I thought, Oh, he really does love me. But a short time later, we broke up. We got into a terrible fight, and it ended with him saying we were finished. I only had my drug habit and myself to blame. But I wanted it to be his fault. I needed to blame someone other than myself. Before I stormed off that night, I took a cross that was one of his favorite possessions.

Later, after things cooled off, he asked if I'd taken it. I said no. I think he knew I was lying, but he didn't press me. I've kept that cross for all these years. Every time I see it I'm reminded of that troubled time when I lied to Michael, lied to so many people, and lied most of all to myself.

14

One Flew into the Cuckoo's Nest

Claudia was dating James Caan, who had been one of Hollywood's hottest and busiest actors since his sizzling turn in *The Godfather* in 1972. He was also an enthusiastic partier, with an appetite for fun that matched his gregarious personality. He and Claudia met at the Playboy Mansion, and I subsequently joined them for weekends at Jimmy's ranch in the Las Vegas desert, where we got obliterated.

I fell in love with actor Gregory Harrison. It was love at first sight. He was my type: dark, handsome, and good-natured. He liked sports, played guitar, and was incredibly romantic. Our affair was hot and heavy. I actually thought he was the one I would marry. But once again my drug use got in the way. Some days were lovely, and other days I was like a cyclone tearing through a house. There were times when I was so coked out of my mind I wouldn't let him into my apartment. I also blew off dates. I can still picture a time when he stood downstairs at the front desk and had security buzz me over and over, pleading with me to let him up. I wouldn't.

He ended up walking away from the relationship. I didn't admit that drugs had ruined a serious relationship. Instead I told myself that I needed to chill out, take some time to recover from the breakup, and get healthy. So I went to Hawaii with my brother Kevin.

Now in his mid-thirties, Kevin was still trying to figure out what to do with his life. Psychologically, his swings were bigger than mine. His drug use was heavier, too. My mother, who'd wanted to get him professional help since he dropped out of high school, began openly worrying he might kill himself. Both of my parents were scared he might do something crazy.

I felt a strong kinship with him, stronger than I can rationalize. It was just that the more lost he seemed, the more empathy I felt. After we landed in Hawaii, our first stop was the health-food store. We picked up a load of fresh fruit and juices, vowing to cleanse our systems. We ran on the beach, lay in the sun, and played guitar at night. Somehow we reasoned that doing mushrooms also fit into this regime.

The theory was that mushrooms opened the doors to a deeper, clearer understanding of life. We hiked to the seven sacred pools in Hana, where we'd heard that mushrooms grew in cow paddies. It had rained recently, and the mushrooms were all over. We brought a bota bag of wine, which we used to clean the 'shrooms before we ate them.

We tripped for several hours while gathering more mushrooms. I remember being down on my hands and knees and feeling connected to the earth as I dug through the soft, moist ground. On the way down the trail—there were only a couple trails in and out—other hikers asked what we were doing and I was so joyously high that I told them about the mushrooms.

"They're the greatest thing in the world," I gushed. "You have to try them!"

We met two gay guys on the trail, and I gave them a handful of hallucinogenic truffles. A few hours later, Kevin and I saw them again at the general store. They still had a bit of a glow in their eyes as I asked if they took them.

"Did we take them?" one of the guys said, rolling his head back as if he were surveying the sky.

His boyfriend hugged me and said, "God bless you, child."

Kevin and I made subsequent Hawaiian getaways for the same purpose. Each one was intended for getting into shape. I wonder how many times I would've had to go there before I realized that I returned more strung out than I was when I arrived. It was a different kind of exhaustion. I looked great physically, but my brain was fried.

After returning from one so-called vacation, I went to work on the movie *Skatetown, U.S.A.,* which starred Scott Baio, Flip Wilson, Ruth Buzzi, and was billed as "the Rock and Roller Disco Movie of the Year." Like a disco, there was a lot of cocaine being done on the set. Many people were open about it. Unable to resist temptation, I fell back into my same old routine. Soon I was missing days on the set. Few people in Hollywood were so straight that they made a stink about actors getting high. But God help the person who cost the production money by not showing up.

I didn't think I was above such behavior. I simply didn't think. My friend Carin's uncle Bill Levey was directing the movie. Ray Stark, who'd produced my first play when I was a kid, was the producer. He had become one of the most powerful men in the business. He also had one of the more explosive tempers. I was nervous every time he was on the set.

Plus I was already self-conscious from having to do most of my scenes wearing tight short shorts and a tube top. To ensure that I was superskinny, I did coke and popped diet pills. I got below 110 pounds, which was too thin for me. But I was of the opinion that I couldn't be too thin.

I thought I was doing a good job keeping myself together, but I was only fooling myself. Bill Levey covered for me when I showed up late or flaked altogether. But it got to the point where the whole set talked openly about my erratic work habits and unreliability. One day Ray took me aside and said he wanted to take a walk with me. We went around the corner from the soundstage. Then he stopped and turned toward me.

"Maureen, I know what you're doing," he said.

"You do?" I said, scared and trying to hold back tears.

"This is a business," he said.

"I'm sorry," I said. "I'll do better."

"It's not about doing better," he said. "Listen to me carefully. I want to make sure you understand. You aren't showing up for work. You're behaving irresponsibly. If you don't go get help, I'm going to make it so you never work another day in this business."

He paused to let the thought of losing my livelihood sink in. I didn't know what I'd do if I couldn't work.

"Do you understand me?" he asked.

"I do," I said.

I didn't know what to do. Nor did I know how to get help or who to turn to for advice. I felt trapped. I couldn't lie or pretend my way through the situation as I had done every time up to that point. With so much at stake, I turned to Carin's parents, both of whom I respected. They made calls and found a hospital in the Valley that treated drug problems. Then they did what I was too scared and ashamed to do myself: They told my parents.

I can't imagine the devastation my parents felt, especially my mother. They knew that I wasn't in good shape, but this was confirmation that their daughter was plagued with the kind of problems that had cursed various members of our family. They didn't say anything; privately, I'm sure they cried. But to me, they offered nothing but support. They closed ranks and let me know how much I was loved.

On top of the guilt I felt for causing them pain and worry, I was frightened to death by the reality that I was going someplace for treatment. I came up with umpteen excuses to get out of it. Except I took

Ray Stark at his word. I knew not going was the end of my career. Without my career . . .

I didn't want to think about that.

I drove myself to the small psychiatric hospital in Van Nuys, parked my car in the lot behind the building, and broke down. I was scared and sick to my stomach. My fear that I might one day go insane had finally come true. I thought of how my grandmother had died in a mental institution after losing her mind. I had a sense of inevitability, like I had arrived.

The staff was waiting for me inside. It was more proof of inevitability; they were expecting me! I was shown into a room where a nurse went through the bag of clothes and belongings I had brought even though I insisted I wasn't hiding anything. It didn't matter. Everything was taken away from me. Next, a doctor examined me, wrote down the drugs I said I'd abused (coke, diet pills, quaaludes), and then nodded blankly when I said that I hadn't done anything for two days.

I stayed for a week. Even though I was assigned a private room, I was aware that almost everyone knew who I was. They whispered and talked about it openly as if I didn't have ears. One day we took a field trip to a park in Pasadena. As we stepped off the bus, several mothers pushing strollers stared at me. I immediately asked to be allowed to get back on the bus lest someone ask for an autograph. When the attendants refused, I felt like I was losing whatever scrap of dignity I had left.

Just like in the movie *One Flew Over the Cuckoo's Nest,* a nurse gave us meds twice a day in a little white cup. I had no idea what they were, and when I asked, the nurse simply said they were to help me. I called home from a pay phone in the hall and expressed concern to my parents. But they'd been called separately by the hospital's doctor and told that I was still doing coke, which wasn't true. It made me feel like I really had lost my mind.

On the day I checked out, I drove myself from the hospital to the Santa Monica pier, where *Skatetown* was shooting scenes. I assumed everyone knew where I'd been, and I was given a warm welcome back. Many, including Bill Levey, expressed their concern and hope that I felt better. I wanted to keep it quiet and move on. My first scene was with *Welcome Back, Kotter*'s Ron Palillo. We were in a car and about to run through our first take when he took hold of my wrist.

"Maureen, you still have your hospital bracelet on," he said.

"Oh my God!"

I stiffened, mortified. Then Ron burst into his unmistakably Horshack laugh. Hearing that right in my ear, I laughed, too. Everyone offered support. One day, Bill Levey brought Richard Dreyfuss to the set. The thirty-one-year-old actor, at the top of Hollywood thanks to winning a Best Actor Oscar for *The Goodbye Girl,* was starring in the hit *Close Encounters of the Third Kind,* and had his own struggles. He shared those stories with me.

I related to those stories. I also respected Richard. He managed to hit a note in me that others missed. At his urging, I attended a couple of AA meetings.

I started to think that maybe I could stay sober. It was a daunting task. The people who were rooting for me were the same people with whom I'd gotten high a couple weeks earlier. Most of them were still getting high. But I made an effort, and my willpower seemed rewarded when I auditioned for a small part in the movie *The Idolmaker,* a drama about music's Frankie Avalon era.

The buzz in Hollywood on the film was that it was a hot project. Taylor Hackford was making his directorial debut, and Ray Sharkey was already cast in the lead as a rock Svengali who turned hot guys into stars.

Hundreds of girls interviewed for the same role as me, but the casting director asked me back the next day. I prepared by talking to several reporters at fan magazines who used to write about me during the *Brady* days. I wanted to be great. Then I went in the following afternoon and nailed my audition. I had never been better, or prouder of myself. Afterward, I called my agent, Sandy Bressler, and gushed, "I really can do this. I really can act."

However, in the interim between the audition and filming, the lure of old habits proved too strong, and I started doing coke again. My need to do it, and do it in greater quantities, seemed to be more powerful than before. I stayed up for three nights prior to my first scene on the movie. I remember looking out my apartment windows and seeing the sun come up. Nothing was worse than knowing I had to be someplace in an hour and feeling wasted from not having slept or showered for days.

I only had two full days of work on the picture, so I didn't let myself think about bailing. Somehow I made it to the set and did my scenes opposite Peter Gallagher, who was making his first feature-film appearance. If he knew I was blitzed, he graciously didn't mention it. Neither did Ray Sharkey, who spent time with me off camera that day. He was probably having problems, too. But I was paranoid that everyone knew I was messed up, and I got pissed off at myself for blowing an opportunity.

Nearly a week passed before they needed me again. Although I was straight and rested that second day, I've always believed Taylor Hackford was disappointed in the performance I gave compared to my audition. Why didn't I have more self-control even when I knew my behavior was self-destructive? I had no faith in myself—no faith, period.

In that frame of mind, I chose guys for the wrong reasons. I was at a party when I spotted writer-actor David Ladd across the room and knew I wanted to be with him. I felt like it was love at first sight.

But I confused lust with love, which explains why we didn't last. I didn't want a real relationship as much as I wanted a man who would keep me company *and* keep the party going.

That explains my relationship with an older, talented, and very accomplished man in the music industry. For the purpose of this story, I'll refer to him as Colin.

We met through a mutual friend, a girl I knew from Frank's, and we had instant chemistry. It wasn't just physical, though that was nice, too. He was slightly over six feet tall, with longish, Rod Stewart–like hair, and he spoke with a British accent. But with Frank as our common denominator, we shared an even more potent attraction, and on our first date it was pretty clear from what we did in the back of a limo that both of us were into coke.

I was just as intoxicated by his world. A master at making records, he slept late, worked at night, and seemed to live in either the back of a limo or at the console in a recording studio. At the time we got together, he was working on albums with four or five well-known bands. All were FM-radio superstars. The music was phenomenal, and the drugs were better. The two were inseparable.

And so were Colin and I. We hung out at night and returned to his place in the wee hours. He sent me home in a car the first few times. But it wasn't long before I went inside with him and stayed the rest of the night. We got close quickly. We told each other stories. We shared secrets. We also shared each others' bad habits. We were like lights that never got turned off.

He took me to parties at homes rented by some of rock's most famous personalities, and I hung out at recording sessions. I liked this world. Rock stars were fun, and they tended to let pretty girls get away with anything. I remember getting obliterated in the studio, sniffing lines off the engineering board when no one was looking. I also sang background vocals on several songs.

To me, this was the epitome of the good life: talented people, great music, and lots of coke. It wasn't real life, which made it even more attractive. I almost hated to interrupt the fun by going off to work on the movie *Texas Lightning,* kind of a redneck love story about a macho truck driver who decides to turn his son into a man by taking him on a hunting trip. Then the son fell in love with the waitress at the local honky tonk—my character—and the notion of manhood took on an unexpected twist.

It was a difficult role for me. I'd never tackled such a sexy or adult role. I had to bare equal amounts of skin and emotion, and both caused me anxiety.

My friend Gary Garver was the director. He helped give me the confidence I needed to set aside my inhibitions and good girl image. I took risks that still shock me when I think about them, just the way I allowed myself to cross a line emotionally in front of the camera. As a result, I think that movie still has some of the best work I've ever done.

But I was emotionally raw when I did that film. I didn't realize the high wire act I was living. I wasn't acting as much as I was letting everything show.

After the movie, I returned to Colin's with a sense of relief of being spirited off to the land where nothing mattered but getting high. He wasn't involved with any projects at the time, and so we locked ourselves up in his house and stayed awake for days. Colin liked to do coke and have sex. As long as there was coke around, I didn't care what we did. I just wanted to maintain the buzz.

During this period, my agent arranged for me to audition with Steven Spielberg for his new movie *Raiders of the Lost Ark*. Although Steven was looking at many actresses, it was still a big deal to get a meeting with him. However, I was so messed up that I missed my appointment with him. I don't know what excuse my agent gave them, but he managed to set up another meeting and made me swear to show up.

I managed to get there, but I was pretty messed up when I sat down across from Steven. It's amazing how I deluded myself into thinking I was prepared. I'd been up for several days. I probably looked drawn and tired, but thought makeup covered it. What no amount of makeup could conceal, though, was my inability to function like an actress who cared about her craft.

It was obvious I was fried. At one point, as I struggled to answer his questions, he gave up, pointed to a bowl of fruit, and asked if I wanted an orange. It was a polite way of saying you need to take better care of yourself.

And he was right, of course.

But I didn't pay attention. I wanted to keep going even when Colin went out or fell asleep. I snuck through his house, looking for more dope. I remember searching his coat pockets for coke. I rifled through the clothes in his closet, his desk, and even his bathroom drawers. I knew all of his hiding places. It's funny to think back and realize he had hiding places from me.

It's worse to realize I spent time looking for it.

It was inevitable that Colin and I would graduate to a more powerful high, and we did. We started to freebase, meaning we cooked our coke into a potent concentrate, let it harden into a rock, and then smoked it in a pipe. A few months earlier, Richard Pryor had set himself on fire while freebasing. Lucky to escape with his life, he joked that he'd caused an explosion by dipping a cookie in two different kinds of milk. It wasn't funny. Basing was extremely dangerous—and not just because you could catch yourself on fire. Once I did it, I was hooked. I thought of nothing else but doing more.

Colin's appetite for the drug was just as ravenous as mine, except he pursued it more indulgently and hedonistically than I did. Whereas Colin liked to get high and have sex, my favorite place to get high was in a closet by myself. Since I only cared about access to the coke, I obliged. It was like we were chasing two highs.

I remember Colin wanting a change of scenery after we'd literally gone into hibernation in his house. He ordered a limo to take us up to San Francisco, and we sat in the back doing base and having sex the whole drive. We checked into the nicest hotel, hung up a DO NOT DIS-TURB sign, and didn't leave the room for a week. God knows what the people at the front desk thought when we checked out.

At some point during this up and down rollercoaster, I began to suffer from hallucinations. It was always a variation of the same theme: the cops were about to bust into the house. I was convinced they were outside. The time of day didn't matter; they were always there. Watching every move I made. Even when I sat in the closet, I thought they could see me. Sometimes I was so scared I crawled through the house. Other times I was so tweaked and tired I thought, what the hell, let them come get me.

I shudder when I think about the way I felt back then. Only one thing was certain and I wasn't even aware of it: I was teetering on the edge, totally crazed—and about to crash.

15

A Brady Bride Is Fried

When I first heard about *The Brady Brides,* a two-hour movie that had the Bradys reuniting for Marcia and Jan's double wedding, I said no way. I thought it was stupid. I was a million miles away from the world of Marcia Brady, and, as I told my agent, Sandy, I didn't consider that a bad thing. It was 1981, and I was twenty-five years old, and I had been through so much—and was still going through so much—that wasn't Marcia-like that I didn't want to think about returning to the *Brady* fold.

In a way, it was like facing family, and that scared me in the shape I was in at the time. Colin and I had once spent a weekend at Barry's beach house and I had rummaged through the house until I found some coke in a kitchen drawer. I did all of it. Barry had never said anything, and I was too embarrassed to risk a confrontation. But Paramount knew NBC saw the movie as a pilot for a potential series and the money they offered kept growing until it was impossible to resist.

I know the same was true for Barry and for Eve, who had married a policeman and lived in a cute old bungalow in Manhattan Beach. Some of us spoke on the phone beforehand. A nice spirit emerged as the entire original cast signed on, including Florence, Ann, and Bob, who surprised the Schwartzes by agreeing to the projects. The money was the motivator, of course, but Bob also reportedly said he wouldn't let anyone else give away his girls.

Casting our husbands was a top priority for Sherwood and Lloyd. They looked at hundreds of guys. After whittling down the list, they scheduled screen tests for me with more than a dozen actors, the same way they had cast the original *Brady Bunch* in 1968. There was one huge difference, though. Instead of showing up on the set that morning, I blew it off. I was at home, getting high, as I'd done for days.

Around noon, I heard a banging on my door. Someone yelled my name: *Maureen!* I ignored it and moved into the bedroom, closing the door behind me. I sat on the bed and continued to play solitaire, smoke cigarettes, and do coke. I thought if I didn't answer the door whoever was there might go away.

But they didn't. The knocking got stronger and more determined. I scooted off the bed and sat in the corner, trying to move farther away. Then the phone rang. I let the machine pick up. It rang again, and rang and rang some more. I kept playing solitaire, trying to block out the disturbances and burrow deeper into myself.

BAM! BAM! BAM!

I thought the door might break down.

RING! RING! RING!

For a few moments, there was quiet. The knocking and the ringing finally stopped. I thought they might have gone away. But then: "Goddammit, she's not answering . . . I know she's in there . . . Maybe she's dead . . . Shit."

The voice or voices came from outside. It sounded like they were underneath my balcony. I had no idea whether they were imaginary or real. I was on the seventh floor. Although the building pool was on the sixth floor, I couldn't imagine how anyone could get onto my balcony.

"Maureen! It's me! I'm coming up!"

I peeked out my bedroom window and saw a long metal ladder extended from the pool deck to my balcony.

Suddenly my agent burst through the bedroom door. He stopped as soon as he saw me curled up in the corner. He was panicked.

"What the hell are you doing?" he said.

I looked up without responding.

"What's going on?" he repeated.

I shook my head slightly.

"Never mind. I know what's going on." He took off his jacket and threw it on the bed. "Everyone's waiting on you. We have to get you to Paramount right now or else this whole thing is over."

Sandy picked me up, took off my clothes, and threw me into the shower. I stood in the stall, motionless, still high and freaked out. He turned on the water and ordered me to clean up and then get dressed. When I came out in a towel with my hair dripping wet, he was in the living room, barking at me to put on some clothes and brush my hair—my chestnut hair that I used to brush all day long when I was first on *The Brady Bunch*. Now it was too much of a chore.

Sandy took me straight to Paramount. We barely spoke the whole way. I sat in the passenger seat with my head thrown back and eyes shut or else I stared out the window, feeling sick and unable to focus as the buildings and storefronts whizzed by in a blur. When he gave my name at the gate, I let out a groan.

"Do I have to go in?" I said.

"Yes."

He marched me into Sherwood's office. We sat down and I faced Sherwood and Lloyd. I felt like all the air had been let out of me. I was worn out and sick.

And sad.

And ashamed.

And scared.

"I've got a problem," I said, crying. "It's cocaine. I can't stop. I'm really, really sorry."

"Thank God you're okay," said Sherwood. "That's number one. We're going to get you some help."

W ork was always my sanctuary, my safe place. Whether straight or stoned, it was where I could go and feel comfortable. But that wasn't the case anymore. Going to the set for screen tests that day and the subsequent few days made me a nervous wreck. I was embarrassed and ashamed. I didn't want anyone to see me and vice versa. I still felt like I'd rather be curled up in a fetal position in the corner of my bedroom.

I saw Florence first. In a way, it was like seeing my mother. She hugged me, and later, during a more private moment, she said, "I know what you're going through. I'm really, really sorry. If you need me for anything, I'll be there for you." Ann B. Davis set a copy of the Bible in front of me and said, "Whatever I can do, whatever you need." The others also knew I had a problem, but they didn't say anything. I thought it was better that way. Now I wish they had intervened.

Actually, one day I received a note from Florence. I'd sent her flowers for her birthday. She thanked me for them, and then offered encouragement. "I truly admire you as a human being," she wrote. "You've got guts, compassion, sensitivity, and you're a real survivor! It's so hard in this business to retain your sense of humanity, to be forgiving of one's self and others and not to be disillusioned by all the disillusioned people around us."

As promised, Sherwood and Lloyd got me help immediately. I don't know who they asked or what process they went through, but they hired Dr. Eugene Landy, a psychologist who cultivated a reputation as "the shrink to the stars" by treating Rod Steiger, Alice Cooper, Richard Harris, and Brian Wilson. The Beach Boys' troubled genius was Landy's most celebrated patient, and later the cause of his undoing when the Wilson family took him to court amid charges of gross negligence. In 1991, the courts finally forced Landy out of Wilson's life.

Landy practiced a controversial twenty-four-hour-a-day therapy in which he and his so-called therapeutic team assumed complete control of every aspect of the patient's life. As Landy explained to me, that meant he controlled everything from what I ate to where I went to whom I spoke to on the phone. He even said that if I was in a relationship and wanted to have sex, he had to approve it.

"I'm not in a relationship," I said.

I didn't tell him about Colin. The two of us were mostly off by this time, though I had been reluctant to give him up completely.

"You don't have to be in a relationship to have sex," said Landy.

"Right."

"You should know that if you do have sex, I will know about it," he added. "I may even be watching."

I had never met anyone creepier than Dr. Landy, who said such things, I'm sure, to get into my head. He did a good job, too. He was a short, doughy man with longish dark hair. His office was on Robertson Boulevard, in Beverly Hills. At our first meeting, he was wearing running shorts, a corduroy blazer over a T-shirt, and a bright orange hat. My parents were also present. Dr. Landy reminded me of a performer as he explained his round-the-clock therapy. It was like he enjoyed listening to himself talk. He mentioned his famous patients. He left out the fact that Gig Young had killed himself. But he could've said anything and my parents would've been relieved that someone was doing *something* to help me.

He told me to relax so he could examine me. After feeling my wrist and ankle, he said I had a thyroid problem.

"I've never had one before," I said.

"You do now," he replied.

He asked me a few questions about my family, my career, and *The Brady Bunch,* then explained that I'd been screwed up by both my real and TV families, and so on. There was a measure of truth to his interpretation, but it was mostly madness. Dr. Landy sent me straight to his own personal doctor, who confirmed my thyroid problem, then added diagnoses of anxiety and depression, and issued prescriptions for Ascendin, Descendin, Cytomel, and Primitil.

On top of being looped on all those drugs, I was met at my apartment by one of Dr. Landy's so-called therapeutic technicians. She introduced herself as Nancy. She was short, blond, and had a thick, athletic build. She followed me inside and searched my place from top to bottom. From that moment on, I couldn't do anything without her watching me and taking notes.

The next day Nancy supervised as I followed Dr. Landy's orders and destroyed my address books, and then she shadowed me at work. That night Landy himself made a surprise visit to the apartment, and he did so again early the next morning as I was getting out of bed. I never knew when or where he was going to show up, nor what kind of getup he would have on.

One day he walked in with a two-foot-tall, red-and-white-striped *Cat in the Hat*–like thing on top of his head. He also wore a Hawaiian print shirt and sweatpants. He asked to use the bathroom and left the door open, yelling, "So how's everything going? How are you doing today?"

I didn't know how to respond. I thought I was hallucinating.

One day, I heard Dr. Landy and Nancy mention something about microphones they'd planted in my apartment. I didn't know whether or not they bugged my place, but I believed it was possible. I looked under the coffee table and inside cushions. I didn't find anything. Either way, where was the therapy? What kind of treatment was this? Between the prescribed medications, the paranoia, Nancy's ever-watchful eye, and Landy's surprise visits, I really thought that I was losing my mind.

At the end of the first week, during one of the informal therapy sessions that developed when Dr. Landy seemed to materialize out of nowhere, he told me that I could no longer trust my family. He said they were out to get me. They wanted my money, he said, or else they were so envious of my fame—he mentioned my brother specifically—that they wanted to destroy me.

That was news to me. I'd never seen or suspected any such behavior. It struck me as absurd, beyond comprehension. Even in my state of mind, I knew that I was the one who had abandoned my family. It wasn't the other way around. All of a sudden Dr. Landy scared me. I feared that either he was brainwashing me or I was about to lose my final hold on sanity.

So one night I went out to dinner with my friends Pam and Bill. Nancy with me, of course. At one point, Pam went to the bathroom. After waiting a few minutes, I got up to go, too. Somehow I convinced Nancy to let me go by myself. It might've been the first time I'd gone to the bathroom alone in nearly two weeks. In any event, as soon as I saw Pam, I fell into her arms and cried, "Please, please, please help me!"

It was like a scene from a movie.

"You've got to help me," I said. "I don't think I should be in this twenty-four-hour therapy anymore. I'm really scared. The guy treating me is saying my parents are out to get me. They've got me on so much medication I can barely function. I feel like I'm a vegetable. I'm at a point where I'm going to break and lose it."

Before I finished, Pam hustled me out of the restaurant and drove me to her house. I hid out there for the next couple days, until Sherwood and Lloyd, after realizing my anti-twenty-four-hour-therapy hysterics were for real, fired Landy. I immediately quit taking all the medications he'd put me on. Going cold turkey like that made me terribly sick for about a week. But at least Landy was out of my life.

I don't know how it was decided, but I moved in with Lloyd Schwartz, his wife, and their young son. They converted their TV room into a bedroom. No one wanted me living by myself while we worked. They figured they could still keep a close watch on me, maybe not in a Landy-like way, but still close enough; Sherwood and Lloyd also assigned their secretary to watch me every minute I was at the studio.

Away from the studio, I sensed my TV husband, actor Jerry Houser, might have also been instructed to keep an eye on me. But such paranoia lasted only while we worked on the movie, which NBC reorganized into three half-hour shows that ran on consecutive Fridays. By the time we were shooting the series, which the network ordered after the initial episodes proved ratings winners, I realized Jerry's interest in me came from his heart.

Jerry was a solid actor who'd worked steadily since making the leap a decade earlier from Valley Junior College to the movie *Summer of '42,* in which he played fifteen-year-old Oscy. He hadn't been my first choice as Marcia's husband, but we became good friends. If Jerry had had his way, we would've been more than friends. We dated several times and made out once, but I didn't feel the right chemistry was there. To be fair to Jerry, I didn't know how to feel anything at that point.

Nor was I ready to open myself up like that. By the time we began shooting the series, I had relapsed again. The emptiness inside me was too great and the urge to use again was too strong. I didn't have the power or resources to mount a meaningful struggle, and that was because there wasn't any meaning to my life. I tried to find peace in my journal.

> *Stop!*
> *For just a minute*
> *let me show you simple me.*
> *Away from all distractions,*
> *that's the way it's got to be.*

Unfortunately I didn't know how to get away from the distractions. Getting high was the only way I knew to escape.

Through old connections I'd made at Bill's, I scored some coke and got high at Lloyd's one night after everyone had gone to sleep. It was a mistake. The moment I finished, I wanted more. I was an example of the cliché that says an addict can't just do a little. One line was too many, an ounce not enough. I thought of little else until I was in a position to get more.

Until that point in time, I would have denied ever having put myself in a compromising situation to get drugs. But I was desperate, and desperate people get in trouble because they don't think. I remembered the name of a man I knew from the Playboy Mansion. He was an older man who had coke and chased young women. He'd hit on me numerous times at the mansion.

One desperate night when I couldn't think of anyone else, I found his number and called him. He lived in a high-rise not far from my Wilshire address. I went over to his place and pretty soon I was loaded. He had a lot of coke, as I'd thought, but he turned out to be scarier than I ever imagined. Not that I let it inhibit me.

No, my behavior was quite the contrary. Using coke as the lure, he got me to undress and lay on his bed. Then he videotaped me. It's one of the things I am still most ashamed of. I knew it was wrong and disgusting. I knew I had sunk to a new low. But I was powerless. I wanted the coke.

I finally returned to my place, wrecked, and fell into bed. Sometime late the next day, my father awakened me. He'd used his key to get into my place and stood over my bed. I looked up at him through bloodshot eyes caked with sleep. I was still too messed up to react in any manner to his presence. The scene was like a nightmare for both of us, I'm sure.

Shaking his head in frustration, my father didn't mince words. He said he knew what I was doing and would call the police if I continued.

"You can clean up in jail."

Sadly, I knew that threat wasn't enough to make me stop. I used because of a fear that was so much stronger than my fear of jail, and it was going to take something much more powerful to get me to stop.

16

The Vineyard

My relapse instigated changes. I left Lloyd Schwartz's home and moved in with my friends Pam and Bill, who believed they could help keep me clean. On their recommendation, I attended group therapy sessions three times a week after work. They had heard people rave about the benefits of the group and the brilliance of the man who ran it, Dr. Henry Gold.

Dr. Gold insisted everyone call him Henry. He was short, stocky, and wore T-shirts and slacks. He perched cross-legged on an upholstered chair in a room where the rest of us sat on sofas and wooden chairs. It felt like a club. Most of the others were in the entertainment industry or related businesses. I was the only actor, and the only person with a public persona. I was scared of revealing too much of anything in case someone talked about it outside the room.

Nonetheless, I was lured in by the problems other people confessed. Soon I dropped my guard slightly and began to open up. I liked participating and hearing people comment and offer suggestions. Pam and Bill gave one of those see-we-told-you reactions when I said it felt good to have a place to go and talk.

But then one night, during one of the groups, someone made a re-mark about me and later followed it up with a question to me that made me wonder if they might be trying to find out information about me for another purpose. Maybe the *National Enquirer*. I didn't know for sure. But I was wary and uncomfortable.

I forced myself to keep going. Then one night after the group Henry took me aside and suggested I try LSD. He explained that he believed the drug opened people up to deeper thoughts they couldn't reach any other way. He said he used it frequently. He said he thought it would help me learn about myself. He even offered to help me, privately.

I said that I'd think about it even though I had no intention of tak-ing him up on the offer. I never went back to the group either.

I fared much better talking to Jerry Houser. Jerry and I had moved past his effort to start a romance and settled into a close friendship. We went out to dinner almost every night after work and talked. He was one of the few people in my life who didn't seem to want any-thing from me other than my company. He made me feel comfort-able. He seemed to accept me for the crazy, imperfect young woman I was.

One night after dinner, we were in his car, parked someplace, and I told myself that it was time for him to get to know the real me. Of course I had a skewed notion of what I meant by this. I had recently bought some coke. I had a little left, and I wanted to do it.

"Jer, can I do anything with you?" I asked.

"What do you mean?"

"Can I do anything?"

"I don't know what you mean by that," he said.

"I mean anything. As in *any-thing*."

Jerry hesitated. "I don't know."

I reached into my bag and took a tiny stash bottle known as a one-hitter. I looked at Jerry, then put it up to my nostril, and inhaled deeply. When I turned back to him, Jerry was staring at me with the kind of reproving, concerned look that I subconsciously wanted. The vibe in the car was suddenly awkward, and it caused me to scoot back against the door.

"I don't feel comfortable around that," he said.

"I'm sorry," I said.

Jerry took a moment before saying anything. He turned down the radio. "Can't you stop?" he asked.

I shook my head. "Deep down I think I can," I said. "But, Jer—and I've never said this to anyone before—I'm afraid of what I'm going to feel if I don't get high anymore."

Jerry said that was one of the saddest things he'd ever heard. He gave me a hug that was so affectionate I thought he might break my ribs. About a week later, Jerry came by one night and we took a walk through the neighborhood. He asked if I was high, and I said no. I'd been straight for the entire week, I explained, but it had been a struggle.

He offered encouragement, and we kept walking along the tree-lined streets, enjoying the night. We turned on Coldwater Canyon Boulevard and ended up in front of what both of us at first thought was a cottage behind a white picket fence. Upon closer inspection, it turned out to be a church, the Little Brown Church to be exact. Later, I learned former President Reagan and his wife Nancy were among the many couples who'd been married there since it opened its doors in 1940.

"I wonder if it's open," said Jerry.

We turned up a short stone path. Both of us reached for the door at the same time. It was unlocked and appeared to open almost on its own as soon as we touched it. Jerry and I looked at each other with the same whoa-this-is-freaky expression. Neither of us said anything, but we were sure it was a sign. We went inside and felt the quiet solemnity of the small, simple room. There were maybe ten rows of pews. We slid into one in the middle.

All of a sudden I felt nervous. I whispered to Jerry that I couldn't remember the last time I had been in church. He smiled, then bowed his head and began to pray. He did it in a way that seemed different, at least to me. He said his prayers out loud. It was strange to hear his voice resonate in the silent room. It was as if his words were being heard by other people, and carried more weight because of this.

And what words! In the most beautiful, sincere way, he prayed for God to help me. When I heard this, it was like a dam burst in me. Tears flooded out. It was such a profound moment, almost more than I could handle. I want to say I felt something greater than me come into my life, though it could as easily have been me giving up the struggle to hold everything inside and keep myself together.

Then, suddenly, I began to pray out loud. The words came out of my mouth as if they'd been there all along, waiting for me to let them out. I can still hear myself asking God to come into my life and help me, to give me strength, courage, and purpose to get myself on the right path and stay there.

Since then, I've come to believe that we know and reflect God through our actions not our words. My faith is rooted in the knowledge that I will help other people when they're down because I want to believe that others will help me. That's God's way. And luckily for me, it was also Jerry's way.

Jerry was extremely involved in his church, and as I got to know him during the three and a half months *The Brady Brides* was in production, he talked to me about God. Sometimes he was obsessive about it, even "witnessing" between scenes on the set. By the time we finished the series, which wasn't picked up because of low ratings (and dismal scripts), he really pressed the issue. Despite my resistance, he must have felt I would come around. His intuition was correct. All it took was the right time.

About a week after that night at the Little Brown Church, Jerry got me on the phone and said he wanted to take me to a place.

"What kind of place?" I asked.

"A church," he said. "But it's not your ordinary kind of church."

"This is your church, right? The one you talk about all the time?"

"Yes."

"I don't know, Jer."

"Why don't we just go and you can see what it's like."

"No, I don't think so."

"Good. I'll pick you up next Sunday."

Per Jerry's suggestion, I was dressed casually in jeans and a T-shirt when I got into his car. He drove us to Santa Monica, stopping a few blocks from the ocean. When I didn't see a church, I asked where it was. He pointed to an old movie theater. I wasn't good at walking into strange gatherings where I felt on display and out of control. I also didn't like it when people dropped by unannounced. I was like my mother in that way, and I'm sure years of cocaine use had exacerbated it.

With Jerry holding my hand, we entered the theater. It was crowded. As he said hi to people, he introduced me as his friend whom he was bringing to the Vineyard for the first time. I was greeted with a mix of handshakes and hugs and an abundance of warm feelings. I felt a good spirit and energy. The people there impressed me. The majority appeared to be in their mid to late twenties or thirties, and nearly everyone had a Hollywood-perfect look. They were pretty or handsome, tan, with great hair and better clothes. A few looked familiar, maybe famous.

If such superficial observations shaped my initial impression, the service was full of substance, way more than I could honestly handle. I thought it was bizarre when people became so moved by the joyous infusion of spirit that they stood up and lifted their arms. I had never witnessed this before. But I connected with the sermon, and the biggest part of the service was music, great music, which I thoroughly enjoyed. It turned out the charismatic worship leader, Tommy Funderburk, was one of the leading background singers in the record business, and the band and choir were industry pros. Jerry also pointed out some notables in the seats, including Bernie Leadon of the Eagles.

As amazing as the experience was, I felt uncomfortable. I tried to explain this to Jerry, who wanted my impressions. I couldn't articulate it other than to say that I felt like everyone knew something that I didn't.

After the sermon, Funderburk said there would be several people at a table outside the theater to speak with anyone wanting to learn more about the Vineyard. It was at that table that I met Fred Walecki. One of several people manning the table, he started a conversation as I looked at some of the pamphlets. We exchanged numbers and he gave me a Bible, promising me light and love would enter my life if I read it.

"We'll see," I said.

I was not an easy or quick convert. Though Jerry continued taking me to the Vineyard on Sundays, and though those Sundays turned into weekday discussion groups, gatherings, sermons, and sing-alongs, and though Fred began showing up whenever I showed up, I still didn't believe in God. I enjoyed the community and the music, but the religion sailed over my head or at best caromed off me without making a dent. As I told both Jerry and Fred, I had too many doubts and too little faith.

What I didn't say—because I didn't know how to—was that I was personally and spiritually empty and lost. "I took a walk outside today," I wrote in my journal. "Although in the city, I was a million miles away." However, judging from other entries I made at the time, I was searching inside myself. "Reflections of my past dwell deep inside my soul—like a strobe alternating between war and peace."

> Love for life—it's there inside
> When wrappers they unveil
> Happiness must come from within
> Even when the skies seem kind of pale

When I looked at myself in the mirror, I saw vacant eyes staring back at me. I looked like that person I'd told Jerry about, the person who had successfully blotted out all feeling. Self-destruction is an ugly, lifeless process. Would I be able to turn on the light again? Many of the people I met at the Vineyard had similarly dark pasts, some with stories much worse than mine. I was different, though. I didn't believe. As I told Jerry, I wasn't able to embrace God, and that made me uncomfortable.

"Don't quit," he said.

"That's not it," I said. "I like the sermons. It's like my old drug dealer or one of my friends is talking to me. But nothing's happening in a spiritual sense."

Jerry scratched his head.

"Do you pray?" he asked.

"No."

"Why don't you give it a try?"

I didn't make any promises then. But I began to pray at night—always saying the same thing. *God, if you're real, please show me. I don't believe, but I want to believe. I need a sign that You're real. Please send me a message.* I suppose it was more of a request than an actual prayer, which might have been bending the rules. But at least I had opened a dialogue.

This went on for several weeks. I told Jerry and Fred that I'd started to pray, but I kept it from everyone else. Then one afternoon I was with Carin and another girlfriend in Westwood. The three of us had gone shopping after a meeting at the Vineyard. We were walking out of a clothing store and starting down Westwood Boulevard when suddenly and without warning I was thrown to the ground. Literally thrown. My knees gave out, a force pushed me from behind, and I went down.

What happened? To this day, all I can say is that I had no control over my body. Some other, more powerful force was in charge. The next thing I knew, I was on my knees and my arms were lifted toward the sky. I looked and saw two hands reaching down from the sky toward mine. It was Jesus. As crazy as it sounds—and I still can't tell this story without thinking I'm a little nuts—I knew it was Him. After pushing me to the ground, He was picking me back up.

Overwhelmed by emotions, I burst into tears. People stared and whispered, "Isn't that Marcia Brady?" I didn't care. Carin knelt down, put a comforting arm around me, and asked what was wrong.

"I wanted a sign God was real, and I got one," I said.

"What?" she asked.

"I was pushed down . . . then arms came down from the sky."

"What are you talking about?"

I sat there and filled my girlfriends in on the details. If they commented, I didn't hear it. I could only describe what had happened to me. They helped me stand and took me around the corner to a Christian bookstore, where I recounted the experience to some people. It was quite a scene. Some of them handed me little pieces of paper on which they'd written verses of Scripture. One woman who looked to be about my mother's age took my hand.

"God bless you, dear," she said.

"Thank you," I said in a soft voice.

"How do you feel?" she asked.

I thought about how to answer. I mulled over the possibilities. "Changed."

That seemed appropriate and accurate. But was I? I didn't think it could be that easy—and it wasn't.

17

Much More Than a Hunch

Though I distanced myself from my family during my heaviest drug years, they had always been there when I needed them, and after the experience in Westwood, I wanted them back in my life. I told them what had happened to me. I was almost embarrassed to tell the story. I had no idea what to call it—a profound event, a rapturous moment, God reaching out to me, Jesus knocking me down and lifting me up. But afterward my father wrapped his arms around me.

He couldn't have been happier. He asked if I remembered his own experience seeing Jesus when I was little. When I nodded, he hugged me again.

My mother was thrilled that I'd found something other than drugs, but the scars she bore from years of watching my self-destructive behavior made her skeptical. She'd been through this with my father. Talk was fine, but she wanted to actually see me look and behave healthier.

I attended various Bible study groups several times a week. I took my father to the Vineyard, and I followed up by taking my brother

Kevin, who was still directionless and involved with drugs. My parents and I hoped he might find inspiration and purpose there, too. Unfortunately, that didn't happen. But I continued to move back into the family fold, and I had Fred to thank for that—and for much more.

In the L.A. rock world, Fred Walecki's name wasn't as well known as that of his famous friends Don Henley, Linda Ronstadt, Warren Zevon, Bonnie Raitt, and David Crosby and Graham Nash. Fred owned Westwood Music, a local institution. It was the musician's music store. He had every kind of instrument imaginable and advice for any situation. He was the guy people turned to whether they needed a mandolin or money.

Fred and I started to date about a month after I met him outside the Vineyard. He was in the process of breaking off an engagement. It was a weird situation that made us a mutual support team. We shared an appreciation for old and vintage things, which provided openings for deep conversation as we scoured antiques stores and garage sales. As sweet and concerned as he was for me, my feelings for Fred weren't clear until I took him home to meet my family and saw the way he interacted with Denny. He was the first guy I ever dated who paid attention to Denny and treated him like a human being. He even took him out to lunch.

How could I not have feelings for him? Fred's prized possession was a sailboat, and we spent many afternoons on the water, frequently with friends of his, including singer-songwriter Peter Cetera and his wife. Since I was a fan of Peter's group, Chicago, I was impressed. Through Fred, I also met Linda Ronstadt, Bernie Leadon, and other musicians. They lived my fantasy. I was in awe of them.

He gave me beautiful gifts that I still have, including a silver toiletry set and a small, custom-made Martin guitar that he inscribed on the inside. After about six months, it seemed as if we might be together long-term. He had a gorgeous piece of property in Topanga Canyon, and we planned on building a house and living there. But one day Fred said that he was going to have a room in the house for his mother. I thought, Uh-oh, this isn't going to work.

However, I didn't say anything in case I was wrong. It was early 1982, and I was relying on Fred way too much to think about breaking up. He was my rock, the first person I called when I needed help, and thus his was the number I dialed late one night when I woke up after dreaming that my brother Kevin had died. He was lying in the middle of a baseball stadium, and I was shaking him, saying, "Kevin! Kevin! Wake up! Get up!"

He didn't move. And I remembered looking into his eyes right before he died. One of his eyelids fluttered up and down, like a spasm, opening and closing rapidly, so that I couldn't tell if he saw me. It was a gruesome, awful feeling to think of him as dead.

I called Fred, who picked up the phone and said he had just gotten home after spending time with John Belushi and several others at the On the Rox nightclub in Hollywood. He heard how shaken I was as I explained the dream, and he came to my Wilshire condo. Even though it was the middle of the night, he insisted on driving me to my brother's.

I had an eerie feeling as we pulled in front of the same Woodland Hills complex where I had my first apartment. We knocked on my brother's door. It took him a while, but he finally answered. He said we hadn't woken him up. I immediately noticed that the eye that had looked weird in my dream was bloodshot; the other was white and normal, though slightly glassy. I explained that I'd been worried about him, that I'd had a funny feeling.

When we sat down, I saw that Kevin's girlfriend, Susan, was there. She came out of the bedroom. Both of them were in a strange mood. I don't remember how it came out, but Kevin said that they had been getting high, shooting up heroin and coke, which I had no idea he was into, and he'd been about to give himself a hit that could've killed him when Fred and I knocked on the door. That gave me the chills. Maybe I had saved his life.

Fred and I talked with Kevin and Susan for a long time, making sure they were all right. They didn't do any drugs while we were there.

Later that morning Kevin called Fred and asked how he could've been with John Belushi earlier in the evening when the actor had died late that night. Fred was stunned. Neither of us had heard. My brother said it was all over the news. Belushi had OD'd at the Chateau Marmont Hotel, where he'd been doing speedballs, which is a mix of heroin and cocaine.

"Just like me," said Kevin.

That summer Fred and I went on a cruise in the Virgin Islands. On the way, we stayed overnight at his concert violinist sister's fancy New York City apartment. It was all first-class and romantic, but midway through the cruise, I looked at Fred, who had hinted about marriage, and realized that I couldn't spend the rest of my life with him. It was a gut feeling, one that didn't translate into words, and I couldn't bring myself to tell him. Not there in the middle of paradise. But I felt terrible.

Then I became extremely ill. Fred took me to the hospital, where I was diagnosed with dengue fever. Of course Fred took wonderful care of me. The timing was impeccable. I figured it was God bringing His hammer down on me for being such a terrible person. I wondered if I was heartless.

It got worse back in Los Angeles, where Fred proposed to me one day while we were at his mother's house. He gave me an exquisite engagement ring, and I gave it right back. It was the moment I had most dreaded, and was horribly difficult. I didn't want to hurt him. But I thought marrying such a good man when I knew in my heart that he wasn't "the guy" would end up hurting even more, and so following many anguished conversations, we broke up.

Heartache is always tough to handle, but I kept myself busy with going to the Vineyard. I was so grateful to Jerry and Fred for ushering me into that community of caring people. I learned that people like to help, and I found myself trying to do the same thing. Between the

Sunday services, Bible studies, socials, and concerts, I had enough structure and support to keep me sane and straight. And thank goodness, because the breakup had occurred while my career was at a standstill.

There was no work and few auditions. I thought it was because word had spread in Hollywood that I was a born-again Christian. Being a drug addict was fine, but heaven forbid you find God. No one wants to hire you. I was clean. But battling the urge to use again was a daily struggle. I didn't know how to deal with depression, loneliness, despair, low self-esteem, worry, and anxiety. Each day, it was like being caught in a current that wanted to drag me out to deep water, and I had to kick and flail my way out of it.

I never knew whether I was going to be up or down. One night early that fall when I was at the Vineyard for a concert featuring Lynn Kellogg, Tommy Funderburk, and Bernie Leadon, among others, and I was in my seat really feeling the music lift me out of the doldrums, I turned around and saw this guy behind me. I'd never seen him before. He had dark hair, a great build, and chiseled features. I looked straight into his eyes and thought, This is the man I'm going to marry.

Much later I learned that when he looked at me, he said to himself, "Now, that's the kind of girl I want to marry." But at that moment—and it was a real moment where we connected—neither of us said anything.

After the show, people milled around and talked in groups. I was with Carin, another girlfriend, and some guys we knew from the Vineyard. Little did I know that across the hall, Michael was with his friends, surreptitiously pointing at me and asking if any of them knew my name. They looked at him as if he'd just come from Mars. Was he serious? How could he not know my name?

Michael was serious. He had no idea who I was!

His friends asked if he'd ever heard of Marcia Brady from *The Brady Bunch*. Of course he'd heard of the show. He just hadn't seen it.

"That's her," he was told. "She's Marcia Brady."

"Okay," he said. "What's her real name?"

"Maureen McCormick."

"Is she still an actress?" he asked.

"Yes."

He groaned. Prior dating experiences had soured him on actresses. He was also disappointed when he saw me smoking in the parking lot as he walked to his car. He wasn't keen on cigarettes either.

In the meantime, I secretly watched him as he said good-bye to his friends. I fantasized a whole relationship starring the two of us. Then I went to work making it happen. Before we even met, I learned his name, Michael Cummings, and ingratiated myself into his circle of friends. I started going to the same Bible studies, sitting near him on Sundays, and accidentally crossing paths, so there was a familiarity by the time we formally met.

We had a mutual friend at the Vineyard in Bob Pierce. I told him about my interest in Michael, but he didn't respond positively when I asked him to arrange a formal introduction. He didn't think Michael and I would be a good match. Instead he offered to fix me up with a friend of Michael's who had been one of the leads in Walter Hill's film *The Warriors*.

No thanks, I said. I liked Michael.

A short time later, Bob was offered a part in a low-budget Christian-themed film called *Shout for Joy,* the story of legendary surfer Rick Irons's successful quest for a world championship and the events that led him to his faith. The Vineyard's Erik Jacobson was the writer and director. Erik also cast me, and then he landed Miguel Ferrer although he dropped out before the movie was completed.

I didn't know that Michael had been offered the lead, but turned it down because he thought the script needed work. He was at a point in his career where he was getting noticed and needed to make the right choices. He had appeared in the feature *Miracle on Ice,* several movies of the week, numerous commercials, and even started his own theater company.

But Bob convinced him to take on a supporting role by promising they could rewrite their parts. He said the three weeks of shooting in Hawaii would be like a paid vacation. And he mentioned that I was in the movie. He knew that Michael, despite his reservations about dating actresses, was interested in me.

From what I heard later, Bob worked that angle with Michael. He emphasized my skill as an actress. He said that I drew from an incredible emotional well and could tap into it at will. Michael was quiet as his friend went on about me. But Bob knew that he had him.

In early November, they flew to Oahu and went to work on a very tight schedule that had no time for vacationing. With funds for only about three weeks of filming, the goal was to finish before Thanksgiving. The weather posed another challenge. As shooting got under way, a huge storm in the Pacific churned up the waves, darkened the sky, and delayed production at least once a day because of rain.

Disaster struck the day before I was due to arrive when the storm hit the island. It caused so much damage across Oahu that production was shut down indefinitely. Bob called and told me not to get on the plane. I didn't have to dip into that well of emotion to express my disappointment. He said that more money was going to be raised and shooting would start up at some point after the first of the year.

That was good news, I said. But it wasn't the part that bothered me. I'd been looking forward to getting to know Michael. Now I had to come up with another plan.

A few days later, Carin and I were at the Christian bookstore in Westwood. Carin wanted to have a holiday party at her house, and along with another friend of ours, Susan, we discussed the details. While Carin talked about food, decorations, and music, I wondered how I was going to get Michael there. The three of us were hatching schemes when something by the front door caught my eye. I glanced over and saw three guys walk in, including Michael.

Talk about providential!

They came over to say hello. With my heart pounding, I invited Michael to the party—and he said yes.

At the party, I worried that he might not show up. I kept my eyes on the door until I saw him walk in. Then, instead of saying hi, I made a beeline to the bathroom to check my hair and makeup. I kept an eye on Michael from afar, and I think he did the same with me. We crossed paths several times without saying anything of consequence; we were always talking to someone else. But wasn't it funny how we kept running into each other?

I felt the tension build.

Finally, we met by the door leading into the backyard, as if it were time or inevitable or both, which it was. We talked for a few moments. Then we moved to a tiny bench outside in a nook by the garden. Quiet, romantic, pretty, I thought it was a perfect setting for our first real conversation. As we settled into talking, everything felt right and good. I wanted to know everything about this good-looking man, and it turned out there was a lot to know.

He was from Minnesota, the second of three children. He'd begun acting in plays in junior high school and continued through high school and college. In 1971, he won an award as the top actor in the state. He took a year off from college to backpack through Europe. He spent time in England, Sweden, Denmark, and Norway, where he settled down, translating a play and putting together a show that toured several cities.

His great build was not for nothing. In high school, he'd lettered for three years in gymnastics. In college, he took up diving. He also wrestled, ran track, studied karate, and he had danced in ballet companies in Minneapolis and Los Angeles. I glimpsed a deeper, thoughtful side when he said his refuge from the ups and downs of work was writing and camping.

"Not the kind of camping where you drive your car in, put up your tent, and pull out your grill," he said. "I'm talking about the kind where you load everything into your canoe, paddle for a couple of days up various lakes and rivers, and portage a number of times, working to get into the wilderness."

"I can't imagine," I said.

He smiled. "You'll have to try it. That's when you really feel like you're living."

I worried when Michael mentioned that he had once bartended part-time at the Sunset Strip club Carlos'n Charlie's. I'd gone there many times when I was loaded, and I prayed he didn't recognize me from those days. He didn't. I considered that a minor miracle and quickly changed the subject to the Vineyard. I found out he'd been going there for about six months after experiencing what he called a dissatisfying restlessness at another church.

When he asked how I'd gotten into show business, I told him that as a child I used to put on puppet shows for the other kids on my street. I also gave him a short history of *The Brady Bunch,* laughing often because he seemed to be the first person I'd ever met who hadn't watched the show. I knew such people existed, but how ironic was it that I'd fall for such a guy?

Then again, if I wanted someone to fall in love with me rather than with Marcia, it made perfect sense.

But I had little patience or interest in telling my story. I wanted to hear more from Michael. His voice was deep, calm, and strong, like a massage. Listening to him made me feel good. Despite sensing his interest and letting him know the feeling was mutual—I didn't want to jinx myself by thinking we'd had a connection—I had no confidence that someone as together as Michael would call me again.

I was wrong. The phone rang the next day. It was Michael. He asked me out, though he wouldn't tell me what he had planned—only to be ready at six-thirty. He took me to a tiny theater on Santa Monica Boulevard. I thought we were going to see a play. It turned out to be a puppet show. It was more elaborate than the puppet shows I'd put on as a kid, but I adored the thoughtfulness of his choice.

I've always said he could've taken me to Paris that night and it wouldn't have been as romantic. That puppet show was my Paris.

Afterward, we went to a coffee shop and talked until four A.M. Although this was technically a first date, I knew it was going to turn into something special. As a result, I found myself opening up to Michael. I revealed things about my family and myself that I hadn't mentioned to anyone. In fact, I marveled at the things I heard myself say. I even opened up about my drug problems.

As soon as I heard myself mention cocaine, though, I regretted it. I thought it was going to be a deal breaker. Why would someone like Michael want to date, and who knows, maybe one day marry, a drug addict?

I kicked myself under the table.

Actually, I did more than that. I articulated my fear and I went as far as describing Michael as "straight," as in "why would someone as straight as you . . . ?" He took offense and corrected me by saying he thought of himself as "focused." To him, *straight* meant someone who hadn't tried and didn't want to try things beyond a narrow set of accepted behaviors.

But he had, he told me, experimented with much of what the world offered and chose to reject much of it.

I understood what he was saying—and liked him even more because of it.

Women talk about falling in love with a guy's sense of humor, his gentleness, the way he spoke to their mother . . . something. With Michael, it was the sense that I could trust him. Throughout that first night at the coffee shop, I found myself wanting to tell him so much and find out even more about him. It was as if we were playing catch-up with each other's life, as if we were supposed to have known each other all along.

With him, I felt like I had nothing to lose by telling him the truth—and perhaps everything to lose by hiding it. I thought if Michael Cummings was really the guy for me, the guy I'd been waiting for, he had to know everything about me—the good, the bad, and the really, really ugly.

He had to see it all—and boy, did he ever . . .

18

Shout for Joy

We didn't kiss at the end of our first date, but that only stoked the yearning we had to be together again. After dinner again a few nights later, we were parked in his yellow Datsun pickup truck, talking, and as if on cue, both of us were unable to withstand the urge any longer. Already close, we leaned in and finally kissed in a way that left no doubt we shared the same thoughts. It was the most romantic kiss in the whole world, and it went on and on and on.

We were engaged about thirty days later.

Yes, it was quick and passionate—but those four weeks were also fraught with difficulties. Michael tried to establish a sense of intimacy beyond immediate attraction by telling stories and sharing his beliefs, but I repeatedly frustrated him by shutting him down. I didn't want to reveal anything more about myself. It was, as he often said, like waiting out a storm.

Michael was just so present all the time that it was new and unnerving, exciting and frightening, and, well, different. To one degree or another, drugs had always been part of the equation with every other guy with whom I'd been serious, so emotions were either masked or mixed up. Not with Michael, who barely drank. In addition, he made it clear that he didn't want to sleep with a woman until he was married. I was shocked at first, but then I warmed to the idea and remembered my similar pledge from years ago.

Besides knowing that in my heart I'd always believed I wouldn't go to bed with the man I planned to marry until after the wedding, I was comforted knowing our burgeoning relationship wasn't based on Michael getting in my pants. On the other hand, it scared me to death. Despite my protestations, I ended up exposing way more of myself than I would have by taking off my clothes. Both of us did.

One day we had a terrible argument. It was week two of our relationship, and we were engaged in a marathon, all-day conversation about love, forgiveness, compassion, and understanding. All sorts of personal revelations punctuated the discussions. At one point, Michael brought up his previous girlfriend, an actress with her share of personal issues who liked him far more than he ever liked her. But he was trying to make a point about how he still cared for her in a certain way, "a platonic way," he said.

All I heard was that he still had feelings for this woman, and I flipped out. No amount of explanation helped. He couldn't reach me. He thought he was going to lose me. I feared I might not get him back.

A few days later, the buzzer rang on the security intercom in my condo. It was Michael, calling up from the lobby. He said he was in the neighborhood and thought he'd stop by. It was so old-fashioned, so warm and friendly, so Michael, and so not me. I wasn't used to people dropping by unexpectedly. I didn't like being surprised. I grew up in a home where people didn't come over. The house was always a mess. My brother Denny was unpredictable. My mother lived in a perpetual state of fear of being "found out." If someone knocked on the door, people freaked.

And that's the way I reacted when I heard Michael's voice from downstairs. But I also had another reason. Following our fight, I'd relapsed, and at the time the buzzer sounded, I was doing coke. I said I wasn't able to see him; something along the lines of "sorry, I'm very busy right now." The tone of my voice was different, distant, and one he hadn't heard before.

"No problem," said Michael. "Sorry for not calling first. I just thought—"

"I'm just doing laundry and stuff and I'm not ready for anyone," I interrupted.

"Don't worry," he said. "I'll come by another time."

I felt like I had narrowly escaped a horrible situation. An instant later, I realized the truth, that I might have created one. I panicked. Something he said hit me. *Sorry for not calling first.* There was something about the sound of his voice that unnerved me. I panicked. Who tells the person they love and want to spend the rest of their life with that they're busy?

I had a feeling that if I let Michael walk away, he was going to walk straight out of my life and I would never see him again.

Did I want him to see me, though? I was stoned out of my mind. I had been up for a couple of days. Finally I said to myself, "Maureen, just let him in. This is the man you're going to marry. Let him see all the ugliness. Let him see the truth."

I clicked on the intercom.

"Michael?"

There was no answer. I tried again.

"Michael?"

All this had taken place in less than a minute. Now he wasn't there. With tears streaming down my face, I dashed downstairs. After not seeing Michael at the phone opposite the security desk, I looked across the lobby. He was stepping out the front door. It hadn't yet closed. I caught up to him a step or two later. He was startled to see me. I grabbed him as if I didn't want to ever let him go and began to apologize.

"I didn't mean to turn you away," I said. "I want you to be here. I'm glad that you came by. You can always come by. You don't have to call. It's just that—"

I started to sob and couldn't get the words out. Michael pulled me tightly against him, as if to give me some of his strength.

"Sometimes I'm just crazy," I said. "Sometimes I'm nuts. I don't understand why I say the things that I do. But I'm really glad you're here. I think it may actually be perfect timing. I have something to tell you."

I took Michael upstairs and told him everything, including my fears about syphilis and going insane. He was amazing. He took me in his arms, pulled me close, and let me feel his strength. He said that he was glad that I'd let him back into my apartment; he wanted to know all of me.

I was glad, too. I also knew that I'd lose Michael if I ever got high again. And if I lost this man whom I loved more than anything else in the world, this man who gave me peace and a sense that things were okay, I'd lose something else he gave me—the chance for me to love myself enough so that I didn't have to get high again.

Two weeks later, he came over to my place, got down on one knee, and asked if I would marry him. He handed me a Troll doll from a collection he'd started when he was a child. This was his favorite one, Pookie. I started to laugh. Then I saw a gorgeous diamond engagement ring on Pookie's arm. It fit me perfectly. Michael also gave me a silver heart locket that had belonged to a great aunt of his. Inside was a letter that was the most beautiful thing ever written to me.

Michael explained that he probably would have walked away from our relationship two weeks earlier if I hadn't come for him, but thanks to what he felt was a divine sense of destiny in us being together, he was able to see "a genuine, wonderful person, with a beautiful heart, who nonetheless had a huge battle going on inside of her," and he felt like he couldn't abandon me in the middle of such a fight. Nor would he abandon me ever. Whether I realized it, he said, I made his life better and brighter.

After we celebrated, Michael insisted on asking my parents for their permission to take my hand in marriage. Of course I had told my parents about him. My father had also come to the church to meet Michael. But this was different. We drove to their house in Westlake Village. I warned him about the mess and everything else he might encounter upon meeting my family. He wasn't concerned.

However, I was dying as we sat down with my parents in the living room. I hadn't explained why we wanted to speak to them, but they didn't have to wait long as Michael got right to the point. He said he was in love with me and had already proposed, but he wanted their permission—their blessing, as he put it—to marry me.

My parents were stunned. I saw their mouths drop open. They recovered, though, and my father mostly asked Michael numerous questions about his background, his family, his career as an actor, and his plans for supporting me and any children we might have. For my father, who was always a softer touch than my mother, it was a pretty severe grilling, which Michael withstood with a poise, character, and politeness that made me proud.

We discussed our plans to marry that summer. My parents advised us to slow down, get to know each other better, and let time be our first test.

"No, we're getting married six months from now," I said. "I wish it was even sooner. I'd get married tomorrow if I could."

Michael put his arm around me in support.

"Well, we'll see," said my mother, who'd barely spoken till then; her terse comment only served to underscore her skepticism.

Michael understood that she was merely raising a cautionary flag. He expected it. Just not so severe. My mother really gave him the cold shoulder that day—and for a long time afterward. It was because she had concerns about my well-being. It wasn't that she didn't trust Michael. No, he was straighter than her Iowa upbringing. Her issue was with me.

Although she never verbalized it, I was the one she didn't trust. She also wanted to make sure Michael was up to the challenge of taking care of me.

"You've got a lot of proving to do," she told him before we left.

That got under his skin.

Afterward, in the car, he said her remark had offended him. He didn't feel like he had to prove anything. He knew who he was. He knew that he wasn't after me for money, fame, or any reason other than the right one. He loved me.

"If your mother doesn't like it, that's her problem."

"I don't think it's that," I said. "I think she's afraid that she can't trust me. She probably doesn't believe that I'll ever be straight or get my act together."

"Maybe when you believe in yourself," he said, "she'll believe in us."

Easier said than done. I didn't know how to believe in myself, and the insecurity this created in me triggered an overwhelming sense of anxiety. I wanted everything to work out so badly, and I wanted it instantly. I ignored the fact that life is a process. I ignored it because I couldn't deal with the uncertainty. And so it was like the floodgates opened, and I found myself flailing around in a pool of uncertainty, anger, and fear that things wouldn't work out.

I reacted by lashing out at Michael. I turned the first four months of 1983 into a living hell. Although I desperately wanted to get married in June, I pressured Michael about money. I wanted him to tell me how he planned to support me when his income from acting and bartending didn't add up to what I thought I needed. How did he think we were going to have a family?

I demanded answers, and when he wasn't able to give me specifics, I got angry at him. Angry and then angrier . . .

He realized my fears had to do with trust. I didn't trust myself. How could I trust him? God only knows where he got his patience and ability to forgive. Or where he got his ability to see the goodness in me, which he swore to me was there even when I cried that I couldn't see it. To relieve the pressure, I turned to an old vice: throwing up after meals. I made numerous secret trips to the bathroom. It made me feel more in control.

In the spring, following a six-month interruption, *Shout for Joy* started production again, and we returned to Oahu. The change of scenery and the tropical air were the perfect tonic for our troubles. We were put up in separate houses—all the guys in one, all the girls in another—and Michael and I weren't able to spend much time with each other since we didn't have any scenes together.

Things quickly fell back into place. We shared some nice moments at night after work and managed several romantic walks on the beach.

One afternoon I was on my way to meet Michael. He had a couple hours off and we wanted to take a stroll. I was walking down the beach, heading to the spot where we'd arranged to meet, when I came across a beautiful piece of driftwood. I saw there was a piece of paper stuck into a hole. Curious, I pulled it out and to my amazement found a touching romantic story written on it. Talk about fate! It gave me chills. I ran down the beach to find Michael and show him.

Naturally, he was waiting for me, acting all innocent. When I showed him the paper and began gushing about the story, he grinned. He'd written it earlier that day and planted it on the beach, knowing I'd find it.

"And if I didn't?" I asked.

"I knew you would," he said,

That kind of self-confidence got Michael into trouble a few days later when he went surfing early in the morning. The conditions were too dangerous on Oahu's legendary North Shore for experts, let alone for actors portraying surfers. An offshore storm had turned the waves into monsters. But Michael, who'd been trying to learn to surf for the movie, wanted to develop proficiency beyond the norm, and so he was all about practicing as much as possible.

He and a couple of production assistants paddled out into the huge breakers. They planned on taking their time and picking manageable waves. In a matter of seconds, though, they found themselves in the wrong place and had to commit to a wave that was way beyond their ability. They wiped out, got slammed into a coral reef, and then got caught in a riptide that took them far out into the ocean.

Somehow all three of them managed to hang on to their boards, though they ended up far away from one another. Michael later told me that he'd never felt as humble and insignificant as he had when he was being sucked out to sea.

In the meantime, back on shore, Bob Pierce was looking for him. He wanted to work on a scene they were shooting that afternoon. He arrived at the girls' house, thinking he might find Michael and me together. I was drinking coffee and studying my lines when he came into the kitchen and asked if I knew Michael's whereabouts.

"He went surfing with Joe and Lucy," I said.

"What!" Bob exclaimed. "Have you looked outside? Have you seen the waves? Nobody goes out on a day like this. There's a major storm headed here."

Minutes later, the entire cast and crew had run to the beach and located Michael and the other two surfers. One of the crew guys had a pair of binoculars, and all of us took turns looking at them. Two lifeguards arrived on the scene, but refused to go in the water, saying it would be suicidal. The Coast Guard figured they'd have to send for a helicopter, which they eventually did. I ran up and down the beach, feeling sick that I was so helpless.

After about two hours, Joe managed to make it to shore, followed by Lucy, who was taken to the hospital with severe lacerations from the coral. Michael needed another sixty minutes before he managed to get himself to safety. He said it was only after he resigned himself to whatever God had in store for him that he felt a sense of inner calm and renewed strength in his arms, enough to catch a wave that took him out of the riptide and up the coastline. Then he caught another one that brought him toward the shore.

We watched from the sand, cheering him on, shouting encouragement, and crying tears of hope. Finally, mashed and bruised, and also utterly drained after nearly four hours in the ocean, he emerged from his ordeal. I was in the water, waiting for him when he got to a place where it was only knee-deep. We hugged for a long time. It was my turn to share some of my strength.

At that moment there was no question in my mind that both of us were survivors.

19

Tears in Heaven

After a romantic dinner before leaving Hawaii, Michael and I were standing on the balcony outside a restaurant, talking as the waves broke nearby in a rhythm that was like music, when suddenly he reached out, drew me close, and kissed me. To this day, twenty-six years later, I can still feel the emotion in that embrace. In the moonlight, I felt like we were the only two people in the world.

Back in Los Angeles, with our wedding date looming less than six weeks away, the clarity and calmness we enjoyed in Hawaii evaporated and we fell back into our bickering ways. This time, it grated at Michael, who finally said, "Look, I don't think we're ready. Let's postpone the wedding."

To me, that meant, "You're crazy. Let's cancel this thing." I kind of freaked out until his ability to stay focused ("Maureen, listen to me: I still want to get married, but we can't get married with this kind of disconnect") got through to me. Gradually, I saw it made sense. Once I calmed down, both of us felt a sense of relief. The pressure was off to perform, so to speak, and we could get to work.

We needed to find out why two people who loved each other ended up battling so frequently. Like many churches, the Vineyard required counseling sessions for members planning to marry. The idea was to identify each other's strengths and weaknesses and raise awareness of potential trouble spots. Michael and I filled out questionnaires designed to highlight our compatibility. Nervous, I wanted to back out before I finished. I thought the church would try to talk Michael out of marrying me.

My fears were extreme but not unwarranted. We flunked the test. According to the results of our questionnaires, we weren't compatible in any areas. Zero.

"Zero?" Michael said, taking my hand.

"What do we do?" I asked.

"You can't take these answers too literally," the counselor said. "Marriage, like daily life, isn't a black-or-white, yes-or-no thing."

"So we can still get married?" I asked.

"If you want," he said. "It's your choice. As I said, these are just indicators."

We continued weekly sessions with Cedric Johnson, a therapist recommended by the church's counselor. Cedric was an empathetic man with a large build, glasses, and a slow delivery. We liked him right away. He had Michael and me talk about our differences. I was a Democrat, and Michael was a Republican. I was Catholic, and he was a Presbyterian. I was emotional, impulsive, easily frustrated, hot-tempered; he was thoughtful, careful, reserved, analytic, and blessed with more patience than Job, which I tested daily.

"See, nothing in common," I said.

"Is that what you think?" Cedric replied.

"Well, we love each other very much."

"That's a start." He looked at Michael. "Does he pick up his towel in the bathroom?"

"Yes," I said.

"That's good, too."

We worked with Cedric for a few months. Then I quit. I was done. Michael thought we were just getting started, though. We were talking and listening to each other without any manipulation, he said. He was right. In hindsight, we were making progress. But I was still done with the therapy.

Michael wasn't. He went to a couple of sessions by himself. At one, Cedric said, "Your relationship is like a stick and pot. That's all you have. Why do you stay?" Michael didn't have an answer. "You don't have to have one," Cedric said. "I just want to make sure you think about it."

Then Michael and I signed on to work together in the musical *Shenandoah* at a theater in Raleigh, North Carolina. We put our problems on hold; the show seemed like an adventure, and it was. We shared a room in the same hotel. After performances, we went out to dinner with the cast. On weekends, we did our laundry at a Laundromat called Suds. At the end of the run, the promoter had everyone to his home for an old-fashioned Southern-style dinner.

When we left Raleigh, Michael and I felt full in ways that had nothing to do with all the fried chicken, okra, and black-eyed peas we'd eaten. The trick was to sustain that sense of well-being, trust, and compatibility.

To supplement his income between acting jobs, Michael signed on with a company that sold early versions of desktop computers to businesses. He started off as a typist and quickly worked his way up, then changed firms for a better position and more money. He didn't particularly want to do that kind of work. But he wanted to calm my fears and quiet my criticism by proving he could support us.

He implored me to understand that he was more concerned about living his life in a way that felt right than he was about living it to make money, and to him, acting felt right. He was confident that the bigger things would eventually work out. I wish that I had been able to trust him. How could I, though, when I didn't trust myself? As a result, my put-downs continued.

I can't say why Michael hung in, but he did. Not only that, he pushed me to reconnect with my family, particularly my mother. His instincts were good. From her quiet and fragile perch on the sidelines, my mother had taken great pride in my accomplishments as an actress. Likewise, she had worried through all the years I struggled and needed help.

She was more thrilled than anyone to see me in a better place. But she still didn't trust it. Besides her doubts about me, I think my quick romance with Michael recalled her rapid engagement and marriage to my father and the years of turbulence that followed. That Michael was a Christian also reminded her of my father—and not in the best way. Of course Michael's faith manifested itself very differently from what we had witnessed with my father. She'd see that over time.

I know there's one reason that Michael and I managed to stay together through all the heavy-duty ups and downs: our faith. The two of us had faith that our love, despite all of our problems, was real, strong, durable, and worth sticking around for. Our faith made us believe our love was real. We had faith in God. And we had faith that there were people to whom we could turn during the worst of times. Those people were our friends at the Vineyard, and they played a vital role in keeping us together as a couple and individually. They provided peace and comfort during the worst times, and they raised us up even higher when life was good.

Without the Vineyard, we probably wouldn't have survived. It was a giving, nourishing community. Being there made me feel better about myself. It gave me a place to go and find company, comfort, and understanding when I felt alone—and in the middle of 1984, I felt alone way too often.

Work was scarce and auditions weren't any more plentiful. Like many actors, I felt unwanted. I didn't understand why my career had slowed. It was made even harder when strangers wanting an autograph asked what I was working on and I had nothing to say. They got their autograph or photo, told me they had as a kid either wanted to be me or date me, and then I walked away wondering why I wasn't working if I was loved by so many people.

Then Michael's truck was stolen. It was another unpleasant thing we had to deal with. But he managed to turn a lemon into lemonade by arranging to buy his father's old car and drive it back to Los Angeles, which meant traveling to Minneapolis, and he invited me to go with him. We needed an adventure, he said—something that would get us out of town and out of our routine.

It sounded good to me.

Michael's parents lived in a large, Cape Cod–style house outside of the city. The rooms were decorated with antique chests and chairs, old beds, and quilts. The house had a comfortable, family feel. His father was an electrical engineer, and his mother was a stay-at-home mom. They impressed me as nice, solid, conservative people—good Midwestern stock, as they say.

I felt like they were wary of me, this young woman who'd grown up on TV. I didn't think they were impressed. In reality, I was deathly afraid Michael's parents would find out about my past, both my drug problems and my family issues, and that would be the end, they'd put the kibosh on our relationship.

Michael and I spent some lovely, romantic days on the water. There was a large creek behind his house, and we got into his canoe and paddled for hours. We explored numerous small lakes where we seemed to be the only two people on the planet. I appreciated the solitude and beauty, as well as Michael's skill and competence. It thrilled me to see how adept he was in the outdoors. He'd grown up spending summers camping and canoeing these lakes. Sometimes he went days without seeing another person. That sounded nice to me.

I found the time we spent outdoors calming, as I did the time I spent with Michael. I felt as if I'd exhaled for the first time.

After a week, we began the drive back to Los Angeles. We didn't plan a route or a schedule. The point was to take our time, get lost in the drive, see the sights, eat in small diners, stop to look at salvage shops and antiques stores, explore the countryside, and then check into hotels along the highway.

The longest road trip I'd ever taken was a two-hour drive with my family to San Diego when I was a kid. Otherwise everything in my life had always been planned. This was the first time I'd ever gotten in a car and said okay, let's see what happens today. It was freeing and fun. Michael said he enjoyed being with me away from Los Angeles. He said he was able to see a different side of me.

He also got a kick out of watching people react when we walked into diners and rest stops. Inevitably someone came up and asked, "What are you doing here?" I could've said "having the time of my life." Or I could've said I was falling in love with Michael all over again. Both were true.

Little things were such fun. At one hotel, I tried the "Magic Fingers" massage bed for the first time. I giggled *and* jiggled till my quarters ran out.

Each day—no, at various junctures throughout the day—I relished how reliable and resourceful Michael was in every kind of situation. He had such confidence and so much ability. One day, as we drove through the desert, I got to thinking about the two of us. Maybe it was the picturesque scenery outside the window. Maybe it was everything. But I realized how foolish and narrow-minded I'd been to judge him solely by the money he earned as an actor.

He was a great guy, *the guy*. I was lucky to have him.

One day after we returned to Los Angeles, we were walking into Westwood when I stopped, put my hands on his chest, and looked up into his eyes. I'd had a revelation about us, or rather about him, I said. I no longer cared how much money he earned. If he wanted to work as an actor, I would be behind his effort 100 percent. If he wanted to do something else, I would support that enthusiastically, too.

The bottom line was that I loved him, and believed in him, whatever he did.

"I'm going to trust you," I said.

I really meant that I was going to trust myself. I had so little faith in me; I needed to convince both of us. Indeed, Michael asked if I was telling the truth or saying something I thought he wanted to hear. I stressed that it was the truth. He took me at my word and said he hoped that my behavior would prove it.

Calmness prevailed, and we began to plan again for a wedding. Michael's career also took off. He was cast in a production of *Richard II* at the Mark Taper Forum. Then he landed a handful of commercials. Nestlé flew him back and forth to New York umpteen times before signing him to a multiyear spokesperson deal and shooting an elaborate TV spot on location in the Smoky Mountains. Although they spent millions on the commercial, it never aired.

There was so much activity that our wedding seemed to sneak up on us without warning. I couldn't figure out where the time went. And as was my way when things seemed out of control, I panicked slightly. I felt the need to make everything perfect; that was impossible; it was a control issue. I was struggling when Michael's family came into town. There was so much to do. On top of the wedding, Michael needed to pack up his apartment.

We were on pins and needles at the idea of our families meeting. They were extremely different. There was no telling what my brother Denny might blurt out. On the day before our rehearsal dinner, Michael felt like he needed to tell his parents about my past drug problems, what he called the elephant in the room. Until then, he had avoided most of their questions.

I was devastated when he told me that his parents knew. I shut myself in the bedroom and felt like I'd never come out.

Then my mother blew up at me because she'd heard the club where we were holding the reception was anti-Semitic, a problem since most of my guest list was Jewish. At first, I said I didn't care since I wasn't ever coming out of my room, but the truth was, I did care, and upon further investigation, I found out it wasn't true.

Despite everything, I left my bedroom, everyone had a good time at the rehearsal dinner, and by four o'clock on March 16, 1985, the small red-brick Presbyterian Church in Brentwood was filled with my family, Michael's family, my *Brady* family, and about two hundred other close friends and relatives. Ready or not, we were getting married.

I had never seen my mother look more beautiful. She wore a new dress that showed off the weight she'd lost for the occasion, her hair was done, and she added a tiny sparkle with heirloom jewelry. My bridesmaids—Carin, Pam, and Michael's sister, Carol—were also gorgeous in off-white gowns, as was Michael's niece, Jennifer, our flower girl. As for me, I went for an understated Princess Diana look in a simple, off-the-shoulder white dress and carried a mix of white stephanotis and gardenias. When Michael and I kissed, everyone in the church cheered.

At the reception, my father made a long, emotional toast and a friend of Michael's performed a comic song he'd written about Michael's life that had everyone laughing and singing along. Our first dance to Stevie Wonder's "You Are the Sunshine of My Life" was supposed to showcase the dance lessons Michael and I had taken for the occasion, but we forgot everything we learned as soon as the music started.

No one noticed—or cared. The dinner turned into a party that went way past the time any of us anticipated, which was fun until three-quarters of the way through the night Michael and I remembered there was still one more momentous event left to the evening. It was our wedding night. We were finally going to consummate our relationship. With that realization, I knew we'd turned the corner, that all the preparations, anxiety, and tears had been worth it, and the rest of the night was about the two of us.

Or it would've been if I hadn't blabbed about my nervous excitement to Barry and Eve, who got the entire *Brady* crew to follow us back to the Hotel Bel-Air, where they decamped in our honeymoon suite and, thanks to several bottles of champagne, stayed . . . and stayed . . . and stayed . . . None of them wanted to leave. We would have felt the same way if not for something else on our minds. Eventually I said that I wanted to slip into something more comfortable and far too revealing for any of them to see, which got a laugh and our first moment alone.

As memorable as the rest of that night was, Michael topped it the following day when he read me something he had written while I slept. He said that he'd read someplace that marriage was like two tributaries merging and, after some turbulence, forming a single great river. "That's us, you and I," he said, adding that we hadn't quite gotten to the river part yet, but he looked forward to the adventure. And he was sure it would be an adventure.

Indeed, "our whole relationship to this point is kind of a blur, except for the exact second when our eyes locked," he continued. "That instant will forever remain like a tattoo in my memory, recallable at will. You're a once-in-a-lifetime person. An impish confluence of celebrity and innocence that danced into my life, upsetting the applecart I'd created for myself, answering questions I never asked, pulling and pushing until I thought I might go crazy.

"But crazy in a good way. I just kept adjusting and readjusting until that day I came to a decision because there was really no choice. I got down on my knees, prayed to God that He wouldn't abandon me, and then prayed to God that you, like me, would also say, 'I do.' And it will be forever."

Part
Three

20

For Better and For Worse

After the wedding, Michael and I were exhausted. One day, as we walked into Westwood, I joked that we were holding hands to keep each other from falling down. Although neither of us would've objected to a relaxing honeymoon in Hawaii we spent the next week helping at the Special Winter Olympics in Park City, Utah.

Inspired by my brother, I'd participated for years in both the summer and winter Special Olympics. As Michael realized, it was exhausting to run around on the slopes all day, assisting special kids and adults and visiting with their families. But it was worth every ache and pain.

Most of the special Olympians recognized me as Marcia. Some of them got very excited when they saw me and called out, "Marcia Brady." Those were the few occasions when I didn't try to distance myself from my TV character. Through Denny, I knew how hard it was to reach people with special needs. So I understood and appreciated the connection being Marcia helped me make with them.

I also loved seeing the joy in their parents' eyes when the kids recognized me and came out of their shells, expressing genuine excitement, affection, and love.

Unfortunately, the producers and casting directors with whom I met in my professional life also recognized me as Marcia, minus the love and affection. Despite the varied work I'd done since *The Brady Bunch*, they still saw me as Marcia, a grown-up version. As a result, I couldn't get work. It was the longest drought of my career. It frustrated me to no end because I didn't know what to do. No matter what, I couldn't be anyone else.

Michael's career also slowed down, but he was still feeling his oats and buoyant compared to me. One day he suggested taking advantage of some of the money we'd saved by moving temporarily to New York.

"Why don't we give it a try?" he said.

I wasn't against it, but I wanted to understand why.

"Just to try the acting life there," he said. "Change the scenery, change the type of work, and maybe change perceptions."

"Change is good," I said.

We went for nearly a month and got a room for $65 a night in a bed and breakfast. It was actually a four-story brownstone on the West Side, and the room we had redefined small. We were on top of each other whether we were laying down or standing up. Only one of us could get dressed at a time. Despite the inconvenience, the city was full of excitement and things to do. We had a great time sightseeing, going to theater, and living the New York actor's life, as we'd intended.

None of my auditions worked out, but Michael got numerous bites. Right before we were scheduled to return to Los Angeles, he was asked to read for the daytime soap *All My Children*. We didn't have a place to stay, so I flew home while he looked around for another room.

There was a hotel across the street from the brownstone, except rooms were $250 a night and up, way too steep for us. But Michael really liked the place, as well as the convenience. He struck up a quick friendship with someone at the front desk, who took pity on him, or simply liked him, and let him have a room for the same rate we'd paid at the bed-and-breakfast. It was a great room, too, with a view of Central Park. Just an incredible deal.

One day, as Michael tested again for the part—the choice, he found out, was between him and two other guys—I was out doing errands and ran into a guy I knew from an acting class I'd attended years earlier. As we caught up, I mentioned it was ironic to see him after so long since he'd once had a role on *All My Children* and now Michael was in New York with a seemingly good shot of getting cast on the same show.

We laughed. However, it turned out that neither Michael nor the other two actors got the part. The guy I ran into ended up getting rehired. Did he make calls as a result of the tip I'd given him? Was there funny business behind the scenes? I don't know, but it left a bitter taste. I'd sensed that Michael was going to get the job, we were going to move to New York, and life was going to be different. As I told Michael, I was ready for that kind of change.

Instead Michael returned to Los Angeles, disappointed but not defeated—not until we got home and played the message on our answer machine. We walked into the condo and saw the light blinking. We had one message. It was from Chris Viores. He managed both of us. "I hope both of you are sitting down," he said. Then there was a pause. I turned to Michael and smiled, figuring there was good news about one of the auditions we'd gone on in New York or something else. "Seriously," he continued. "Because this is not good news. Mo, your agents let you go, and Mike, you lost your agent, too. Guys, I'm really, really sorry. We'll have to regroup and start over."

I wasn't able to regroup. I was lost, confused, and emotionally unstable. My bulimia flared up again, as it did when I couldn't get a grip. Between throwing up and swimming, I looked healthy and good. My skin was clear, my body was still in shape, and my hair was the same blond mane I had brushed so assiduously as a teenager on the *Brady* set. Internally, it was another story. Without work, my sense of self was in free fall, and it took everything else with it.

Life was an up-and-down cycle again, my moods seemingly deter-mined by forces as varied as the weather, the moon, the sound of a door slamming, or a plate being set on the table too hard. Each day was random and unpredictable. I had no idea what was going to set me off. I had no patience. I expended so much energy keeping myself to-gether that the littlest things caused me to lose it.

Michael and I were always on top of each other. My small condo didn't leave us much space for ourselves. We had one bedroom, one bathroom, a living room, and a kitchen. At least he got to enjoy a change of scenery after getting a part-time job selling office equip-ment, an activity at which he enjoyed success and received positive feedback. There was no escape for me. I was Marcia Brady's hostage, one half of a love-hate relationship with myself. I was trapped by my past, something I desperately wanted to break free from—and yet break free to what? And become whom?

Many years earlier, I had hired two guys to decorate my condo. They'd turned it into an ultrachic bachelorette pad done entirely in pink. Michael sometimes referred to it as the Pink Palace. I used the term, too, but in a negative sense, as it was anything but a palace. As my mood faded to black, I began to abhor the constant sight of pinks. Colors radiate emotion, and the pink was unrelenting. I was never in that mood. I remember sitting in the living room on one of bleakest of days. I was perched on my pink sofa, looking at myself in the wall-size mirror and feeling like a piece of something or other that had landed in a vat of cotton candy.

What was I doing there?

What was I doing, period?

I melted into a deep, unstoppable cry. Sometimes I cried for an en-tire day without letup. At that time, I felt like I had a big empty hole inside me, and I cried whenever I thought about it.

In some ways there is no hell greater than a once-popular child star in her thirties trying to figure out a direction in life and recapture the sense of purpose that was so intense and clear years earlier. How could so many people come up to me in stores and on the sidewalk and say they loved me, say they'd always loved me, when I had no such feelings for myself? Why didn't the right people in Hollywood love me?

I cried myself to sleep most nights. I remember lots of anger and deep-down sadness. I was terribly depressed. I think part of it was everything I'd been through, part was genetics, and part was the years of drug use and abuse. I should have gotten treatment. I didn't.

One day I fell into a bad place. I compared it to being caught in the same kind of riptide that had pulled Michael out to sea four years earlier in Hawaii. I stewed in silence all day at home. After Michael got home from work, I got worse. Something about his presence pushed me in even deeper. Suddenly I went from silence to rage. I swung at Michael, needing to lash out. It was ugly. At the peak of our fighting, I stripped off my clothes as if shedding my skin, walked onto the balcony, and screamed that I was going to jump.

In that state, I desperately wanted relief, and I saw it down below on the pavement. Did I want to kill myself? No, not really. Would I have done it? Yes, most definitely. I was out of my mind. However, Michael grabbed ahold of me and hauled me inside. Although I struggled and fought, he used his considerable strength to wrestle me into submission. He was literally my rescuer. Thank God he didn't let go for the longest time.

Looking back, I should've sought professional treatment immediately after what was such an obvious and desperate cry for help, but Michael and I accepted such volatility as part of our relationship. Then, in early 1987, I landed a part in the movie *Return to Horror High*, the story of a movie crew that makes a documentary about a high school once beset by a serial killer—and guess what happens? Yes, members of the movie crew begin to disappear.

On the plus side, it was work. I played a police officer with a ghoulish fascination for blood. On the negative side, I knew it was a B movie and it made me feel as if I might as well stop dreaming of ever getting parts that would earn me respect. Michael encouraged me to have fun. I wish I'd had a better attitude. Only now can I look back and appreciate that I was in a George Clooney movie—it was one of his earliest films—and wish I could try it again.

Michael and I entered another rough period where we fought often and hard. I should clarify: I fought often and hard. Several times I provoked and pushed him to the point where he spent the night elsewhere until I cooled off. He would have been justified if he'd walked out for good, but he didn't. I know that he wondered what he had gotten himself into. He'd asked himself that question before we got married, and he was still asking it four years later.

Why did he stay?

Much later I actually asked him, and Michael said that he'd made a life-long commitment and decided he was going to work at it until it's unworkable. He thought child stardom had arrested my development, and in many ways he was right. He also sensed that I might be suffering from a sort of chemical imbalance or some kind of mental illness related to depression.

It was not in my nature to be a cruel or mean person. My moods seemed to take me captive, and the swings from high to low were extreme and beyond my control. Thank goodness Michael never lost sight of the person he saw when he fell in love with me. Because I frequently lost track of that person and when that happened I also lost track of what I thought of as normal.

In early spring 1988, we celebrated Passover at a friend's Seder dinner. It was a large gathering, with upwards of 70 people. About a week earlier, I found out that I was pregnant, and I wanted to tell Michael in a special way. We hadn't been trying, but a baby was always in the picture and so I was bursting with excitement. I wanted to be a mother in the worst way, and I knew he would be an exceptional father.

I decided to break the news to Michael at the Seder dinner. I don't know why I felt like I needed that kind of group cheer, but I did. I thought everyone would help us celebrate, and I thought it would be wonderful for Michael. Needless to say, it wasn't. As dessert was brought out, I gave Michael a bouquet of helium-filled balloons that said "Congratulations! You're a Dad!" and said, "I'm pregnant."

Michael didn't know what hit him. His expression changed from disbelief to shock to anger and finally to confusion and hurt. He muttered something along the lines of, "Why are you telling me like this?"

At home, he tried to figure out why I had surprised him like that in front of all those people with such personal news. I felt like he grilled me unfairly and went into attack mode. It wasn't pretty, and we stayed mad for several days.

About two weeks later, I suffered a miscarriage. It was my eighth week and there was no real reason for the miscarriage other than the pregnancy didn't take but I chose to believe that God was punishing me for every stupid thing I'd done. Devastated, I couldn't get out of bed or stop crying.

This time it was my mother who came to my rescue. She stayed by my bed and confided that she'd miscarried her first pregnancy, something I didn't know, and, though she didn't directly mention her syphilis she described the emptiness she felt after losing the baby, her worries that God was punishing her, and her fears that she might never be able to have a child.

I related, and opened up about my own similar feelings. All of a sudden we were talking, I mean really talking, as women, as mother and daughter. In that bleak moment, it was as if we were reaching out for each other.

"You'll try again," she said.

The advice wasn't new or earth shattering, but coming from my mother, it made an impact. She also shared some thoughts about making the unfairness of life beside the point, rather than *the* point, something that resonated in me for the way it poignantly related to both of us.

I began to realize that life, despite moments of happiness and joy, is really about discovering priorities and dealing with unforeseen vagaries, differences, obstacles, inconveniences, and imperfections. I remembered *Saturday Night Live*'s late, great Gilda Radner as Rosanne Roseannadanna saying "It's always something. If it's not one thing, it's something else."

Nevertheless, from those talks I had with my mother, I got the sense that something good was going to result from all these tears.

21

The Story of a Lovely Lady

Michael and I woke up one day and knew we had to get out of the Pink Palace. Space was the primary issue, but so was our sanity. I had piles of stuff everywhere; the clutter was beginning to resemble the interior of my parents' home. If we didn't move, we were going to lose our minds.

My mother urged me to look in a nice part of the western San Fernando Valley, close to home, as she said. She felt like I had fallen in with the wrong crowd on the West Side. Even though Michael and I looked in all parts of the city, she was the one who found the two-story, Cape Cod–style home we bought. It was in a development in the foot-hills of a stretch of mountains known as the Santa Monica Preserve.

Michael and I fell in love with it right away. The down payment was a stretch, but Michael borrowed money from his parents and I pitched in the rest. The neighborhood was full of other young couples starting out. Some had babies, and I noticed a few women were preg-nant. One night I joked that there was something in the water. Mi-chael didn't stop me from drinking it.

In August, I woke up several mornings feeling sluggish, like I couldn't get started, and considering I'd always been a morning person, I thought it was strange. About a week later, I discovered it wasn't at all strange. It was a new life growing inside me. I was pregnant. Given the miscarriage, I regarded it as a miracle.

I couldn't wait to tell Michael. This time, I told him in private, and we enjoyed a lovely celebration in our new home. We kept the news to ourselves until the end of the first trimester, about the time I signed on for another turn as Marcia in the CBS TV movie *A Very Brady Christmas*. Everyone returned except Susie (she was newly married and honeymooning in Jamaica). All of them celebrated my good news.

I was the first among the *Brady* kids to get pregnant, and I appreciated the love I got on the set as I told people, like Sherwood and Lloyd and Ann B. Davis, all of whom commented in ways that left no doubt they were proud of me for getting past my drug problems and marrying such a steady guy. Then there was my TV husband, Jerry Houser. Without him, I wouldn't have met my real-life husband and father of the child growing inside me. As I said, it was family time.

That also meant there were the usual complaints from Bob Reed about the script, though there were much fewer since he'd gone over it scene by scene before shooting began with Sherwood and Lloyd in order to avoid fighting during production. Still, he cringed at the end when the family's rendition of "O Come, All Ye Faithful" helped rescue Mike from a construction-site accident. What did anyone expect? Though it was a movie, it was still the Brady bunch!

The ratings were enormous, nearly a forty share, and so naturally talks began again about another *Brady* series. By then, I was past the grueling morning sickness that hit me during the first three months, and though I felt wonderful physically throughout the second trimester, I worried about whether the baby would be born healthy. With all the drugs I'd done, the way I'd mistreated my body, and my family history, I convinced myself the chances were abnormally high that I would have a handicapped kid. I had amnios and sonograms as often as possible.

Each time they came back fine. My doctor told me to relax and stop worrying about family curses and other such nonsense. Only my mother understood my fears, and not only did she listen to me, she opened up about her own life in ways I'd never heard. She shared vulnerabilities that neither of us knew existed, and as a result we grew truly close—closer than we'd ever been. It was wonderful.

One time she called me up on a Saturday morning and said she was stranded. Since she didn't drive, I asked where she was, thinking I had to go get her someplace. She laughed and then asked if I wanted to take her to garage sales. She ordinarily did this with my father, but for some reason he was busy. Well, that began a routine the two of us wouldn't stop for years. My mother and I went out every Saturday and Sunday morning, looking for treasures or, as we joked, things we didn't need but couldn't live without.

It turned out she was a tiger. I saw where I got my addictive tendencies. She went through the papers, marked out a route, and then we hit every frickin' antiques store and yard sale in Southern California. I'm not exaggerating. We drove hundreds of miles every weekend, talking nonstop. I was amazed at how much we had to say to each other; then again, I wasn't. It was on these drives that I finally learned about her childhood, details about her syphilis, and stories that cleared up things I'd always feared.

I had spent so many years embarrassed about her, yet I realized how similar we were in ways. Shoppingwise, tastewise, we shared a mutual love of old things. That was because both of us enjoyed things that were real, solid, and full of character. We appreciated the test of time, things that survived and aged. We looked at, and bought, the cutest chairs and tables, rugs and knickknacks. At one point, Michael had to hang tables and chairs from the vaulted ceiling in our garage. I could've opened a furniture store, that's how much stuff I had.

Yet my mother and I continued to hunt for the perfect Windsor chair. Then we got into clocks. Oh my God, we loved clocks. Then we switched to quilts. Each item we got into prompted a new recollection from my mother, and that was great. One day she gave me two quilts that she'd had in storage; they'd been made by my great-great-grandmother and her friends and relatives in the 1800s. They had quilting parties, then passed the quilts down to subsequent generations. My mother put her hand on my rounded tummy and said one day I'd give them to my child.

I gave up when it came to food and indulged in cravings for milk shakes and french fries. The result was sixty extra pounds. I shrugged them off, telling myself that this was my time to get fat and not feel guilty about it. Maybe that's why pregnancy is called a miracle; it's the only time you can eat whatever you want. Michael and I turned a room into a nursery. Lloyd Schwartz and his wife hosted a baby shower for me at their house, and everyone laughed as we told old *Brady* stories.

But as I got deeper into my third trimester, and especially toward the end of it, I began turning into a different person. The lightness of being that had defined the past three months disappeared. My fears returned—would my baby be healthy, would we be good parents, what if there was an accident—and it was like a fist clenching inside me as I tried to keep the demons in check. The transformation in me was slow and excruciating. There were times when I didn't feel like me, and yet if I'd been asked what "me" felt like, I wouldn't have known how to answer.

No, that's not true. I felt fat.

And big.

And I got bigger.

At one point, my doctor said, "Maureen, you'd better start watching how much you eat." It wasn't only food, though. I suffered from edema, a condition where I retained water. I was so swollen and uncomfortable I didn't want to move. In fact, I didn't move; I sloshed. And it was painful. My feet ballooned, and I had to cut the backs of my shoes out.

I stared at my due date on the calendar, waiting with hope, excitement, trepidation, and utter fear. I don't know about other women about to give birth, but I reached the point where I couldn't wait to get that baby out of me while at the same time I was scared to death about what I was going to do when that happened. My mother said other women felt the same. She told me about giving birth to each one of her four children, and how each one had been a different experience.

I prayed for a good delivery. But then as my due date came and went, I just prayed that I'd *have* an experience. I went seven days past my due date. Then nine days. It didn't seem like I would ever have the baby.

I'd seen my doctor every couple days, but when I went for an exam on the tenth day past my due date he informed that there was no more amniotic fluid. He said that my water must have broken without me knowing it. He sent me to the hospital. Michael spent the next three days with me, sleeping in a chair, the two of us waiting for something to happen.

Finally, on the morning of May 19, I was wheeled into the operating room, and underwent a C-section. The next thing I remember is hearing a baby's cry, and then I saw my doctor, cradling a newborn in his arms, by my side. He said "Maureen, I want to introduce you to your daughter."

Suddenly my whole life changed. I was a mother. I was deeply relieved when the doctor announced that she was beautiful, perfect, and healthy. I still counted her fingers and toes. Then I kissed and caressed her, and did all those little things that mothers do when they first see the child that's spent the previous nine months inside them. I was so pleased when she nursed without any problem. I was like, "It works! It works!"

Everyone laughed. I had tears in my eyes. I was really and finally a mom. It was the role I'd always dreamed of and I looked up and said, "Thank you, God."

S everal members of my *Brady* family came by the hospital, including Susie. Florence was among those who sent flowers celebrating our newest addition, to whom we gave the name Christine, which is what my mother had almost named me. My whole life I had preferred the name Christine over Maureen and vowed I'd use it if I had a daughter. But a funny thing happened once we got her home. One day Michael and I looked at her and I said, "She doesn't look like a Christine, does she?"

Michael agreed. He'd never felt like the name Christine was quite right, but his goal during my difficult third trimester had been to avoid fights at all costs, so he kept his opinion to himself. But he was delighted to help pick a new name, one that fit. After staring at our beautiful sleeping infant, we decided on Natalie.

My mother was amused when we told her about the change. But she agreed that Natalie suited the baby perfectly. I'd never seen my mother as happy as she was when helping me with Natalie. She admitted that she'd hoped I'd have a girl. She shared my joy when I gushed about the feeling I got breast-feeding Natalie.

Unfortunately, such highs were countered by equally extreme emotional lows that were beyond my ability to control. Some days I was unable to get out of bed. Other days I was a shrew. I felt powerless against my body chemistry. As Michael recalls, my moods were unpredictable and inconsistent. It was a constant struggle and something we dealt with, praying the better days would outnumber the bad ones.

I can't say that they did. Despite being offered a ton of money, I turned down the offer to reprise Marcia Brady yet again in the new series *The Bradys*. Sherwood and Lloyd Schwartz tried to change my mind. My TV husband Jerry Houser also chimed in. My agent called every other day with a new and bigger offer.

But the script was absolutely awful, and I didn't want to do it. I had a deal with Blake Edwards's production company to develop my own sitcom. Though nothing would come of it, I had high hopes. It was also too soon after Natalie's birth for me to go back to work. I didn't know how I would feel from one day to the next. Unless something fantastic came along, I wanted to stay home.

Good thing, too. I heard Bob Reed nearly got in a fistfight with Sherwood during production. He also made sure all the Paramount and CBS executives knew he thought the show was garbage. Bob even traded words with Florence and Ann B. That was sacrilegious. They were among the nicest pros in the business.

I've learned there's usually a reason when people behave out of character, and this time was no exception. Although he kept it to himself, Bob was HIV positive and battling for his life. His anger was the outward manifestation.

In the meantime, Michael and I worked hard to start our own production company. Neither of us had any experience running one, but we had passion. Our first project came from a story we saw on *60 Minutes* about Donna and Ricardo Thorton, a white woman and black man, both of them intellectually handicapped, who met in an institution, fell in love, got married, and had a normal child.

It was actually a follow-up to a story that had been broadcast four years earlier, in 1986. Michael and I were moved to tears. Our first thought was that it would make a great movie; suddenly we wanted to make it. We acquired the rights and then shopped the project around Hollywood. We pictured Forest Whitaker as Ricardo. But our inexperience prevented us from pulling it together.

Eventually Kirstie Alley's production company took over the rights. The movie, titled *Profoundly Normal,* aired on CBS in 1983 and starred Kirstie and Delroy Lindo. Although I wondered how different our version might have looked, the film was as good as we'd imagined: touching, sad, funny, provocative, and ultimately an example of how the human spirit is able to triumph over incredible odds.

Michael and I wanted to believe that would happen in our own lives. There was still so much fighting, darkness, and pain in our marriage. Sadly, I refused to deal with the fact that I was sick—and all of us paid the price.

22

Insanity

Florence called and told me that Bob Reed was extremely sick. I gasped when she said he had AIDS.

I'd heard he didn't look good during production of *The Bradys,* and I wasn't surprised to read years later in Barry's book *Growing Up Brady* that Bob had been undergoing treatment for AIDS-related illnesses at that time. He started telling close friends about his condition in 1991. From what I heard, he thought he would be able to beat it. His spirits were upbeat when I spoke to him.

About a year before he died, Barry asked him to write the introduction to his book. They met at Bob's house, and Bob gave him all of the vitriolic memos he had written to Sherwood complaining about the *Brady Bunch* scripts.

I loved that. It was like a passing of the torch to his oldest son. *Here, take my thoughts. Remember my passion. Keep the flame burning.*

We knew Bob was a great actor. He wanted us to remember that he'd cared about the quality of the work, too.

Toward the end of his life, he was taken care of by his good friend Anne Haney. He was in the hospital the last time we spoke. I called him essentially to say good-bye, though I never uttered those words. We talked about other things. It was extremely emotional. I tried not to cry. Then I reached a point where I just didn't care, where it wasn't worth trying to hold back. I told him what really mattered, what I really wanted him to know—that I loved him.

In a weak voice, Bob said the same to me: I love you, too.

He passed away less than a week after we spoke, on May 12, 1992, in Pasadena. He was fifty-nine years old. Barry called from Chicago with the news. The entire *Brady* cast gathered for a service at All Saints Episcopal Church. I hadn't seen most of them since Natalie's birth nearly three years earlier. I cried through the memorial Barry arranged at the Pasadena Playhouse. It was terribly sad.

Afterward, the press hounded us. Reporters approached us outside the church and playhouse, and our phone was ringing when Michael and I got home. It continued to ring for days with reporters asking me to comment on Bob's homosexuality and confirm that he'd died of AIDS. It was ghoulish. I hung up each time without saying a word.

However, it eventually came out that Bob had lived a tortured life as a gay man; he'd hated his homosexuality. His death was sad enough, but knowing he was so unhappy in his life made it even sadder.

I battled myself just as ferociously, although for different reasons. I took my anger out on Michael. I never knew what would set me off. It could be a look, a comment, the rattle of a dish, a blanket out of place—anything that upset the norm or threw off my fragile sense of balance and control, which often seemed like almost everything. Consider the following.

Michael's parents visited shortly before Natalie's first birthday. It was their first trip to see us since our wedding. I was on pins and needles before they arrived. One day Natalie was crying furiously in her room. As I tried to calm her, Michael's mother stood in the doorway of the nursery, watching me. She made a comment, which she intended as a joke. But I didn't get the humor and went ballistic. Michael extinguished that fire but I continued to rage out of control in numerous other situations.

Michael took a job as a dialect coach for a theater in the Valley that was staging an Ibsen play. Since he was trying to establish himself in a different aspect of the business, he didn't charge them. I blew up at him. How could he not get paid?

Then he signed on to do a reading of a new play, and the same thing happened. He did the work for free. We argued the whole time he should've been preparing; he wasn't ready for the performance. I'd never seen him as angry at himself.

On the day after the reading, we were still fighting as we drove around doing errands. Suddenly Michael lost his temper, one of the rare times, and in blunt language he stated that he wasn't the one who had put a quarter of a million dollars' worth of coke up their nose. The rage in me was such that I smacked him in the face. I didn't even think. It was that automatic.

Between the blow and the shock from it, he momentarily lost control of the car and swerved out of our lane. Fortunately, he regained control before we caused an accident or injured anyone.

Another time, Natalie, two years old, spilled some water and a couple of red grapes on the carpet in her bedroom. It left a tiny, faintly red stain about the size of a quarter. But that was exactly the kind of blemish on my orderly little world that set me off. I saw it and began yelling. When Michael tried to calm me down, I focused my rage on him. What's interesting when I think back on it now is that deep inside I wasn't angry. I was scared—scared of my world falling apart.

Michael was stunned by the attack, and justifiably so. My upset about that one little stain turned into a list of grievances about him, about me, about us. Everything boiled down to money, or the lack of it, and truth be told, my fear that we were going to lose everything.

He looked more shocked than he had when I hit him in the car.

"What the—" He caught himself about to swear. "What does all that have to do with Natalie's dropping a grape on the carpet?"

"You don't fucking get it!" I hissed.

"Why do you have to swear?" he protested.

"Fuck you!" I screamed.

I grabbed Michael. I wanted him to fight back. He tried to restrain me, but I jerked free and hit him. He froze.

Natalie was right there, too. At that moment I didn't care.

"You don't fucking get it, do you?" I yelled.

Actually Michael did get it. Knowing I'd be a basket case as long as the carpet wasn't perfect, he spent every night for the next few days on his hands and knees, scrubbing the carpet until the stain was gone. At one point, he used a toothbrush to clean individual fibers.

That scene was repeated a few months later when Natalie broke a cup in the bathroom. I didn't know what it was; I just couldn't handle it; when something like that happened, the string that held me together broke.

When Natalie was almost five years old, Michael left me. It wasn't the first time. Sometimes he spent the night in his car; other times he slept on a buddy's sofa. But this time we'd fought in front of Natalie, and it was bad. I later found out that Michael snuck back into the house, found our daughter, and said, "Daddy will never, ever, ever leave you."

At her school the next day, he found her on the playground and reassured her that he was still present and would never leave. He was probably reassuring himself, too. I didn't make it easy for him. He later told me that he always returned because our fights followed a pattern. After a cooling-off period, I was contrite and sorry. For the next few days, I was normal and enjoyable. Then the pressure built until both of us were on edge, waiting for the next explosion.

I knew I was at fault. That part was clear to me as the smoke and dust rose over the battlefield. When Michael returned, I confessed my problems and swore that I would get help. But that never happened. We never broke from the status quo. Not even when I was embarrassed publicly, as happened once when we fought in front of Natalie's preschool, which was at our local Presbyterian church. When I picked Natalie up the next day, one of the teachers started a conversation with me.

"It's amazing what we as teachers hear from the kids," she said.

I felt my face flush. Natalie or another kid must have heard me in front of the school the day before.

"Really?" I said.

"They're little sponges," she said.

At that point, I knew she was referring to me. I thought it was best to apologize for my mistakes, the same as we taught the kids.

"I know," I said. "And I'm very sorry. I had a bad fight with my husband yesterday in front of the school, and I screamed 'fuck you.'"

She looked at me, puzzled, then shocked.

"What?"

"Yeah, I told him to fuck off."

"But I wasn't talking about you," she said.

Oh my God, I wanted to die. I needed help. Michael was constantly pleading with me to find a therapist. He suggested couples therapy. He was willing to share the responsibility; anything to improve life, to make it less of a battle. I refused. Sometimes I was calm about it. Other times I screamed and kicked. I was afraid of the diagnosis. I didn't want to be told that I was insane. I didn't want to end up like my mother, or worse, my grandmother.

The irony was that I was worse than my mother ever was, and while not as bad as my grandmother, I probably could've used quiet time in an institution. One time I asked Michael why he hadn't left me for good. He said something like he wasn't going to leave until God changed the locks. Marriage, he explained, was about more than attraction and emotional ups and downs. It was about commitment.

He'd made a commitment to me, he said—to us, and to our child—and he wasn't going to abandon it. I put that resolve to its most severe test when his parents came out for Natalie's fifth birthday in May 1994. As always, I was against it. I spent a week letting my anger build, and after they left, I exploded. In the heat of battle with Michael, I lost control and again slapped him across the face. It's one of those moments that still makes me sick whenever I flash back on it.

Michael left the house, slept in his car half the night, and then crept back in after I was asleep and made himself a bed on the downstairs sofa. At wit's end, he needed an outlet, someone to talk to about our situation, and he confided in a friend who offered to come out to the house and talk to us.

Michael thought he was doing the right thing, a good thing. But when I heard he'd let the secret out of the house, I felt betrayed. I said that I wanted a divorce.

"You're serious?" Michael asked.

"I want you to move out," I said firmly.

I stormed off to the bedroom. Michael stood by himself, shaking his head. He was resigned to throwing in the towel. He realized we were locked in a pattern that was not going to change and that was most likely insane—that is, if your definition of insanity is doing the same crazy thing over and over again, and expecting different results. And me, I think deep down I knew that something had to give or he would give up and I would . . .

Well, I didn't want to think about what would happen to me.

23

Get to the Heart

Work was always the best tonic, but not much came my way. Other than playing myself on the sitcom *Herman's Head* and a similar cameo in the movie *Dickie Roberts: Former Child Star,* which had me uttering the line, "If one more person calls me Marcia, I'll bust his f-ing head," my career was at a standstill. It was hard to take. It made me even more insecure. I remember getting mad at Michael for using a big word in a conversation. I thought it was condescending.

That summer I took singing lessons from Florence Riggs, the wife of celebrated vocal coach Seth Riggs. I liked to sing, and it was a way to stay busy. Michael, though he was forging a new career in sales, continued to hone his acting skills. He encouraged me to do the same.

One day, as I waited for my lesson, the door to the studio opened and the student before me came out. It was Rosie O'Donnell. She saw me and stopped.

"Oh my God!" she squealed. "Marcia!"

I turned red. I was a huge fan of hers. Funny, I didn't even mind that she called me Marcia. After all, she was Rosie.

"Hi."

"I can't believe I'm meeting you," Rosie said. "I'm the biggest fan. *Marcia, Marcia, Marcia!*"

She pantomimed me as Marcia getting hit in the nose by a football. Ow. Then she sang snippets of one song after another from the old *Brady* albums.

"I know 'em all," she beamed. "I could be a long-lost Brady."

I laughed. I felt an immediate kinship to Rosie. She was so present, so right there in the room, and so friendly. In a few minutes of conversation, she revealed that she knew more about *The Brady Bunch* than I did. Her memory about the episodes and trivia went beyond encyclopedic. She was a riot.

She was preparing to star in the musical *Grease* on Broadway. What I subsequently found out about Rosie is that she's one of those people who pours herself into a project, but once she does it that first time, it's pretty much over and she's ready to move on to the next thing. She's not someone who wants to stay in a play for months and months. One day, after she'd been in the play for a while, she called me from New York and asked if I wanted to fly there and audition for the part of Rizzo.

But Rizzo was her role. I was confused. I thought she was under contract. It turned out she was, but Rosie explained that she also wanted to get out of her obligation. When she'd mentioned this to the producers, they'd asked who could replace her and she'd brought up my name.

So I flew to New York, sang the songs, did a monologue, and got the job. It was one of those coincidences that made me wonder if there are accidents in life or if it's all about fate. Why had I been taking singing lessons? What were the chances of me meeting Rosie? Maybe Rosie's an angel; she's certainly a generous woman.

In any event, I hadn't worked seriously in years, and boy, as Rosie warned, and then as I found out, starring in a musical was serious work. It was the fall, and I had barely two weeks to relocate to New

York, learn the songs and dances, and get myself into the kind of condition needed to perform eight shows a week. It was a huge undertaking and an equally large upheaval in our personal lives. The production didn't give me the support I felt I needed to learn my role. I felt on my own, insecure, and lost.

I thought I was going to have to tell the producers at the last minute that I couldn't do it. I wasn't getting it, and I didn't want to embarrass myself. One night, before one of Rosie's last performances, which I'd watched every night, I went into her dressing room and wailed.

"I can't do this," I said. "I'm going to leave tomorrow. It's not working."

"What's the problem?" she asked.

"I don't know what to do," I said. "I haven't had a director the whole time I've been here."

She stood up.

"What? Do you think I ever had a director?" she exclaimed.

"But—"

"No buts," she said.

"But this is Broadway."

"And that's exactly why you aren't quitting, why you're going to do it, and why you'll do great."

"Oh my God," I said. "Do you think?"

"I know."

Sometimes all you need is someone believing in you, and things work out. This was one of those times. I made my way tentatively through opening night. I spent more time looking at the other actors than I did at the audience. I wasn't quite sure what came next. I just wanted to get through the first show—that was my only goal. Afterward, I felt like I got rid of a hundred pounds of anxiety. Michael and Natalie sent me flowers and called. About halfway through the week, I began to feel like I knew what I was supposed to do, and by week's end, I performed with confidence.

The only part I didn't like was being separated from Michael and especially Natalie. It was the first time I had been away from my daughter, and it was hard. I had moments throughout the day when I wanted to see her, pick her up, or just hear her run into the room and say, "Mommy!" Phone calls were a poor substitute. I always felt like something was missing.

My parents came to see me and that was probably the most special part of the six weeks I spent in the show. They never traveled and never spent any money on themselves. My poor mother arrived with a terrible cold and spent the first few days in bed. She was so frightened by the big city that I think she worked herself into a nervous state that wiped her out before she even arrived. But they pulled themselves together and let me take them to all the sites, including St. Patrick's Cathedral and Rockefeller Center.

Michael and Natalie arrived the following week. Aside from having them there, the highlight for me was how cute my daughter looked in her coat and hat. I felt like I had my little dress-up doll back. We also saw *Beauty and the Beast,* walked through Central Park, shopped at FAO Schwarz, and enjoyed eye-popping chocolate concoctions at Serendipity. Natalie, though initially frightened by the crowds and commotion, fell in love with New York. She didn't want to go home. Nor did I want her to.

A t the end of my six-week run, I was nervous about returning home. I looked forward to being with Michael and Natalie, but I didn't have work lined up. After nearly two months of nonstop activity on the play, I feared my empty calendar. Like many actors, downtime scared me. It was when I thought too much about myself, always negatively. What was positive about not working? It created a dangerous void.

I told Michael that I wanted to have another child. We'd had this discussion umpteen times in the past. He always said the same thing. With the number of problems in our marriage, he didn't think we could handle another child. Nor did he think it would be fair to the child—or to Natalie. I didn't look at the situation that way. I was only concerned with what I needed, wanted, and what I thought would make me feel whole. That was at least one more child and maybe two.

Hearing him tell me no angered me. In January 1995, I forbade his parents from visiting us. We fought off and on through February. I couldn't get a grip. Unable or unwilling to confront my own issues, I punished him. After he came back from a business trip late that winter, I barely spoke to him. I also hid a letter from his parents, telling him it hadn't come. He found it in my purse.

A year later, I was still unhappy, still stuck in a bleak place, and I continued to take it out on Michael. I didn't have a good reason. In order to support our family, he set aside his acting career and got a job in corporate sales, working his way up the ladder. By the mid-nineties he was among the company's top national salespeople and earning a good living. Nonetheless, in August 1996, I still picked at him, this time criticizing him for being too conservative.

"I like to get tipsy, swear, and have fun," I said. "And you don't."

"That's because someone has to be sober and pay the bills and make sure things get taken care of," he said.

I wasn't working at this time, and it grated on me in numerous ways. As it turned out, that idle time gave me the opportunity to meet and get to know some of the other mothers in the neighborhood, women who had children Natalie's age. One worked part-time, another was a housewife, one was a doctor, and another was a teacher. They made me feel like I had friends for the long haul. They weren't part of the business. They were part of my life.

One of the revelations I had later on was how similar all of us were. Every once in a while, one of the women would let something slip about an issue at home. I was the same. I might say something about Michael or Natalie. Rarely if ever did I mention my own anger,

frustration, or depression. That was still forbidden territory. But sometimes I wonder how much misery I could have avoided if I had been
able to open up, if I had been able to ask for help.

That would come.

Late that fall I was cast in an episode of *Touched by an Angel*, the
hit CBS series starring Roma Downey, Della Reese, and John
Dye. I flew to Utah, where the show was filmed. It was an episode of
clips from past shows tied together by a story line in which Monica
(Roma) is in the doghouse and has to earn her angel privileges back. In
the process, she encounters my character, Jodi, a troubled woman (talk
about typecasting) who's comforted by stories of the angel's past
deeds.

If only that had happened in real life. I was a bundle of nerves and
anxiety on that job. It was one of the hardest of my career as a result of
a discussion I'd had a few weeks earlier with my new manager, Mark
Teitelbaum. The two of us had spent the day going to meetings. In the
course of driving across town, we'd talked about many things as we got
to know each other, and he'd sensed more about me than I was willing
to admit. At one point, he made a carefully worded suggestion that I
get help.

That got the pot simmering. By the time I arrived in Utah, I was
convinced that everyone could tell I was screwed up. I thought my face
was like a billboard that said DRUG ABUSE, SYPHILIS, AND FAKE! My first
morning, I had a panic attack. I'd never had one before. I got to the
set, went through makeup, and then sat in my dressing room, thinking
I hope they don't call me. I'm the worst actress in the world. I'm going
to blow it.

The confidence I always had on a set was gone. So was the joy I'd
felt since childhood about working. I felt like whatever talent had gotten me to this point in my career was gone. I phoned Michael. He
heard me trying to catch my breath and asked what was wrong.

"They're going to find out I'm no good," I cried.

Then came the knock on the door. I don't know how I got through those scenes. The whole time I was convinced that everyone on the set knew I was a former drug addict. Even as I performed my lines, I heard the alarmed voice in my head saying, "They can see. They know who you really are."

If only I'd had the courage to simply say to myself, "So? So what if they know?" In reality, they probably did know—and didn't care. I don't know of an industry as forgiving as show business. By and large, the work is based on exploring the frailties of being human.

No, the fear I had of being found out was due entirely to me. At forty years old, a milestone I'd accepted with a shrug, I was at a place in my life where, like it or not, I began to acknowledge (I'm not going so far as to say confront) the things in my past that I'd spent my life trying to forget. It wasn't a conscious, purposeful effort. It was a process. Issues were bubbling up. I was like a kid peeking out of the covers in the dark to see if monsters were in the room. Eventually I'd see if they were real or imaginary.

After *Touched,* my manager realized I had never done a TV movie of the week. He arranged meetings at all the networks. Soon after, I met with Jerry London about a TV biopicture he was directing about country-music superstar Barbara Mandrell. I also met with the movie's writer, Linda Bergman. Based on Mandrell's autobiography, *Get to the Heart,* which opens up with her taking the stage again two years after her miraculous recovery from a 1984 car crash, and then flashed back to her youth as a multi-instrument-playing prodigy determined to rise up the ladder of country-music stardom, first with her sisters and then on her own.

It was the best script of my career. I identified with many aspects in Barbara's life: the way she started out as a child performer and how she enjoyed being the center of attention. She had her share of emotional struggles, too. Then of course she had to find new levels of strength and determination in order to come back from the car accident that resulted in multiple fractures as well as memory loss and speech problems.

Michael and I went with the director, writer, and producer to meet Barbara in Las Vegas, where she was performing. We met before the show and visited backstage afterward. Later, I spent much more time with her there and on the set, observing and talking. Her talent aside, I was fascinated by the number of people in her world and the way she was always at the center of it.

On a more personal level, I was inspired by the strength she'd summoned at every phase of her life, whether she was a child pursuing a dream or a young woman doing the same, and especially by the way she rebounded from the accident. She told me about its devastating affect on her and her family, yet how, ultimately, after much prayer, reprioritizing, and hard work, it brought all of them closer together.

One time Barbara and I were talking on the phone. I'm someone who says "oh my God" more frequently than I probably should (hey, even grown up, I'm still a Valley girl), and I blurted the words out in response to a story she told. Barbara said, "Maureen, do you have to use the word *God* so much?" I cringed and then said, "Oh my God. I'm so sorry."

Barbara didn't like being on the set, but she made sure her concerns were known. She offered suggestions. I don't remember specific criticism from her, but I was insecure about my acting. Although not as bad as on *Touched*, I still needed time by myself at the start of every day as I transformed myself from a scared doe into a country-music superstar.

Cameos by Dolly Parton (the director was smitten with her, as was I) and Kenny Rogers added authenticity, as did the presence of Barbara's daughter playing the youngest Mandrell sister. Michael and I watched the movie after it was finished. A harsh critic of my work, I cringed during moments where I thought I pushed it too far, where I tried too hard. But there was one scene in which Barbara was running a business meeting and took control of people in a way I couldn't imagine myself doing. While shooting it, I felt like I stepped outside myself and into her skin, and I was thrilled to see it played that way on the screen, too.

The lessons I'd learned then were still resonating in me when the movie aired at the end of September 1997. Helped by good reviews, it was CBS's highest-rated TV movie that year. More important, I felt good about myself for stretching as far as I ever had in my career, and succeeding. It had nothing to do with Marcia Brady either. In fact, somehow, through a long, bumpy, circuitous route via Barbara Mandrell, I rediscovered Maureen McCormick, actress.

And I didn't stop there.

24

Mo' Better

After finishing *Get to the Heart,* I looked forward to spending time at home with Natalie, her friends, and their mothers. Some of Barbara's message about reprioritizing had rubbed off on me. One morning I walked outside with my coffee cup and had a conversation with one of my friends in the neighborhood who was walking her dog. We waved at Michael as he drove to work. I told her about the difficulties he was having at his job because of undependable suppliers.

Once I was back inside, I realized how much I liked where we lived; the house and the neighborhood felt right, like we were supposed to be living there. I appreciated being able to walk outside and talk to a friend. I liked being part of this world of moms, this cozy community that bonded through shared experiences. All of us had raised our children together. We went out to dinner once a month, and sometimes we let our husbands come with us, though we preferred the girls-only nights.

Over time, without realizing it, I revealed many of the things I'd always kept private. Sometimes I realized what I was saying; other times the stories came out of my mouth before I knew it. I would gasp and say to myself, did I really say that? But I needed to get those things off my chest. I trusted those women. And the truth was, after so many years, they knew me better than I knew myself.

And they knew what I needed. One afternoon I was sitting on the porch with my friend, Janie. She was the mother of three children, and a doctor. She lived around the corner and down a few doors. As we talked, I started to cry. I didn't know why. It was a feeling, I said, like a sadness that came over me. I said I thought there was something wrong with me.

"Do you feel like that often?" she said.

I shook my head yes.

"Gray and blah," I said.

"For any reason?"

"Sometimes, yes. But most of the time, no."

I explained that the sadness was always with me. I said I didn't know what was wrong with me. I had a beautiful home, child, and husband. I had great friends, too. I had everything a person could want. Yet . . .

"It's like there's an insanity brewing inside me."

She reacted to my choice of the word *insanity*. I had to explain that what I meant was complicated, difficult to share, and even harder for me to articulate. I tried to explain the sad, scared, tenuous feeling I'd had for as long as I could remember, since I was a teenager. Even on good days I felt like it was always just beneath the surface. And on bad days, it consumed me. It filled my life with dark skies and rough water. The feeling came and went on its own accord, affecting my moods, which in turn affected my marriage.

"It scares me to know that I'm not in control, that I could go insane if I let it consume me," I said.

I cried.

"I don't even know why I'm telling you," I said.

"It's okay," she said. "I'm glad you are."

"I feel like I'm at war with myself. There's all this stuff that I've kept in me and it wants to come out. I feel like I'm going to go crazy if I don't tell someone."

I explained that I was at a point where I couldn't go on, where I wanted to find out what was wrong with me. She handed me some tissues. I apologized for breaking down and burdening her. I also thanked her for being there and listening to me talk. Just talking seemed to relieve some pressure.

"Maureen," she said, "I think you could be depressed. You could possibly be bipolar. I think it might do you a world of good if you were to go see a doctor, get diagnosed, and maybe get on some medication."

"I know," I said.

"Have you done that?" she asked.

"No. Michael has begged me to go for help."

"And?"

"I'm scared."

"What about, medication?"

I shook my head no and explained that my past problems with drugs, which had provided escape and relief until they almost killed me, scared me off anything stronger than an Advil. She asked if I'd heard of Prozac and said it sounded like it might make a positive difference in my life. She surprised me by describing some firsthand experience she'd had in her family dealing with depression.

I related to many of the things she said. At various times, she could've been describing me. It gave me the courage to reveal my deepest, darkest family secrets, from my mother and her mother to my brother Denny. I told her everything. I tried to make connections for her: how I was passive like my mother, subject to swings like my father, and . . .

"I fear that I might be insane like—"

"You don't have to go there," she said, and stopped me. "You aren't insane. You're a wonderful, special person carrying around a lot of pain."

I kept going.

Billy Hinsche of Dino, Desi &
Billy and me.

Bill Levy, director of *Skatetown
U.S.A.*

Eve and me, 1989.

Our friends Dup and Bob
Pierce. Bob helped introduce
me to Michael. Bob also played
my husband in *Shout for Joy* in
Hawaii.

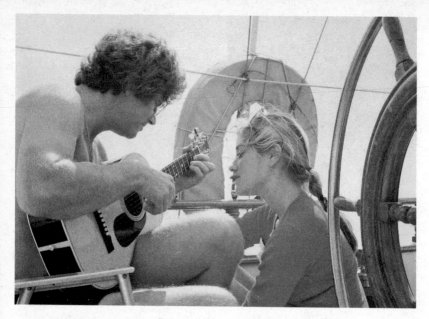

Harmonizing with Fred Waleki, 1980.

Thanksgiving, 1984. Just after Michael and I were engaged.

During *Shout for Joy,* our prenuptial honeymoon, 1983.

Our wedding, 1985.

I finally have an excuse for
not having a flat tummy.
Eight months pregnant in
1989.

One precious little girl and
two tired parents, 1989.

Natalie is seven months old! Spending Christmas in Minnesota

The family, 1991.
Top: Dad and Mike. *Bottom:* Denny, me, mom, and Kevin

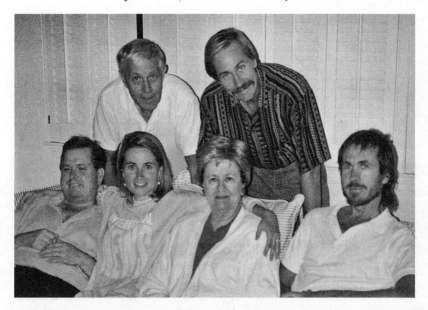

Mother and daughter, 1991.

Natalie likes chocolate.

Natalie and Kona.

Lloyd Schwartz and me during *The Brady Brides*, 1981.

Cybil and me, 1995.

Easter with Bill and Hillary at the White House, 1995.

Mike and Natalie visit me on Broadway during *Grease*, 1994.

As Rizzo in *Grease*.

Natalie watching Mom signing autographs after a performance of *Grease*.

Natalie and me in Central Park in New York during *Grease*.

The family. *Top:* Michael, Kevin, and Denny. *Bottom:* Dad, Natalie, mom, and me, 2000.

Shooting *Get to the Heart: The Barbara Mandrell Story*, 1997.

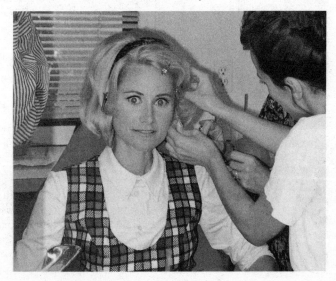

Director Jerry London, Barbara Mandrell, me, writer Linda Bergman, and producer Tom Patricia, 1997.

With Christopher Atkins, costar on *Title to Murder*, 2001.

A promotional shot for my album taken by my friend Carin, 1995.

With Wayland Patton, dueting on "When You Get a Little Lonely," 1995.

Florence
Henderson and
me, 2003

Me on the set of
Scrubs, 2003.

Touring with *When You Get a Little Lonely*, 1995.

On the red carpet. The Rascal Flats are so amazing and down to earth, 2008.

My favorite pic. Our
little trio, 2007.

Mary and me in Africa,
2008.

The more I said, the better it felt. It was a true purge.

I cried and cried and cried.

What I discovered at that moment, though, was how badly, how desperately I wanted help. I had all this fear inside me. And anger. And hatred. Hatred for what I'd done. For what I'd put my parents through. Hatred for the way I'd treated Michael. For being selfish and self-destructive. For being Marcia. For expecting things to be perfect. For not having my career go the way I'd imagined it.

I hated everything.

And I was tired of it!

I was tired of hating!

I just wanted to be me, Maureen, and appreciate that. I wanted to appreciate the things I had, not what I thought I wanted.

At Janie's suggestion, I went to my doctor and asked for a prescription for Prozac. My internist was a wonderful man whose daughter sometimes babysat for Natalie. It was very hard for me to sit in his office and admit that I was depressed and then have to provide him with my family's and my own medical history, which I did without crying too much.

He was wonderfully understanding, though. He even made me smile after I apologized for crying and said I was embarrassed to admit I had a problem.

"Maureen, I'm a doctor," he said. "People don't usually see me unless they have a problem."

He wrote me a prescription, but a couple weeks went by before I filled it. Given my history of drug abuse, I was wary of taking anything. I was also scared of medication that was going to alter the way I felt in my head. Hey, I was embarrassed of just going into a bookstore and asking the girl at the information desk to point me toward the self-help section. I also worried what people might think if they saw me reading a book on depression. It was silly.

Michael and I sat in bed at night, poring through the literature. He also did research on the Internet. Soon I told some of my other close girlfriends what was going on. After years of not talking about anything, I was suddenly telling everyone. I realized my friends would still love me, warts and all, and they did. They were incredibly supportive.

After deciding to start on the Prozac, it was almost anticlimactic. I didn't feel any effects from it. Granted, I didn't know what to expect. But I thought I'd experience something. It actually took about two weeks before I felt the drug starting to take affect in my system, and it wasn't pleasant. I felt hyper and amped up. My mind wouldn't stop racing. I was unable to concentrate.

I complained to Janie, who explained the unpleasant side effects were part of the process. She encouraged me to stick with it.

I stayed with it only because I trusted Janie. But about six weeks into the course of treatment I felt the beneficial effects. It happened so gradually that one day I noticed I didn't feel jittery and unfocused. I'd grown so accustomed to the nagging side effects that I had to stop and think when they were no longer there. In their place, I felt different. Actually, I realized that I felt good.

And once that happened, it was like a wonderful awakening, as if I'd been rewired in such a way that I no longer felt the pain and fear that had given a foreboding texture to my life since I was a teenager. I was aware of it, but I felt released from it. The same was true of the anger that had made me a tinderbox of emotion through most of my adulthood, especially in my marriage. A weight lifted off of me. I was like a plane breaking through the clouds into blue sky.

I remember telling Michael it seemed like I could finally let go. I didn't know how else to explain it. I kept waiting for it to disappear and the old feelings to return. They didn't. One morning I found Michael and told him the chattering in my head responsible for much of my confusion and conflict was gone.

"It's quiet!" I said, beaming.

The feeling was that dramatic, and so were the changes in my be-havior. Around that time, Michael left his job out of frustration with unreliable suppliers. In the past, such a change would've caused me to panic. I would've taken my fear out on him. We would've fought for days. Now, not only was I supportive of his decision to leave and efforts to find a new job quickly, but I found myself at a party talking to friends about his situation, asking if they knew of any openings, and speaking highly and in fact boasting of his special ability to deal with people.

Michael said he appreciated having the person with whom he fell in love present most if not all of the time. I wasn't perfect by any means, but my better attributes were present and accessible every day, no lon-ger like tantalizing phantoms he had to hope and pray would return and stay. After my husband had given so much to me, I tried to give back. I apologized endlessly for all the irrational craziness I seemed un-able to control for so many years of our marriage. I marveled—both of us did—at how I was no longer fighting myself or Michael.

Like my marriage, my mothering improved, too. Now that I was more in control, I didn't lose my temper if Natalie spilled something. I didn't go to the extreme where I saw my world fall apart just because she broke a glass or messed up a room. I always loved my child, but I enjoyed being a mother more than ever.

As I'd told Michael, I was able to let go. I no longer felt the need to control everything for fear it would fall apart if I let my guard down.

Even with the change in me evident my mother remained skeptical. She needed to see over time that Prozac wasn't another drug that was going to cause me problems. I gave her that opportunity. We went to garage sales two or three weekends a month. I picked her up early in the morning when the best stuff was still available, and we stayed out until the late afternoon. We talked the entire day. I always made sure she knew how good I felt.

Sometimes she asked tentatively if the pills were still making a dif-ference, and other times I told her without waiting for her query. I could tell she was more curious and accepting. One time, while we were searching for a garage sale, I told her about the pain I'd been in for so many years, as well as how I thought the cocaine I did was a way to escape all that hurt and fear. I had tried to run away from my problems, nearly destroyed myself, and been a poor daughter.

I apologized for not dealing with it better. I'd been sick. I should've gotten help sooner.

"But I feel so much better now," I said, suddenly trying to inject a more upbeat note to the conversation.

My mother took my hand and squeezed it.

A little while later, as we walked through the yard sale, she gave me a hug. She had a tear in her eye.

"It's a miracle," she said.

My father remained dubious. He was influenced by Kevin, who seemed to resent me for feeling better. He accused me of being on mind-altering drugs. I felt bad for Kevin. He was a bitter man. He still lived in the same apartment my parents had gotten for him years earlier. He didn't work. Even though my parents provided him with money each month, he blamed my mother's syphilis for all of his hard luck.

I found it nearly impossible to sympathize with him the way I did when we were younger. I had no patience for his criticism and lack of ambition.

As this was going on, I worked on *Teen Angel,* a sitcom about a teenager who dies from choking on a hamburger and is sent back to earth as his best friend's guardian angel. I had fun. I was in the best shape of my life and feeling good about myself, and my work. The regular hours of a sitcom were also convenient for planning around Natalie's schedule. But the show struggled in the ratings, and after eleven episodes I was let go.

I'd never been fired before. The producers called me into their office and tried to soften the blow by explaining that it wasn't me. They blamed it on the network, explaining that sometimes when a show doesn't work, executives tear it apart, try to fix it, and bring in other actors, which was what happened. I was cast off and they brought in Jerry Van Dyke as my replacement.

I held myself together until I got to my car and then I broke down. No matter the explanation, it was still me being rejected. But I handled it. I cried within the normal range and then talked it through with Michael. It was the first major test of my emotional stability since I'd started Prozac. If I hadn't been on the antidepressant medication, I probably would've killed myself.

Work was still sporadic. What I realized is that after thirty years in the business, I needed to work my way up from the bottom again. It was a sobering challenge, but one I met by gritting my teeth and taking the necessary baby steps. In 1999, I was in *Baby Huey's Great Easter Adventure*, a children's movie directed by my friend Stephen Furst, a wonderful, funny guy who'd lost more than a hundred pounds in the twenty years since he appeared in *Animal House.*

Next I appeared on Nickelodeon's *Amanda Show*, a clever and fun series amalgam of sitcom and variety starring Amanda Bynes. Mine was a tiny role, something I had to remind myself was part of the process of taking baby steps. But Amanda was a breath of fresh air, a genuinely lovely kid, and a big fan of *The Brady Bunch.* She asked all sorts of questions about what it was like to do that show; everyone on the set did. The people I met more than compensated for the size of the part, and I realized I could have fun just working.

I also guested on the WB's *Moesha,* the hit sitcom starring Brandy, who was twenty at the time and in love. It was sweet to observe. Her mother was on the set, as was her brother, Ray J. Being around Brandy and Amanda, I couldn't help but reflect on the years I'd spent growing up on the set. After the taping, Michael and I went to a restaurant, where I talked about the emotions and memories that were flooding my head. I cried as I remembered all the pain I'd grown up with, the way I'd covered it up with a smile, then with cocaine, and through it all the impossible effort I'd put forth to try to keep any cracks from showing.

All those years I had wanted simply to be me, but I'd either been too scared to do that or too lost to figure out who I was. Now, as I told Michael, who was thriving in a new job and was on his way to becoming the company's top national salesman, it was different. Our lives for the first time were stable and real. As a result, I wanted to know and understand more about me, which led in a predictable direction.

Whether directly or indirectly, my mother had always been the biggest influence in my life. Over the years, there had been several reunions on her side of the family in Iowa. She'd asked me to go, and I turned her down. I was either too messed up, too scared, too angry, or all of the above. But now I was done treating life like a multiple-choice exam. I knew that I'd missed opportunities.

First I told Michael and then my mom that I wanted to go to Iowa and walk on the ground that my mother had walked on, go into the house where she had grown up, and feel the place that nurtured the woman who gave life to me. My mother didn't feel up to going back—despite previous reunions—but Michael suggested a family trip, and I thought it was a fine idea.

"Maureen, you don't want to go back there," my mom said.

"I do."

"There's nothing back there."

"Not true," I said. "Your childhood is back there. Your family is back there. I want to find out about those things."

My mother rolled her eyes. I laughed.

Michael, Natalie, and I flew to his folks' place in Minnesota. After a few days, we drove to Burlington, Iowa. The decision to travel by car rather than plane wasn't intentional, but the time it took to get there (and that didn't count the years I needed before I was ready) heightened the anticipation. I realized that time can be a good thing. God gives you nine months to get used to the idea of having a baby. You get twelve years to prepare for having a teenager in the house. Hopefully you get a long life to learn from your mistakes. In my case, it was forty-four years.

Burlington, known as the "the world's backhoe capital," is a small town located on the edge of the Mississippi across from Illinois. We checked into a local hotel, called my relatives still left in town, and found the house where my mother grew up.

I stood outside the two-story home and tried to picture my mom as a little girl. The house was well kept. There seemed to be a relatively fresh coat of white paint. What I really liked was that it was still in the family. My mother's aunt's daughter lived there.

They let us in, and as I stopped in the entry, I again tried to picture my mother as a girl. It wasn't hard. The house was decorated with antiques, which helped take my imagination back in time. As I walked up the stairs to my mother's old bedroom, I held on to the handrail and imagined her hand on it.

The entire two days we spent there were imbued with emotion as I connected with relatives I'd heard of but never met. I met my mother's mother's sister. Though she was in her late nineties, I felt like I was almost with my grandmother. I spoke with one of my mother's cousins, a woman who'd grown up with her. I spent hours asking questions. Even when she described the pain my mother endured throughout her life, the bus trips to the hospital to get shots, and how her syphilis was considered a dirty, shameful thing and hushed up, I felt my soul fill up.

I broke down many times, but at one point in particular, she stopped and asked if it was too much for me. I said no, I wasn't crying because of the stories. I had tears because for the first time in my life, I was seeing my mother for who she was: the greatest, strongest woman I'd ever met.

Later, as we drove back to Minnesota, Michael wondered why I was just having this revelation, why I was only now discovering how strong my mother was, and then he laughingly described what it had been like to stand in front of her steel-gray eyes as she said, "You have a lot to prove."

"You think your father is half as tough?" he added. "No way."

I hoped I could be half as strong as my mother. Michael said I already was. "You get as much strength as you need for the next battle," he added.

Neither of us knew it, but I was going to need more than I'd ever imagined.

Part

Four

25

Coming to Terms

Life was a soap opera—literally.

It was the summer of 2000, and I worked for nearly two months on the daytime drama *Passions*. I played Rebecca Hotchkiss, a wealthy, confused, somewhat kinky, lovelorn woman from a line of conniving, emotional women, one of whom had even arranged for John Wilkes Booth to assassinate Abraham Lincoln.

As for real life, I had mixed feelings about the job. On the one hand, it felt like a step down. On the other hand, it was the hardest work I'd ever done.

Every night I had to memorize a whole day's worth of lines. It was grueling. I admired the actors on the show who were able to do it. Creatively, the work demanded a high level of tolerance. Not much happened. Working a soap was a daily grind. I was saying the same words in the tenth episode as I'd said in the first. My character never left her drama. It was the way I'd lived the past thirty years—stuck in the same role—and I had a hard time continuing even though it was pretend.

I politely declined an invitation to return for another season. I couldn't do it. I knew the bedroom scenes were coming and I thought I'd be better off quitting while I was still ahead. Even so, it was tough to get away from Rebecca. Die-hard fans of *Passions* continued to stop me long after I was off the show and ask questions, as if I were still involved with the characters in the town of Harmony.

My next role had the potential for more drama. It was about six months later, and I was the lead in *Title to Murder*, a small feature that again paired me with Stephen Furst. I played a real-estate-title examiner whose life was put in jeopardy after she unearthed seemingly forgotten evidence about the case of a missing woman. An assistant district attorney (played by Christopher Atkins) provided help as well as romance. No one pretended it was an Oscar-caliber script, but the chance to work on a feature film with nice people trumped the lack of quality.

We shot in New Hampshire. One day I complimented Stephen on maintaining his weight, then added that I felt fat. He studied me for a moment and said I only needed to lose ten pounds. I was like, thanks for nothing, pal. Chris was a cutup, the guy on the set who kept things light, and a pleasure to look at. He came to my room at night, wanting to hang out and talk. At one point, I thought he might've wanted to cross the line. I didn't want to go there. I didn't need to. But as a forty-five-year-old mother who felt ten pounds too heavy, I took it as a compliment.

We shot in a sleepy little town that had one major nighttime attraction, a strip club, and one night Stephen and Chris took me there. It was my first time seeing totally nude dancers. I couldn't believe I was there. I didn't know whether to look and enjoy the women or cover my eyes and run out. I applied the old adage "when in Rome, do as the Romans do." So I let Stephen and Chris order me a drink and I watched the girls. They were beautiful, in great shape, and totally bare-ass naked. They were smooth and shiny in front, too. I'd never seen that on a grown woman either.

Several of the girls asked if they could give me a dance. They were quite open and even giddy about the idea of straddling Marcia Brady's lap. I didn't blame them. I was having a good time. One girl finally persuaded me to let her give me a dance. She led me to a private room. I didn't understand why she wouldn't do it at the table, but she insisted it would be more special in the private room.

What the heck, right? But right before I stepped into the room with this gorgeous naked young woman, I came to my senses. I figured the room was filled with security cameras, as, most likely, was the club. The thought hit me: Oh my God, pictures of me here are going to end up in the *National Enquirer*. In a panic I sprinted out of the nightclub, leaving behind peals of laughter.

A lthough I would've preferred to work more frequently, I enjoyed the jobs that came my way. I guested on an episode of *Ellen*, playing Ellen DeGeneres's best friend from high school. Her courage, poise, and personality made me more of a fan than I already was. She was going through a breakup.

It was obvious she was preoccupied at work. We spent time together outside between scenes, talking about the breakup, and I was amazed and impressed by how she was able to share her feelings openly and honestly. She wasn't afraid to expose her pain. She seemed so evolved to me. It had taken me thirty years to learn how to deal with my problems. At the same time, she was able to summon so much joy and share it through her work. It bubbled out of her on the set despite the upset she was going through. I thought she was remarkable.

I remember going home and telling Michael that I thought she was one of the most beautiful women I'd ever met. He gave me a look.

"Don't worry, honey," I said. "I'm not switching teams."

"Phew," he joked.

"Unless she calls and asks me out on a date. Then we'll see."

Why did I like to torture my poor husband?

It was because we'd survived the worst of times only to come out in a great place. I was going into my fifth year on Prozac and our marriage was better and stronger than ever. My family was a different story. They couldn't take a magic pill to calm things down and straighten everyone out. My parents, in their early eighties, still had their hands full with Denny and Kevin, both of whom were in their fifties and still needed or demanded their full attention.

Remarkably, Denny's spirit was still as pure as it had been when we were children. No one in the world said I love you with as much feeling or enthusiasm. Even as a middle-aged man, his face took on a child-like brightness. He'd gotten older without growing up.

Sadly, the same could be said of Kevin. Despite all his natural ability in various areas, including music and art, he hadn't done anything with his life. My parents argued about it endlessly. My mother blamed my father for indulging him too often, and my father made me feel guilty for not having helped Kevin more, almost as if I was supposed to have found him a career in Hollywood alongside mine.

My father often remarked that I'd blown Kevin's chance at success by not making an album with him. I disagreed.

It was difficult having a brother who was constantly at war with the world, with his family, and with himself. I understood why he frustrated my parents. The potential all of us had seen in him was in the past and instead he had turned into a quirky, angry, and sometimes frightening man. My mother confided to her sister that she thought Kevin might go off the deep end one day and never come back.

I tried to help Kevin. I hired him to take care of several rental properties I owned, but it didn't work out. He said he couldn't paint because the fumes made him sick. He also said he couldn't take care of the gardens because the fertilizers might kill him. I also hired him to give guitar and drawing lessons to Natalie and her friends. But the lessons stopped after Kevin cursed out the daughter of a friend of mine and several other mothers warned there could be a problem.

At one point, he became obsessed with buying a van and driving it through Northern California. He spoke about getting away from things and disappearing where no one could find him. My father thought an adventure would be good for him, but my mother objected. I can still hear her saying she didn't want any of her children living out of a car. She worried he would end up dead.

He ended up staying at home. But around that same time he moved from his condo into a three-bedroom home that my parents had redone before renting out. He claimed his condo was infected by mold. He played my parents a video he'd made, showing what he claimed were the contaminated spots on the walls and floors. He said he could die if he stayed there.

All this drama took a toll on my mother. She began staying in bed, complaining that she didn't feel well. She didn't really complain; that wasn't my mother's way. Instead she needed to rest much of the day. She couldn't pinpoint any specific ache or pain. It was a general lack of energy.

I saw she wasn't herself, and that concerned me. In the early nineties, she was diagnosed with breast cancer and had a mastectomy. Although ten years had passed, my first thought was of a recurrence of the cancer. But I forced myself not to think about that possibility. Our family was only as strong as my mother, and at the moment neither was doing that well.

I t turned out my mother suffered from more than just my father's and Kevin's wild theories. Near the end of 2003, she had on several occasions such sharp pains in her stomach that I hurried over to their house and took her to the hospital emergency room. Despite her complaints of severe pain and nausea, doctors were unable to find anything wrong with her. I pleaded with them to do more tests. Nothing was more frustrating than to hear them say nothing was wrong. Couldn't they see she was sick?

By the new year, it seemed I was taking her to the hospital nearly every other day. Finally, after one episode at the emergency room, I said to the doctor, "Look, I can't take her home unless we find out what's wrong with her. You can see that she has something wrong with her. Isn't there anything else you can try?"

For whatever reason, my alarm got through to this doctor. He ordered a certain kind of X-ray, one that I guessed the insurance company didn't ordinarily pay for, and when it came back the radiologist let me see the film. It showed a mass on my mother's kidney. The doctor said it was cancer. I pressed a hand against my eyes to stave off tears, stared at the X-ray, and asked him a question.

Was he sure?

Yes.

Was she going to die?

There were things they could do to fight it.

Could I give her the news?

Yes.

Good. I wanted to tell her in my own way.

After the doctor left the room, I hugged my mother and told her the bad news in the most simple and straightforward words I could muster without breaking down. After a point, I couldn't help myself anymore. I cried. But I assured her that we would get through it together.

She handled the news much better than I did. At home, she walked inside, saw my father, shook her head, and went to bed. My father asked several questions, then paused. Clearly overwhelmed by the situation, he asked what we were going to do. I said, "Whatever it takes."

I knew that fell on my shoulders, but hey, it was my mother. Given my family, I wouldn't have had it any other way. Neither would Michael, who helped me prepare a list of questions for the doctor. The next day my mother and I met with a specialist and a few days later she underwent surgery to remove her infected kidney.

I stayed overnight in her hospital room and then brought her back to my house to recuperate. I'd already prepared Michael for that, and he knew it was pointless to say anything to the contrary when I said we would give her better care than my father and brother. He set up a room for her and helped tend to her with the same warmth and love that I gave her. In fact, one day I walked into her room shortly after he'd spent time with her and my mother was crying.

Alarmed, I asked what was wrong.

"Maureen, you're the luckiest woman in the world," she said. "You have the greatest husband. He loves you so much."

I already knew that, but it made my heart soar to hear that she'd finally changed her opinion about Michael and discovered the man I knew as the love of my life. After nearly twenty years of marriage, he had proven himself to her. That likely happened years earlier, but this was her first time articulating it. She let me know that my greatest achievement was marrying—and staying married—to Michael.

After three weeks, she returned home. Sometimes I look back and wish I had never let her leave my house. It's one of those things I would do differently if given the chance. But she came through the surgery and was well enough to be around her own things at home, as she desired. But I saw her every day and took her to her chemotherapy treatments, which was time we used to talk about everything.

One day I remarked that about five years earlier she seemed to have let go of all her old worries about syphilis, insanity, and the rest of her past. Yes, she said. She'd started to relax and enjoy life when she saw my life come together after I began the Prozac in the latter nineties.

She said it was me. I seemed to come into my own, and she felt good about my family, my husband, and my life. Like I was out of danger.

"You'll watch your daughter the same way," she said.

"I already do," I replied.

26

How Much Time?

Aserious illness unfurls in stages, with pauses that can either make you believe life is back to normal or make you wonder if life will ever be normal again. Unfortunately, with my mom's cancer, it was the latter.

Even when my mom was well and as far back as I could remember, my parents' home was a mess. My mother was a world-class hoarder who didn't throw out a thing while collecting more and more stuff. Their place was filled to overflowing capacity by decades' worth of furniture and knickknacks and even newspapers my mother simply refused to throw away. As she got sicker, it seemed suffocating and dangerous, like the past was closing in around her until life was squeezed out. Plus, with Denny there too, I knew it was no place to convalesce.

I wanted her to be closer to me. I insisted, really. And after some back and forth, she and my father agreed to move into the place where Kevin lived. It had three bedrooms and plenty of space. But I was shocked and disturbed to learn that Kevin kept two bedrooms for himself—one to sleep in and one for high-tech camera equipment he'd purchased—and my parents and Denny shared the master suite.

I didn't know what to make of the situation. Denny slept on a foam mattress on the floor. Sometimes he woke up in the morning covered in ants and spider bites. Kevin refused to let anyone use pesticides. He threw a fit when I wanted to hire an exterminator. But then he'd also been against my mother receiving chemotherapy, arguing that would kill her quicker than the cancer.

Again, one of the biggest regrets of my life is that I didn't take my mother out of that situation. I considered it. I desperately wanted to set her up in our house, where I knew she would be comfortable and well cared for. But she refused. She was as stubborn sick as she was when healthy. She wanted to remain in her role as wife and mother, even though my father and brothers were all grown men.

Still, it scared me to know she was basically dependent on my father and two brothers, one of whom was intellectually handicapped, while the other one often spoke of life as the fifth dimension, like when he said, "Maureen, the floor is not really here. This is all an illusion."

It wasn't an illusion—it was a nightmare. One day my mother called and said, "Maureen, I feel like I'm in prison with your dad and Kevin."

She said the two of them sat around the house and talked nonstop about conspiracy theories, like how the government controlled the population through prescription drugs, how ordinary food was dangerous (hence his devotion to health foods), and how it was likely they were being watched.

"Watched by whom?" I wondered.

"I don't know," my mother said.

When I asked my brother such questions, he always gave me the same response. "You'll see. You'll find out."

"I come out of the bedroom, listen to them, and it makes me sicker," my mom told me. "It's easier to just turn around and go back to bed."

I was at their place as much as possible, almost daily, and still I beat myself up for not doing more. My mom still refused to leave. I hired a nurse who came highly recommended from friends. She reassured me that I was doing everything possible and said she would make sure my mother was well-attended to when I wasn't able to be there.

But Kevin fired her a week later. I brought in another nurse, and he fired her, too. It was maddening to me. It seemed unconscionable. But he had his reasons, he said. Ultimately, I felt like he didn't want anyone else in the house. Kevin turned into a paranoid germaphobe. He picked up a napkin before he touched a door handle. He kept his own special food in the kitchen. Then one day he put blue duct tape on the floor between the kitchen and the living room and stipulated no one could cross it.

I told my mother it wasn't right—I told everyone it wasn't right. *What if Mom got hungry?*

Once again I begged her to come live with us.

As always, she refused.

"Maureen, just take care of your family," she said. "I'm all right here in my home."

At the beginning of the summer, I asked my mother's doctor how long she might have under favorable conditions. He hesitated to give me any length of time, but after I pressed him, he said about six months. I shook my head at that harsh dose of reality. Six months was such a short time.

I started to bargain with God. I asked Him to let her live through the holidays. I just wanted another Christmas with her. Unfortunately, she grew weaker and lost more and more weight. It was impossible to know whether the cancer caused her to whittle away or the conditions in which she insisted upon living. I tried to get her to eat. Friends brought her pots of stew, soups, chocolates, and ice cream, but Kevin ended up putting most of it in the trash.

Kevin and my father became constant companions. My brother set up a large-screen TV and recliner in the living room for my dad, then made blackout curtains and bought more camera and recording equipment for himself. From her bed, my mother called me and complained Kevin was crazy and brainwashing my father. She said she felt like a prisoner.

"Let me get you and bring you to my house," I said.

"No, no," she said. "This is home."

"But it's not a good situation for you."

"I'm just trying to figure out where I went wrong with your brother."

When my mom first got sick, she and my dad wanted to create a living will. Up till then, they didn't have a trust or a will. They asked me to recommend a lawyer. I got some names from friends and let them pick. Afterward, they let all of us know they intended to split everything evenly among the kids. They also made me the executor. No one objected.

At one point during her illness, my mom worried about the rate at which Kevin was spending money on equipment and suggested adding a provision in their trust that gave him his money in installments rather than one lump sum. Nothing like that was ever done, but it showed that even from her sickbed she had realistic concerns.

I echoed these after I saw the blackout curtains go up and more equipment come in. But my father said not to worry, and indeed, there were plenty of other things on my mind. One day I went to my parents' place and learned of a new change. Denny was only allowed to sit in one chair. If possible, Kevin didn't want him touching any doorknobs.

"He's not clean," Kevin explained.

"What?" I said.

Kevin shook his head, angry that I didn't get it. "Maureen, why do I have to spell things out for you? He doesn't know how to clean himself after he goes to the bathroom."

My mother was in bed but not deaf. When I went into her room, she gave me a look that kind of said "you can't believe what's going on here." She seemed to have resigned herself to the worst. Kevin continued to fire all the nurses who were good. I was disturbed but helpless to do anything. One day I found my mother lying in her feces in her bed. My father hadn't changed her. I screamed at him, then tried to clean her up and put on new adult diapers myself. But as thin as my mother was, she was still heavier than I could manage. Both Kevin and my father refused my entreaties for help. My mother rolled her eyes and apologized. I held back tears.

I was frightened a few days later when Kevin spoke about building a contraption to lift my mother up so the person changing her wouldn't have to touch her. I thought he was joking. But he actually built it. That's how crazy things were. And my father boasted about it. *Look at that! Kevin did it all by himself!*

My mother gave me a look that let me know she was petrified, like my father and Kevin might actually put her in it.

One day in early July, my father said he could no longer take care of Denny and asked me to find a home where Denny could live. I was stunned and then heartbroken. We'd never discussed what was going to happen to Denny after my parents were no longer alive, but until then, for as long as I could remember, my mother had been clear. She wanted Denny at home, not in a home.

"Why me?" I asked my father. "Why do I have to do this?"

"Maureen, I can't take care of him anymore. You have to do this."

That didn't sound like my father, not the person I'd known my whole life, not the person who'd taken classes in special-education instruction after Denny was diagnosed as intellectually handicapped. Denny always accompanied my father on errands. They had been pals Denny's whole life. Still, like a good daughter, I did as asked, reasoning that maybe I could find Denny a place where he would feel wanted and be cared for with love and compassion. It took a while, but I found a place.

I decided to break the news to my mother. And because I didn't want her to hate my father, I told her it was my decision. I thought it would be best for Denny, I said. Propped up on two pillows in bed, she turned from me and looked out the window. She knew her world was not going to be the way she wanted it to be when she finally left.

"I promise you I'll always look after him," I said. "I swear. I'll make sure he's okay. But it's going to be good for him to have his own life."

As I suspected, she didn't ask questions. She was too weak. She trusted me to do the right thing, and that was that. My father and Kevin packed up Denny's things. They repeated that they were overwhelmed by having to care for my mother and couldn't take care of Denny, too.

At that point, I said, "Well, Dad, would you like to go see where Denny is going to live?"

We made what was basically an obligatory trip there, and then a day or two later, my father and I moved Denny in. Denny was confused, but he settled down after I promised to come see him the next day. Outside the facility, my father put his arm around me and said thank you.

It was strange. I had the feeling he was saying good-bye to me. And given what I know now, I wasn't wrong.

After Denny went into the facility, my mother took a turn for the worse and we brought in hospice care. That was when I finally began to accept the reality that I was going to lose her. From the time she was diagnosed, I really believed she could beat the cancer. I refused to think otherwise. After all the two of us had been through and shared, I knew how strong she was.

I was wrong. I arrived one day and as soon as she saw me walk into the bedroom she begged for something to drink. After she sipped water, I called an ambulance and had her taken to the hospital. Dehydrated, she was given fluids and she seemed to rebound enough that no one expected her to die anytime soon. But a short time later, on August 1, 2004, my father called me and said she'd passed away.

I couldn't believe it. I'd spoken with her the day before.

And now?

I raced to the house, went into the bedroom, and then came out and stared at my father and brother. My mother was gone. Literally gone. They'd already had her body removed. I wasn't able to see her one last time or say a final good-bye.

I was in shock for a few days afterward. Even so, at my father's request, I made the funeral arrangements. My father waited outside St. Jude's in Westlake, where the service was, for Denny to be dropped off, and right before they went inside he informed my brother that our mother was dead and they were going inside. I was nearby, within earshot of the conversation, and I thought it was the coldest, cruelest thing I'd ever witnessed. Denny's expression melted into one of pained confusion.

"Mom is dead?" he asked.

"Yes," my father said.

"Mom is dead?" he asked again.

"Yes."

"I want to say good-bye."

"You can't," my father said. "She's dead. Let's go inside now. Everybody's waiting for us."

Denny wanted more explanations, more sympathy, more time. None was given him. He was in tears, bawling his eyes out.

I cried, too.

And I would've continued to cry if things didn't take such a scary turn.

27

The Family Trust

Less than a week after my mother's death, my father and Kevin were truly and wholly inseparable, so much so that my father's brother, a retired Air Force colonel, worried that "Kevin will cause my brother to lose his soul." One day they showed up at my house unannounced. They came in full of nervous energy, and I didn't get the sense they came to see how I was holding up.

Their energy was different from mine. It felt like they were on a mission. Kevin certainly was. With my father standing behind him, nodding at everything he said, he let me know that he'd hired a lawyer. To prevent me from screwing him out of his share of money that was due him.

"What are you talking about, Kevin?" I asked.

"You know, Maureen. And I want to say this for the record, the will is no good."

I said, "What?"

"The will—mom and dad's trust—it's no good."

I glanced at Michael, who rolled his eyes. I looked at my father, who was nodding in agreement with Kevin.

"What are you talking about?"

"There's a page missing from it," he said.

We debated that point back and forth. It wasn't true. I understood the real point, though. Kevin had heard from my father that their living trust was going to give him money in increments, and he was freaking out about it. Since my father was still alive, it didn't affect him or any of us. Why he wanted to fight about it now was beyond me. He scared me, and made me scared for my father.

At this point, my father still drove, and the next day he came over and apologized for the previous day's scene.

"Kevin is so sick," he said. "I'm very sorry."

I told my father that he needed to also apologize to my brother Mike in Hawaii. I had to explain that he and Kevin had treated my brother poorly during my mother's illness. They didn't keep him informed about her condition. They didn't let him talk to her. They made him feel like he wasn't part of the family.

"You need to communicate better with him," I said.

At that, he called Mike and said he loved him. He said he was sorry for the way he'd treated him, blaming it on Kevin, who he said was sick and needed help. After the call, my father and I reminisced about my mother. He cried and apologized to me for his own behavior and for Kevin's. He reiterated that Kevin had threatened suicide and needed to see a doctor.

He sounded like my old father again, and I fantasized about getting the family back together. I put my arms around him and promised to arrange for all of us to go to counseling. I said we had to work together in order to come together. My father agreed, but a moment later, seeming alarmed, he asked what time it was and said he had to get back to Kevin.

Alone, I found myself, for the first time, able to think clearly about my mother's death. All of a sudden it hit me hard. I'd always thought I'd be with her as she took her final breaths, holding her hand, comforting her, and making sure the last words she heard were "I love you."

At the end, what else could matter? Unfortunately, it hadn't worked out that way. I was thinking, God, if Mom was only here, none of this would be happening. She was the rock. She was the glue that held us together.

I felt awful that I hadn't been there when she passed. I was angry at my dad and Kevin for not allowing me those moments. They knew how close we were. All of a sudden, as I thought of my mother being gone forever, I was unable to hold myself together. Not that I'd been doing such a good job up to then. But I burst into tears and felt what I was supposed to feel—extreme sadness, anger, and loss.

So much loss.

I remember Natalie coming home and seeing me so distraught. She walked over to me, and without saying a word, my fifteen-year-old daughter wrapped her arms around me. We hugged the way I wished I could've hugged my mother, the way I wished my mother would've hugged me, me taking strength from Natalie, then trying to give back the same to her, and then hearing her whisper, "Mom, I love you so much."

I'd experienced my share of bizarre people and situations, but nothing prepared me for the kind of truly bizarre, un-*Brady*-like craziness I encountered in the ensuing months. The confrontation I'd had with Kevin at my house following my mother's death was merely a warm-up. At the end of the summer, I was looking over some financial documents and accounts when I came across a bank statement that had my name on it as well as my parents'. It was an account of mine from years ago that my mother had monitored, as she did all of our finances.

I was surprised. The sum was significantly larger than I'd thought. I left a message with my father, asking what he knew about it. The response I got floored me. Kevin and my father called back, insisting I needed to sign paperwork canceling the joint accounts. When I hesitated,

Kevin threatened to ruin my career if I didn't comply. I wish I'd called his bluff. Instead, frightened and nervous, I let my dad take me to the World Savings Bank, where I signed everything he asked me to sign—which, in effect, transferred exclusively to him a huge sum of money.

The woman who'd helped with our family's banking for years assisted us with the paperwork. She had been close with my mother and knew all of us, the whole family history. With each form she put in front of me, the two of us exchanged looks and I could tell she was asking if I was sure I knew what I was doing, if I was sure I wanted to transfer that much and take my name off those accounts.

I knew her instincts were right. I shared the same worry. But between the fact that my father was still my father (and still, at this point, behaving like it, sort of) and Kevin's threats, I felt handcuffed. Then the two of them made a quick jaunt to Hawaii, first to Kauai and then to Maui, to look at a couple of investment properties. When my father told me about the trip, I assumed they would also see my brother Mike, his wife, and two boys, Brandon and Colin. My father had always enjoyed a close relationship with his grandsons.

However, when I called Mike to see how things were going with Dad and Kevin, he asked what I meant. He didn't know they were in Hawaii. Nor did he ever hear from them. My father was back in Los Angeles before Mike, deeply hurt, caught up with him. My father explained that he and Kevin had thought it would be too uncomfortable for Kevin and Mike to see each other, so they'd decided against visiting. My father went on to say that he was also upset with Mike for beating him up thirty years earlier.

Mike was dumbfounded. As he told me, he heard this and stopped, shocked. When had he ever beat up our father, hit him, even raised a fist?

Never!

Both of us wondered what Kevin was telling our father. Was he brainwashing him? It sounded like it to us.

Mike was very upset. He couldn't figure out why they'd slighted him in Hawaii or where my father came up with the story of a fight. We talked all the time. He lost sleep. He couldn't figure it out. He assumed the problems dated back to the trip he and Kevin had taken to Europe as young men or the Mine Shaft.

In December, Mike's younger son, Colin, was graduating from the University of Hawaii, and Mike invited my father to the ceremony. Mike reported that their conversation had sounded normal, like old times. My father agreed it would be good to spend time together since he hadn't visited the last time he was there. He didn't mention his accusation about the fight.

All seemed good until the day before my father was scheduled to fly out of Los Angeles. He called Mike and canceled his trip, explaining that Kevin thought that flying would jeopardize his health. In addition, my father said he was hurt after Kevin had told him that Mike's older son, Brandon, who worked in the music business in Los Angeles, had referred to Kevin as a drug addict.

Mike didn't know how to react. It didn't sound like his son. Still. When he phoned his son, Brandon called the accusation ridiculous and said in fact he'd been helping his uncle set up a studio so he could record his own music. He expressed the same kind of shock, hurt, and confusion as the rest of us.

Toward the end of February 2005, I received a certified letter from the Los Angeles County Clerk's Office, notifying me that one of the houses in the family trust had been quitclaimed, or deeded, to Kevin. Then I received a call from the woman at World Savings who helped with our banking. She alerted me to the fact that my father had transferred a large sum of money into an account for Kevin.

A few days later, my brother Mike received a certified letter in Hawaii. It was from my father, who wrote that Mike was no longer to have any contact with him, except by mail. It went on to state that neither Mike nor any other family member was to set foot in any of the

McCormick homes listed in the trust, including the one my father and Kevin occupied. My father's signature was at the bottom.

One day, after the money transfer but before I knew about the letter, Kevin called and insisted I come see my father and him. His voice was stern and clipped; he sounded like the head of some tribunal that had power over me. *We want you to get over here right now!*

I drove to their house, and Kevin let me in. I had a sense he'd been watching for me. The condo no longer felt like my mother had lived there. To be fair, I wouldn't say she ever really had lived there. She'd just been sick there. After a quick glance around, I sat down on the living-room couch. Kevin quickly said I couldn't sit there; he wanted me on the chair opposite the couch, one of two leather recliners.

Suddenly I realized the purpose of his camera equipment, the blackout curtains, and recording equipment. As soon as I sat down in the chair, he ran out of the room, then came back a moment later, studying me intently. It dawned on me that I was being videotaped, and he'd left the room to adjust the camera. Then my father entered the room. He looked at Kevin, as if the two of them were following a plan. Then my father gave me a piece of paper and told me to sign it.

What?

I scanned the paper which was an agreement saying that I willingly relinquished my role as executor of the family's trust because I was mentally incompetent. I refused to sign it. My father and Kevin were irate. They threatened never to talk to me again if I didn't sign. Kevin shouted at me: *Face it, Maureen, you're mentally incompetent. Isn't that true? Admit it, you're on mind-altering drugs. Just state that you're incapable of being the executor because you're a drug addict!*

The more I resisted, the louder he yelled. *I'll tell people about the drugs you take. I'm going to ruin your career.* My father stood beside him, agreeing. When I tried to talk back, Kevin grew louder and more insistent. *You'll never work again.* I felt like I was being punched and bulldozed. Sobbing so hard that I began to gasp for breath, I looked at my father in desperation and bewilderment.

"Dad, why are you doing this?"

"Maureen, you know," he said. "You are sick. You are on mind-altering drugs."

Unable to take their punishment anymore, I crumpled to the ground and curled up in the fetal position. They broke me. Crying, fearing I'd never see my father again, scared by Kevin's threats, I agreed to say whatever they wanted. *Yes, I am greedy,* I cried. *Yes, I did cocaine. Yes, I am incompetent and crazy.*

But I didn't sign the paper.

No matter what they said or threatened, I wouldn't sign.

Deep down, I knew better.

I don't remember how, but I finally got out of there. I saw that nearly three hours had passed. My mind was going a million miles per hour, and I felt like I was about to have a nervous breakdown. My whole body was trembling. I kept replaying everything they'd said to me. I felt like I'd escaped from a cult that had been holding me captive, and it left me traumatized and scared.

I was scared for my own safety; that's how scrambled and out of it I felt. I thought I might need hospitalization to calm me down. I went to my doctor friend Janie's house for help and guidance. She was still at work, but her mother-in-law was there with Janie's children, and she let me in. Still trembling, I called Janie, who told me to climb into her bed and wait for her to get home.

She got there as soon as possible. I stayed for several more hours. I didn't want to leave the doctor's care. I needed her reassurance that I wasn't going insane. She went much further, in fact, saying that my family had imploded since my mother's death, that my father and brother had gone off the deep end, that they had basically abused me for three hours, and that any sane person would respond the same way as I had—they'd feel like they had gone crazy.

My husband had a different response; he wanted to hunt them down and beat the crap out of them. I wouldn't let him set foot out of the house. A couple weeks went by. Then Mike phoned with news of the letter prohibiting him from contacting our father. After hearing my story, he flew to Los Angeles, intent on finding out what exactly was going on with Dad and Kevin.

After he landed, we went straight to my father's house. We knocked on the door even though it was apparent that no one was home. From the newspapers piled up at the end of the driveway, it appeared no one had been there for quite some time.

Concerned, we phoned the L.A. County Sheriff's Department. On their advice, we filed a missing-persons report, and then my husband and I returned to my father's house, where several sheriffs and a social worker from Adult Protective Services joined us on the front lawn. The scene brought out all the neighbors. I heard several whisper my name. I wanted to crawl into a hole.

There were two deputies. They knocked on the door and looked around. One deputy thought he heard something inside. My brother Mike and I said we thought Kevin might be holding our father hostage. The deputies explained they didn't have the legal authority to enter the house forcibly, but they said Mike and I, as concerned family members, could break in to check on our father's safety.

They showed my brother how to kick the door in. Sure enough, it popped open. Mike gave me a surprised look, like "wow, it really worked."

The deputies followed us inside as we looked around. No one was there, but we found Kevin's bedroom padlocked (his camera equipment was inside), blackout curtains over the windows, and a chair wedged against the front door. Kevin and my father had seemingly anticipated a break-in.

I grabbed my husband. I needed support. I was more frightened than ever for my father's well-being. Wasn't this some form of abuse or kidnapping?

The deputies on the scene said there was nothing more they could do. My brother and I spent the next few days pleading with the sheriff's department to take some kind of action. Weren't they able to see something was wrong? But they said it was a matter for the court system, not law enforcement.

Not content to let it rest, I hired a private investigator. Days later, he found my father and Kevin at a hotel in Ventura County. He reported that my father appeared okay and had said that he didn't want contact with any family members other than Kevin.

"How did my father seem when he said that?" I asked the PI.

"Emphatic," he replied.

I was haunted by something. It was all those times Kevin had taunted me by saying, "You'll see, Maureen. One day, you'll see." I never knew or understood what he'd meant—until now.

28

Reality

I f this was a matter for the court system, we clearly needed help navigating those waters, and so on the advice of friends and a therapist I was seeing for the sake of my own sanity, I hired Alex Borden, a Torrance-based attorney specializing in this area of law. My husband sat next to me during our first meeting and calmly filled in details when I was overcome by emotion. I kept bursting into tears—I couldn't help it.

Although fairly young, Alex nodded as if he'd already seen too many cases like this. Indeed, he was way too familiar with such gnarled family situations. He said such stories were more common than most people realized. It was then that I heard for the first time the words *elder abuse*, a term that he said described any knowing or intentional neglect or harm to a vulnerable adult. It could be physical, psychological, sexual, or financial. It was, he added, on the rise.

"It's exactly what's happening to my dad," I said. "What can we do?"

His response was interesting. He spoke about legal measures and fighting for conservatorship, but he emphasized that the best tactic would be to try to resolve the problem out of court, or to use the threat of a legal battle that could result in serious consequences to encourage an outside arrangement. We went that route. At the end of April, we had our first court hearing, at which Alex and my father's attorney, Alan Greenfield, worked out a deal for my father to meet my brother and me, without Kevin present.

It seemed simple enough. All I wanted was my father back. For some reason, though, he failed to show up. Another meeting was set up. My brother and I were to meet my father at noon outside a Mexican restaurant in Ventura. After he didn't show up again, we called his attorney, who said Kevin had changed the plans and now wanted us to meet our father in front of a hotel on the pier.

There were several police cars in front of the hotel when we pulled up. They were, it turned out, waiting for us. Kevin had phoned them, fearing we'd steal my father. After we didn't see my father in front of the hotel, I walked one way down the pier and Mike walked the other, looking for him. I found my father on a bench, sitting by himself. He was like a pawn in this twisted war. How sad.

"Dad, let's go into this restaurant and talk," I said.

Mike joined us as we went inside and got a booth. My father started by saying that he was well but Kevin was dying of testicular cancer and needed $400,000 for treatment. I gasped at the news and asked what could we do, what kind of help did he need? My brother noticed my father was unusually nervous and uptight. He asked who'd diagnosed Kevin's cancer. My father said, "I did."

"You diagnosed testicular cancer?" Mike asked.

"Yes," he said. "Don't you trust me?"

It was a strange response, and the rest of the conversation, while brief, was no better. While we talked about getting a second opinion, my father focused on Kevin's need for the money immediately. When we suggested finding a specialist, my father said they preferred to treat it on their own. Watched by the police, we were able to drive my father back to the hotel.

In the car, my brother turned on a song that he thought my father might relate to, as if it would snap him back to reality. But the moment it came on, he asked Mike to stop, then reached for the door handle and said he had to go. We watched him disappear inside the hotel, where we were sure Kevin was waiting for him. Mike said something about Dad not being Dad anymore. I agreed. That wasn't the man who'd raised me.

W e reported everything to Alex, who called my father's attorney and said we wanted Kevin examined by specialists at one of the large Los Angeles–area hospitals. A few days later, Alex called back with disturbing news. He said that, through his attorney, my father denied ever having claimed Kevin was ill.

In May, we returned to court for another hearing, and outside the building we had a brief family talk wherein we decided upon mediation so we didn't run through everyone's money paying for attorneys. Kevin looked fine, unchanged. When I asked him about the cancer, he said, laughing, "Oh, that was a misunderstanding."

A month later, we were in Oxnard for our first mediated hearing, the goal of which was to gain access to my father. My brother and his son Brandon were there, as were my husband and I, my father and Kevin, our respective attorneys, as well as the mediator. Before the session began, my father passed all the adults, attorneys, and mediator copies of a letter he'd supposedly written. We doubted its authenticity. Still, it created a dramatic moment.

The mediator left the room to read it in private. The rest of us went through it, horrified, in the room.

Over twelve pages long, the letter detailed why I was mentally incompetent and not to be believed or trusted in any capacity. It started out describing my mother as a woman who threw knives and plates at my father, and it went on to say that I suffered from syphilis like my mother, was addicted to cocaine, and continued to take mind-altering drugs. It was heinous.

Yet there we were, a group of adults—family—reading this vile attack on me. My husband's anger was visible. I knew what he wanted to do; thank goodness he didn't. My attorney rolled his eyes. I looked across the table at Kevin. His face was a rapidly changing series of angst-ridden grimaces and contortions, as if he were at war with some internal demon. Everyone saw it.

Finally, the mediator returned, sat down, put the pages of the letter in front of her, looked around the table, paused briefly to take in Kevin's unnerving looks, and in a calm, firm, and dismissive tone said, "Okay, now that we've gotten that out of the way, let's get on with things."

After several hours, all parties agreed to appoint an independent trustee to oversee the family trust. We also agreed, though not in writing, that my father would be open to counseling and regular visits so we could be a family. All I want is to talk to my father alone in a room, I told the mediator. She said absolutely, pointed to a room, and my father and I went into it. There, as if molting out of his strange skin, he hugged me, cried, promised to go into therapy with us, and said, "Maureen, I'm so sorry about this. Isn't it great we're working this out? I love you."

For a moment I had my father back.

Then suddenly he pushed me back and said we'd spent enough time together. Then Kevin asked for equal time alone. Through the wall, I heard him, and I think everyone else also heard him, say, "Dad, she's the sick one! She's the one who needs therapy. She needs a lifetime of therapy."

I doubted those sessions would ever come off, and they didn't. Neither did any of the agreed-upon regular visits.

It wasn't long after this that I was lying in bed one night with my husband, unable to sleep, as usual, because I was thinking about the situation. We were literally in the Twilight Zone. I couldn't believe I'd gotten my life together just to end up in this mess. I muttered something along these lines simply to provoke Michael into talking about it.

He reminded me that I hadn't done what I did just to be able to fight Kevin, which was true, but then he said, "God gives you enough strength to fight the battles you need to fight."

Great, I thought, but does He give you strength enough to win?

What did it mean to win? What was the point?

The fighting was taking a terrible toll on all of us. Denny, the easiest to overlook, was hit the hardest. My father and Kevin visited him once or twice. I saw him every other week, attended every meeting at which the staff provided updates on residents, and had Denny stay with us many weekends and on holidays. After almost a year in the facility, he still didn't understand the arrangement. Every time I saw him, he asked if Mom was really gone and where Dad was. Those were the hardest conversations.

"Is Mom really gone?" he asked.

"Yes."

"When am I going to see my dad?"

"I don't know, Den."

"How is my dad?"

"I'm sure he's fine, Den. He's with Kevin."

"Can I talk to him?"

"We don't have his number, Den. We don't know how to reach him."

After a few rounds of this, Denny stopped asking questions. He looked at me with a confused expression as he tried to process the answers. He looked the way I felt. I always drove away from those visits in tears.

Natalie turned sixteen between Kevin's fake testicular cancer drama and our first mediation. One day I was having lunch with some of my girlfriends at a restaurant in the neighborhood. These women were the bedrock of my reality, the people I relied on for sound advice, good times, and honesty. This was one of those casual lunches of white wine and laughs, until one of them asked what I thought about Natalie's tongue piercing.

I didn't have any opinions one way or the other, I said, because my Natalie didn't have a pierced tongue.

Well, that wasn't what she'd heard from her daughter. Even though I knew we had few family secrets after living as neighbors since our kids were infants and watching them progress from diapers to their driver's licenses, I insisted she was wrong.

"It's not possible," I said. "I see her every day."

"Do you look at her tongue every day?"

"We had an agreement," I said. "When she got her ears pierced, she promised not to get anything else pierced."

"Well, you should check it out," said my girlfriend.

I excused myself from the table and went home. Natalie was in her room. Unable to restrain myself, I yelled upstairs, asking if she'd had her tongue pierced. I was halfway up the stairs when I saw her dart into the bathroom from her bedroom and lock the door. I stood outside the door and asked the question again. Slowly, she opened the door wide enough for me to see the middle of her face. Then she opened her mouth and stuck out her tongue.

"Oh my God!" I said. "Nat—take it out. Then meet me in your room."

My initial reaction foretold the worst kind of knock-down-drag-out, but our talk ended up being pivotal to both of us, and that's because, to my daughter's credit, we actually did talk about it. She came into her bedroom knowing she'd broken our agreement, and she told me everything. She had had her tongue pierced after my mother died. It had been a lark, she said. Amid the chaos that followed my mother's funeral, I'd failed to notice that she'd asked for soft food in her school lunches.

When Michael got home from work, he joined the two of us. Natalie shared more details on her life, things I should've seen or known or wanted to know about my daughter but hadn't because I'd been distracted by the issues with my father and Kevin. As for the piercing, I understood the idea of a good girl wanting to be a little bad. But some of the other stories she told scared me to death. Some brought tears to my eyes. Her openness and honesty impressed me beyond words.

I never shared like that with my parents. It was only after I'd gone home in need of an abortion that I began to open up to my mother, and then it took another twenty years before we really started to talk. I didn't want to go that route with Natalie. I didn't want to imagine the pain I'd feel if she closed the doors to her life to me. Nor did I want to imagine her keeping secrets and battling fears the way I had.

I saw in Natalie a beautiful girl who had a chance to develop into an even more beautiful young woman, and in talking to her, I realized she was even more extraordinary on the inside. Somehow she had survived my faults and lapses. I think all women see themselves in their daughters, or maybe they see an idealized version of themselves. I know my mother lived vicariously through me. In Natalie, though, I saw my baby girl growing up into someone much better than me—stronger, more mature, more together.

And I wanted to keep it that way. At the end of the day, raising a child was the most important thing I'd do in my life, and as we sat there, talking, yelling, crying, and hugging, I thought I'd better get it right, or at least try to, at each juncture. If piercing her tongue was the worst thing she did, Michael and I were going to be two happy parents. But we were a family in turmoil; that was the reality, and it was affecting everyone in different ways, including Natalie.

We needed help. I'd been going to therapy since my mother died, and it had kept me together. I suggested to Natalie that the three of us go to counseling, and she agreed. We went several times. With a therapist directing the conversation in a nonjudgmental and caring manner, we talked calmly and openly. We hit big issues, got beneath the surface, and discovered feelings that might never have come out.

For example, I brought up the hurt I felt upon learning that Natalie had kept a secret from me. Through talking about it, though, I realized I hadn't been hurt as much as I'd been frightened of her keeping secrets the way I did and my mother did and her mother did. As I said, I didn't want her to be like us.

Until then, Natalie didn't know about the sordid family history. Once the door opened, though, I filled in the blanks and provided the backstories. It helped having the therapist there; I think it gave me courage. Without realizing it, as I told the story, I glossed over the details of my own life. I wasn't fully aware of what I had been avoiding until the therapist suggested I tell Natalie about some of the problems I had growing up.

On the one hand, I was like "where do I start?" On the other, I was horrified of exposing all the truly rotten, self-destructive things I'd done and admitting that I wasn't the perfect person I wanted to be for my daughter. At that point, the therapist asked if I really believed she thought I was perfect. I looked over at her. She made the cutest face and shrugged, as if to say, "Mom, you can stop pretending. I know you aren't perfect."

Part of me wanted to laugh at all the effort I'd wasted pretending to be someone I wasn't, especially since it was obvious to everyone but me that I wasn't perfect, and another part of me felt what it must be like when you jump out of a plane when skydiving for the first time. My stomach was in a knot, and I wasn't sure I really wanted to take the plunge, yet I knew I'd be better off for it.

It came down to Natalie. This was my chance to break the pattern, to put three generations of secrets, shame, and personal shit on the table so she would be aware of it, make better decisions, and ultimately be spared having to go down the same self-destructive avenue. So I went for it. I told her about my fear of syphilis, the drug abuse, my two abortions, and more. It was as if I opened a box of keepsakes, but instead of trinkets, glass beads, ribbons, it was filled with pain, misery, anger, embarrassment, shame, and grief.

Telling my daughter those things was one of the most painful experiences of my life, and also one of the best and most profound. When I finished, I felt like my soul was exposed and vulnerable in a way it had never been in front of my child. All the pain, fear, and self-hate I'd ever tried to escape was flapping in the breeze, like laundry on the line. I'd claimed every bit of it. Then I looked into Natalie's eyes for a response. They were as wet and red as mine. Unprompted, she got out of her chair, walked over to me, and gave me the hug of a lifetime.

"Mom, I know you shared all those stories so I wouldn't have to go through the same things," she said. "I understand."

"You do?"

She nodded.

"I just want to say thank you so much. And I love you even more."

That left just one person whose love I needed, and I was working on her.

29

Fifty

Natalie came home from her summer job as a waitress at a popular local deli. She walked into the kitchen and burst into tears the second she saw me. She shook her head and pulled away from me when I tried to console her. It was clear that she was angry with me. When I demanded to know why, she said Kevin and my father had gone into the deli for lunch and told her that I was a vile person and a terrible mother who had beaten her when she was a small child.

She tried to defend me, she said, but they insisted they had proof. They even said they'd seen me hit her.

Now she stared at me, wanting to know the truth.

I told her that I'd done many bad things, but I'd never beaten her as they'd claimed. Nor could I imagine doing such a thing.

Such was summer 2006. In June, my father's brother flew into Los Angeles from his home in Florida to see the family. Uncle John was dying of cancer. He didn't know how much time he had left, but it wasn't long. A year earlier, he'd written the court a letter, warning of Kevin's influence over my father. It was ignored. Now he wanted to say his goodbyes to everyone, especially his brother.

I arranged for the family to get together. I made sure invitations got to my father and Kevin. Neither of them showed up. Disappointed my uncle returned home and died a few weeks later.

That was a blow to the little hope I had left. I didn't know what else I could do to try and bring the family together. I missed my mother's stabilizing presence more than ever. For the past year, I'd compensated by canvassing antique shops and buying things that reminded me of her. If something had the word Mom or Mother on it, I bought it. Small boxes, poems, cups, picture frames.

I tried but never found things with her name, Irene, but I did find all kinds of objects engraved with the word "Iowa," her home state, and I bought those instead. Because my mother had once given me two quilts, I bought dozens of those, too. I knew that with each purchase I was trying to bring her back into my life, and I knew that the effort was painfully futile. It didn't matter. I couldn't stop myself.

I spent a lot of money and time looking for her. I compiled a list of Salvation Army locations from the Valley to Santa Barbara. I had pages with the addresses of antique stores. As soon as Michael left for work and Natalie got off to school, I got in my car and hit the stores. My mom liked teapots, so I had to have a hundred. She liked chairs. I bought ten different kinds.

I couldn't stop. After I filled the house, Michael had to cram even more chairs into the ceiling of the garage. He watched in amazement as the patio and then the backyard itself filled up with enough tables and chairs to host a wedding for more than a hundred guests. Except no one was getting married.

Every so often Michael asked if we really needed another chair, another table, or another half-dozen teacups that said MOM. Finally, toward the end of that summer, he reached his breaking point. It wasn't, he later told me, any one thing I'd bought. It was everything. I couldn't argue that point.

We had piles of things in every room as well as in the hallways. My mother had been a hoarder, saving everything from furniture to newspapers to string, and I seemed to have inherited that lovely trait (or is it a tic?). Michael hired a professional organizer to clean out our house. An understanding woman, she arrived with a crew. Working room by room, they removed everything, put it in the driveway, and returned only the essentials.

I was so embarrassed that the neighbors could see all the crap in the driveway. Of course, over the years, most of them had seen much worse.

I remember surveying all the stuff with Michael. We laughed, cried, and shook our heads in amazement and bewilderment. Most of the stuff went back to the Salvation Army. I suffered a minor panic attack as I watched the truck take away so many things that had, however fleetingly, let me have one more moment with my mother. Michael didn't care. He was thrilled to be getting his house back.

The housecleaning was symbolic of so much more. In August 2006, I turned fifty years old, a milestone I celebrated at one of my favorite restaurants with family and friends, who toasted the way I embraced the half-century mark with good cheer and satisfaction. My response: Why not celebrate it?

Though aging is feared by most in Hollywood, I actually liked it. While a part of me would always be sixteen years old and getting hit in the nose with a football, I arrived at this milestone in real life sans any Botox or plastic surgery. When I looked in the mirror in the morning, I saw the real me staring back. I proudly wore my wrinkles and sags like medals earned in battle.

And a battle it had been to this point. I wasn't perfect by any means, but I had many more pluses than minuses. My marriage was more than twenty years old, strong, and more loving than ever. My daughter was beautiful inside and out. And I felt wiser, better, happier, and healthier than at any time in my life.

What wasn't to celebrate?

Other than the occasional *Brady*-related appearance, I no longer thought about show business. I didn't have an agent. My priorities had changed. I thought more about Denny, Natalie, Michael, Kevin, and my father, and even antiquing than I did about getting a job. Then one day a call came in from Barry Greenberg, an executive at the TV Land cable network. He'd received an inquiry from a producer who wanted to meet me for the MTV show *Celebrity Fit Club.*

I'd never heard of the show. When Barry explained it to me, my jaw dropped.

"Oh my God!" I said. "They want me to be on this show because they think I'm fat."

I didn't know whether to laugh or cry. The ugly truth was, I *had* put on weight. Once my mom got sick, I began to pack on the pounds. My days were spent taking care of her and everyone else, trying to make sure things were okay. Then late at night, after Michael and Natalie were asleep, I crept into the kitchen and wolfed down ice cream, pasta, cake, casseroles, and cookies—whatever I found in the fridge.

It was a high-calorie pity party reminiscent of the binges I'd gone on a decade or so earlier. Except instead of throwing up afterward, I kept it in—and kept eating more. I didn't want to give it up. I needed the comfort that food gave me. I was trying to fill a hole that kept getting bigger. With the weight, I literally carried around my burdens, adding a pound or two with each new upset.

Back when my mother was getting chemo, she hinted that I should lose a little weight. My husband remarked on it a couple times, too. By the time I was offered *Celebrity Fit Club*, my weight had climbed from 115 to 154 pounds, and my dress size had increased from a four to a ten. I remember waiting all day for Michael to get home from work. As soon as he came through the door, I greeted him with a question.

"Am I fat?"

Michael set down the backpack that held his laptop and looked at me. Unlike me, he was good at thinking before he answered a tough or tricky question, and this question defined tough and tricky.

"Well," he said cautiously. "Why do you ask?"

I told him, and then Natalie came home and I went over it with her, too. I was aghast at the effrontery of the offer and said outright that never ever would I go on such a show. I pounded my fist on the table to emphasize the point. Then, agitated, I opened up the fridge and looked for something to eat. Natalie was the one who brought me to my senses, first telling me to look what I was doing—"Mom, close the fridge and come back to the table"—and then suggesting that doing the show might be cool.

"Why's that?" I asked.

"It's a great show," she said.

I arranged to meet with the producer, Richard Hall, the son of veteran game-show host Monty Hall. I picked the Good Earth restaurant to give him the impression that I was healthier than he thought. I ordered fruit, too. During the meeting, he and another producer who also joined us never once mentioned the word *fat* or directly said I was heavy. Instead they spoke in vague terms about getting into better shape, feeling healthier, and losing weight if that's what I wanted to do.

Later on, we laughed at the way they'd tiptoed around the real issue. Nonetheless, they got the point across. I went home, took a long, honest look at myself, and decided this was actually an excellent and timely opportunity for me to get in shape, and to get paid for doing it. My husband was wary of what was required, namely going on national TV and admitting I was not in the kind of shape that most people associated with me. But Natalie was overjoyed that her mom was going to be on MTV.

"I wonder what other fat celebrities will be on with you?" she asked, laughing.

Production began after Thanksgiving, which made my favorite holiday torture. I love to eat and cook. It was the first Thanksgiving I could recall when I only had a bite of pie. Normally I ate to the point where I pushed back from the table, unbuttoned the top button on my pants, and sprawled on the sofa in front of the TV. What I realized instead is that I'm very competitive. I wanted to get in shape for the show, so I immediately cut out alcohol and chocolate.

As hard as that was, my most difficult task came at the start of production, when we had to get on the scale. I don't know what it is about revealing your weight to other people, but stepping up on the pedestal for my first weigh-in was one of the most awful, and scariest, moments of my life—and I'd had my share of those.

It wasn't that I didn't want to see the result. I didn't want anyone else to see. I felt naked. I might as well have been naked. Viewers were going to know at a glance that I didn't have any self-control when it came to Baskin-Robbins chocolate mint ice cream, Famous Amos cookies, and garlic bread. It was similar to the time when I'd panicked on the *Touched by an Angel* set at the thought that everyone knew I'd had a drug problem—except for some reason, this was even worse.

I couldn't have said why other than that this was a public declaration that I wasn't perfect, that I had problems and faults, and that I carried them around my hips and thighs. It was like divorcing myself from Marcia Brady in front of Judge Judy. People were going to see the truth, they were going to see me, the real me, Maureen McCormick, at fifty—heavy, out of shape, and trying to win.

Was that bad?

No, in fact, that was the point!

I reminded myself of that by glancing at my fellow competitors: Tiffany, Cledus T. Judd, Kimberley Locke, Da Brat, Ross the Intern, Warren G, and Dustin Diamond. All of them looked roly-poly and maybe a little soft, but not fat. What I saw were people like me, people who probably ate and overate for many of the same reasons I did, and people who were also risking embarrassment if not humiliation by stepping outside their public image to show they were . . . not fat, but human.

I was okay with being human. It's not like people have much choice—something that only took me thirty-some years to accept. Realizing that, I was able to step on the scale, albeit with my eyes closed and my heart pounding. I fought the urge to rip off my clothes so I'd weigh less than 154. Ah, well.

From there, it was a matter of grit and willpower over the show's hundred-day time span. Dustin was the only clinker among the cast. His jokes and behavior were offensive. I suspected he might have been acting that way in an effort to wrangle his own reality show. Everyone else was wonderful. I spoke regularly to Kimberley, Tiffany, and Da Brat. Warren G referred to me as his sister, and Ross became one of the sweethearts of my life. We walked into every show holding hands.

On the first day of physical tasks, we had to run the stairs in the football stadium at Long Beach City College. I was the worst of anyone. I collapsed after going up and down three times. I was pathetically out of shape. Between shooting days, though, I worked out with a personal trainer and kept careful tabs on my diet. Soon I found myself talking about endurance and upper-body strength. Michael encouraged me to exercise, and Natalie left me notes in the morning saying, "Mom, you look beautiful. Keep it up." They became Team Maureen.

My brother Denny was the most inspirational member of the team. Before one of the weigh-ins, the producers showed a videotape of Denny saying, "Maureen, good luck. I hope you win!" I saw it and burst into tears. I think Ross and some of the others cried, too. As it turned out, I won the competition. I ended up at 117 pounds. I set a record, losing the highest percentage of weight in the five-season history of *Celebrity Fit Club*. I was deliriously happy.

There was a party afterward. Everyone attended, except Dustin. By this time, all of us were close, including the show's host, Ant, boot-camp drill sergeant Harvey Walden IV, and psychotherapist Stacy Kaiser. As we celebrated, people described their favorite *Brady Bunch* episode. As always, I was amazed at the way the show had touched the lives of so many people of every age and background. However, this time I didn't feel at war with my doppelgänger, Marcia. I simply felt blessed.

Why was I no longer at war with her?

Almost a decade of work on myself had paid off. And though it sounds silly, I'd just had one of the greatest experiences of my life on the show. I didn't have to play a character or memorize lines. All I had to do was be myself. *All I had to do.* How long had it taken me to get to that point? But how worthwhile were the results! On the show, I had talked about my bulimia. At the party, I heard someone mention an issue with drugs, and I piped up about my past drug problem. Despite all my fears, I had let it all hang out. After spending my life worrying about what people thought of me, what they might think of me, and trying to present a certain image, I gave up. I was just me. And the darnedest thing happened.

I won.

And I'm not talking about the show.

I won much more than *Celebrity Fit Club*, though losing more than thirty pounds wasn't anything to complain about!

Epilogue: Being Me

Take it from me: Surviving your mistakes, making peace with the past, acquiring some wisdom, and learning to like yourself really does make life better. Hey, wrinkles still appear, things sag, and you may need a few more trips to the colorist. But everything that matters, everything you'd consider a priority, improves. It really does. Still, there aren't any guarantees that life will get any easier, as I sadly and maddeningly found out when the same problems with Kevin and my father persisted into the new year.

Early in 2007, Sandy, the woman my father and Kevin had chosen in court as the temporary trustee of the McCormick Family Trust, urged me to try to get conservatorship over my father. It was a sudden reversal of her position. Till that point, she had been irritatingly non-compliant on certain issues, including our agreement in mediation that he see us and that we go for counseling together. For some reason I still don't know, she came to her senses.

After months of us complaining that we no longer knew where my father and Kevin lived and couldn't even speak to my father, she recognized that Kevin exerted an undue and unhealthy influence over my father. She told us that she felt my father should be separated from Kevin as soon as possible. Well, obviously I agreed. But how were we supposed to accomplish this? After three years of fighting, I was at a loss for ideas. I remember asking Sandy how society could allow something like this to happen when everybody with a clear and sane mind knew what had been going on, including her!

Even more bewildering was how a man who was a loving father and an especially loving grandfather could so drastically change, virtually overnight. We took the fight back to court after Sandy's alarming shift, but that didn't help us understand the situation any better. It was like my father had been abducted by aliens. How did it happen? How was my brother able to take him, and our family, hostage? And why couldn't we do anything about it? Why couldn't the court system do something?

My frustration was such that I almost asked the renowned Dr. Phil for help. I met him when he interviewed me on *Larry King Live*. He was subbing for the CNN talk-show host. I ended up keeping it to myself. But unbeknownst to me, after that show aired, my brother Mike sent Dr. Phil an e-mail, explaining our problem and asking him for help. The show's producers responded immediately, offering Dr. Phil's services if we agreed to tell our story on his show.

I was livid when Mike told me what he'd done. I was shocked. So was my husband. No way was I going to do it. I didn't want to air our family's private matters on TV. It was embarrassing. But Mike argued that we'd tried all the legal options and none had worked. We were desperate. He said going on national TV might actually help our family as well as other people who were engaged in similar battles. We could draw attention to the problem of elder abuse.

The show's producers called me at home numerous times. While debating the pros and cons (going on *Celebrity Fit Club* was one thing, but this was a different kind of nakedness and vulnerability), I wondered how I'd gotten so "lucky" to be the first celebrity in line with the chance to highlight elder abuse. Not that I didn't have my choice of other fine options, including former child TV star, drug addict, and depressive.

Oh my God!

Despite all of my misgivings and fears, I agreed to let Dr. Phil get involved, and my brother Mike and I went on the show. I simply couldn't ignore the possibility, however slim, that he might accomplish the miracle we wanted. Dr. Phil hired a private investigator, who tracked down my father and Kevin in nearby Westlake. Cameras captured me confronting both of them at an outdoor mall. Individually and together, my father and Kevin accused me of being a liar, a drug addict, a sociopath, and a criminal. They also called my brother Mike "abusive" and "demonic" and said they were going after him for elder abuse.

"Kevin makes wild accusations," said Dr. Phil. "Maureen, he says you are crazy. What do you say?"

"No, I'm not."

"He say's you're a psychopathic liar. What do you say?"

"No, I'm not."

"He says he has proof you're a criminal. What do you say?"

"No, he doesn't."

Dr. Phil went over the tapes. He complimented me for standing up for myself and asking the tough questions.

"From my observations, you are right to be concerned," he said.

Following the confrontation at the mall, my father attempted to get a restraining order against me, claiming his "health and well-being are endangered by Maureen's unbridled ability to accost ME at will." The court rejected his petition. He tried again, and was turned down a second time. Ultimately we didn't make any progress. The situation didn't get any less worrisome; nor did our relationships improve.

If there was any benefit to the appearance, it was the outpouring of support I received via letter, e-mails, and people who stopped me on the street. They apologized for bothering me, but said they just had to tell someone about their own family crises and craziness. Like me, they had to constantly prove to themselves that they weren't losing their mind. The number of people with similar stories left me dumbfounded—and strangely comforted.

Comforted?

I know that's an odd thing to admit. But it was partly a realization and partly a confirmation that nobody's life is perfect. Not the people who stopped me in the grocery store, not mine, and not Marcia Brady's. I had the same realization I'd had many times over the past few years: how self-defeating I'd been to think my life could or should be perfect, to pretend it was, and to hide problems that could probably have been solved or maybe even avoided if I'd made an effort to find help.

I found kindred, sympathetic souls in Carnie Wilson and Bobby Brown, two of my costars on the CMT reality series *Gone Country*. I signed up for the reality series in mid-2007. It was hosted by Big and Rich's John Rich, and the premise was simple: he'd help us write and perform our own country songs, and along the way we'd be put through the paces of country life. Since I'd fantasized about being a country singer since playing Barbara Mandrell, and had even made a well-received but little-heard country album in the nineties, the show was like a dream come true.

In addition to Carnie and Bobby, the *Gone Country* cast included Twisted Sister's Dee Snider, *American Idol*'s Diana DeGarmo, Julio Iglesias Jr., and rapper Sisqó. All of us met for the first time on a bus that picked us up around Nashville and took us to an enormous log-cabin-style mansion that had once belonged to Barbara Mandrell. I'd never heard Dee's hit "We're Not Gonna Take It" or Sisqó's "The Thong Song." I felt out of it and old. But I ended up becoming best friends with Bobby.

I was scared of him when I first saw him get onto the bus. I even moved to the back to avoid him. We quickly became inseparable, though. We were two people who'd been through a lot of hard times. It was like we had an understanding without having to talk about it. No one would ever think Bobby Brown and Marcia Brady would end up best buddies, but our souls truly connected.

The same was true with Carnie. We traded horror stories about my old round-the-clock therapist Dr. Landy, who had treated her father, Beach Boy genius Brian Wilson, in the eighties and nineties. She told me her family had finally gotten Dr. Landy out of the picture in the nineties after suing for conservatorship. Once he was gone, their family came back together. That gave me hope.

I was impressed by everyone's song. Mine was called "Being Me." It was a pretty, plaintive ballad in the tradition of soul-baring, heart-breaking country songs. Writing it was like therapy. The words poured out of me, as if they'd been there for years, waiting for me to summon them.

At the finale, all of us rooted one another on. However, people re-marked that there was something about my performance that was dif-ferent from the others. I didn't discuss it, but I knew what they meant. As I stood center stage at the Wildhorse Saloon, I looked beyond (or maybe through) the sea of Nashville fans and off into the distance, where I swear to God I saw faces from my past, my family, and of course that one special person seeming to stare back at me, as I sang:

> *Wish my mom was here to see it*
> *The woman I turned out to be*
> *The long road to here ain't been easy*
> *But that's the price I have to pay*
> *For being me.*
>
> *Lord knows, I'm not perfect*
> *Cast your stones and I bleed*
> *Lay down at night and I wonder*

If it's worth it
That's the price I have to pay
For being me.

I've spent most of my fifty-one years hearing people tell me how I have touched their lives in some way. Many have a story, some want to share memories of their favorite *Brady* episodes, and now I hear people who watched me as a child saying their kids are watching me, too. Recently I met Nicole Kidman and Keith Urban on the red carpet at the Country Music Awards, and I was shocked when both of these superstars (and great people) seemed excited to meet me!

I never would've guessed they knew who I was. But our exchange was typical of so many I've had.

"Hi, I'm Maureen McCormick," I said.

"We know you," said Keith.

"You're Marcia Brady," added Nicole.

"Yes, I am!"

I'll always be struck by how much a part of people's lives Marcia is and always will be, and how, whether I like it or not, I'll always be her, just as she'll always be me. But now I'm not bothered by the connection. Nor do I feel in competition with her or like I want to disown that part of me. Yes, it's still hard for me to go back and see myself as a Brady, but only because I remember the pain I was in and the depression that followed. I feel so different today.

Now I can embrace Marcia, and when people of all ages, walks of life, and ethnicities say they wanted to be me or date me when they were little, like Sisqó did on *Gone Country* when he asked, "Who didn't have a crush on Marcia Brady?" I feel blessed to be that person.

It took most of my life, countless mistakes, and decades of pain and suffering to reach this point of equanimity and acceptance. Is everything perfect? No, not by any means. I wish I hadn't caused my parents so much misery. I wish I hadn't punished myself as severely as I did when I was younger. I wish I hadn't fought as much with my husband.

I wish I had confronted my problems and asked for help instead of taking flight from so many of them. I wish I could spend time with my father and not have my brother Kevin regard me as the enemy.

I also wish that I still wasn't as hard on myself as I am sometimes. I wish that I was still a size three and 115 pounds. I still wish that I could land that special role, one that launches a comeback and makes all of Hollywood say, "She really is talented. What an actress!" Sometimes I wish my life was perfect, whatever that means.

But then I catch myself. I know better. I can honestly say I wouldn't wish to change a thing if it meant trading the person I am at this very moment for someone else. I don't profess to know the answer to the puzzle that is life, but I'm doing better at fitting the pieces together. I'm becoming the best me that I can be.

As I've felt better about myself, I've been able to share this with other people in ways that have continued to make me stronger, wiser, smarter, healthier, and ultimately happier about who I am and why I'm here. That's what's so sad about the way my father and Kevin have shut themselves off from the world and made enemies out of the people who love them. I wrote this book knowing my mother never wanted me to write a book. But one of the things that made it all right was her best friend, Harriet.

Harriet knew our family for more than fifty years and had witnessed the craziness with her own eyes. In March 2008, she died at age ninety-two. She didn't have any family of her own. So when she got sick, my husband and I stepped in. We took care of her for the last six months of her life. I visited daily, brought her food, made sure she got to the doctor, and toward the end arranged for her care and sat with her. She always asked about this book, and when I had doubts she encouraged me to keep going.

One day I was filled with doubts and fears about sharing the stories that my mother, and then I, spent a lifetime trying to hide. Ever the daughter, I worried my mother would be upset with me. Harriet assuaged those concerns, saying that I was wrong, that my mother would, in fact, be proud. In her sweet, soft voice, she said, "You're everything that she always wanted to be—and more."

In April 2008, Michael and I went to Zambia, in eastern Africa, on behalf of Children International, a relief organization that goes to the world's poorest villages and builds centers where children can go to school, eat nourishing meals, and receive medical care. Africa was the last place I ever imagined myself visiting, yet there I was, in this place that was unmistakably far, foreign, and in its own way magical.

One day, as we toured a town in the province of Chibola, I met Mary, a fourteen-year-old girl who'd lost both of her parents to AIDS. She was raising her four brothers and sisters by herself. I was unnerved when we were introduced. The pain and hardship of her life had squeezed virtually every drop of childhood from her face. She had the expression of a forty-year-old.

I was introduced to many people there, but I felt a connection with her. She and her siblings lived in a one-room shack with a dirt floor. They took turns sleeping on a single foam mattress. Their toilet was a hole in the floor. To make money, Mary washed dishes for people in the village. Many nights they went without food. I felt my heart opening as she told me about herself and her life. Soon my arms were opening, too. I reached out and hugged her. She seemed to need someone to lean on, and I said to her, "I hope this feels like a mother."

She leaned into me and tears poured out of her eyes. I cried, too. Months later, I still picture her eyes staring into mine. I can still feel her embrace, the warmth and smell of her skin. I feel like that gave me the ending I'd been searching for, if only because it also felt like the beginning of the next phase of my life. I had spent my whole life searching for me, and there, in a frighteningly impoverished village in Africa, as I opened my arms and my heart to a little girl who needed a hug, I found myself—the real me, not someone else's image or my idealized version. Just me, Maureen McCormick.

And you know what?

It turned out I was perfect—perfect in my imperfections!

From what I've been able to figure out, all of us are here together and we need one another. We must celebrate one another's differences. Learning to ask for help is as important as learning the value of helping other people. I believe all the people in my life have been there for a reason, and I hope I have been in theirs for a reason as well. It's taken me a while, but I feel truly blessed. After all is said and done, I love life. I love people. And I love being me . . . well, most of the time.

And that's the story.

Acknowledgments

I wish to thank and acknowledge the following people, without whose help and input this book would never have come into being. In no particular order they are:

Todd Gold, Harriet Champion, Dennis McCormick, Mike and Hella McCormick, Brandon and Colin McCormick, Leyla Church, Deb Goldfarb, Devin Sunseri, Dan Strone, Lisa Perkins, Laurie Chittenden, Seale Ballenger, Lisa Gallagher, Michael Morrison, Lynn Grady, Tavia Kowalchuck, Michael Barrs, Christine Casaccio, Jennifer Slattery, Josh Marwell, Mike Brennan, Mike Spradlin, Carla Parker, Donna Waitkus, Brian Grogan, Jeff Rogart, Beth Silfin, Kim Lewis, Andrea Molitor, Rich Aquan, Betty Lew, Mauro DiPreta, Lisa Sharkey, Maureen O'Brien, Michele Corallo, Mary Ann Petyak, David Plotkin, Will Hinton, Suzanne Wickham, Rich Fahle, Carin and Paul Pheiffel, Bobbi, Bill, and Richard Abramson, Nancy, Gordon, Brian, Christine, and Sarah Harrison, Janet, John, John Jr., and Heather O'Brien, David Shall, Susan Corzillias, Alexandria, Hannah, and Samantha Shall, Mike, Mary, and Jennifer Garrison, Bob and Dup Pierce, Terence and Carmen Michos and family, Randi Bach, the

Copeland family, the Colclough family, the Higgins family, the Lykken family, the Steinbergs, Mrs. Brooks, the Burnetts, Dave and Vicki Rosemont, the Hogans, Ann Wren, Cindy and Lee Larson, Kyle and Laura Davies, the Ticktin family, the Steiglers, the Skagerberg family, Sandy Peckinpah, Buddy, Robin, and Jenna Singer, Dr. Howard, Pam, and Jennifer Bliman, the Bhowmik family, Kyle and Laurie Davies, Dick and Suzanne Thompson, WPC, Tim and Lori Stevens, Winterhaven, Pat Ring, ARC, Judy Hightower, Mary Shepherd, Tom Militello, Cindy Montgomery, Dr. Greenman DDS, Dom and Kae Oliver, Reina and Magdelena Hernandez, Judy Kaufman, Chris Viores, Carnie Wilson, Bobby Brown, David Garfinkel, Jay Renfroe, Missy Hughes, Cletus, Kimberly Locke, Richard Hall, Brian Shiers, Tiffany, DaBrat, Ant, Harvey, Stacy Kaiser, Diane DeGarmo, Sisco, Julio Iglesias Jr., Dee Snyder, Julie Ross, Wes Stevens, Ross Matthews, Barry Greenberg, Sal Maniaci, Bob Kusbit, MTV, CMT, TV Land, *Access Hollywood*, Mike Lookinland, Susan Olsen, Ann B. Davis, Chris Knight, Bob Reed, Barry Williams, Florence Henderson, Lloyd and Barb Schwartz, Sherwood Schwartz, Barbara Chase, Hope Schwartz, Frances Whitfield, Jerry Houser, Michael and Eliza Gross, Fred Walicki, Tommy Funderburk, Kenn Gulliksen, Desi Arnaz, Alex Bordon, Sarah Hardcastle, Sandra DeMeo, Mindy Johnson, Jessie and Dudy Brough, Mary Wallbridge, Ed and Ronnie Laberthon, Kaiser Hospital in Woodland Hills, David Baum, Cindy Munzlinger, John Jenkins, Pam Pumphrey, Danny Sarnoff, Harry Moses, Claudia Jennings, Keith Jennings, Fredde Duke, Sandy Bressler, Anne Lockhart, Barb and Angie, Lynn and Glenn Braudt, JoAnne and Frank Walsh, Aunt Margaret, Nita McCormick, the McCormick cousins, Ed Laberthon, Mickey and Irene Thorpe, Sandy Chanley, Kim and Dorothy Cummings, Kim and Jeannie Cummings and family, Carol and Don Harvey and family, Tim and Lori Stevens, Mr. and Mrs. Trond Woxen, Cam and Sigi Camereno, Dave and Cathy Thomas, Anushka, Lisa Trunk, Vicki, Kamyi, and Johnson Young, Byron Williams, Mark at Byron Williams, Susan's Healthy Gourmet, Special Olympics, Eunice Shriver,

Best Buddies, Bobby Shriver, Mark Wylie, Jim Murphy, Children International, Northern Lights Direct Response, Touch of Class Pet Salon, Organize This, Mike Kevorkian's State Farm Insurance Team, Timbuktu Marina in Cook, Minnesota, Brad Paisley, Jason Alexander, Eddie Money, Nicole Kidman, Kevin Hooks, Rosie O'Donnell, Stephen Furst, Gail Troberman, Trisha Yearwood, John Rich, Taylor Hackford, George Hickenlooper, Henry Winkler, Barbara Mandrell, Bruce Vilanch, Dr. Phil, Mary Margarette, Matt Ramsey, Billy Lawson, Susy Unger, the Olivers, the Roths, Jeff Auerbach, Dr. Frankel, Diane Lipson, Dr. Arthur Johnson, Dr. Cedric Johnson, Dr. Singer.